ECONOMIC MODELS OF CRIMINAL BEHAVIOR

CONTRIBUTIONS TO ECONOMIC ANALYSIS

118

Honorary Editor

J. TINBERGEN

Editors

D.W. JORGENSON

J. WAELBROECK

NORTH-HOLLAND PUBLISHING COMPANY

AMSTERDAM • NEW YORK • OXFORD

ECONOMIC MODELS
OF
CRIMINAL BEHAVIOR

Editor

J. M. HEINEKE

Graduate School of Business
University of Santa Clara
Santa Clara, California

1978

NORTH-HOLLAND PUBLISHING COMPANY
AMSTERDAM • NEW YORK • OXFORD

ISBN: 0 444 85261 1

Publishers:
NORTH-HOLLAND PUBLISHING COMPANY
AMSTERDAM • NEW YORK • OXFORD

Sole distributors for the U.S.A. and Canada:
ELSEVIER NORTH-HOLLAND, INC.
52 VANDERBILT AVENUE, NEW YORK, N.Y. 10017

PRINTED IN THE NETHERLANDS

Introduction to the series

This series consists of a number of hitherto unpublished studies, which are introduced by the editors in the belief that they represent fresh contributions to economic science.

The term 'economic analysis' as used in the title of the series has been adopted because it covers both the activities of the theoretical economist and the research worker.

Although the analytical methods used by the various contributors are not the same, they are nevertheless conditioned by the common origin of their studies, namely theoretical problems encountered in practical research. Since for this reason, business cycle research and national accounting, research work on behalf of economic policy, and problems of planning are the main sources of the subjects dealt with, they necessarily determine the manner of approach adopted by the authors. Their methods tend to be 'practical' in the sense of not being too far remote from application to actual economic conditions. In addition they are quantitative rather than qualitative.

It is the hope of the editors that the publication of these studies will help to stimulate the exchange of scientific information and to reinforce international cooperation in the field of economics.

The Editors

PREFACE

It has now been ten years since Becker's path-breaking paper which
brought the study of illegal behavior firmly into the domain of economic
analysis. In the ensuing years increasingly sophisticated models of
criminal behavior have been formulated and estimated. And, as is often
the case with economists, the models of criminal behavior which have
appeared in the literature are only slightly less diverse than the number
of researchers involved. For this reason, a portion of the present volume has been devoted to summarizing, reviewing and in general critiquing
the literature (Chapters 1 - 4). The remaining four chapters contain
new empirical studies. The reader will find these studies to be substantially different from those of the past, both in the type of questions
addressed and in the degree to which econometric models have been linked
to the formal constructs of neo-classical theory. A more detailed description of chapter content follows.

Chapter one is a review and critique of the theoretical models of
criminal behavior that have appeared in the literature since Becker.
J. M. Heineke proceeds by presenting four increasingly general models
from which the well known models of the literature appear as special
cases. The emphasis is on identifying the assumptions underpining these
models which are responsible for their widely differing comparative static
properties.

Chapter two is a review of recent developments in the econometrics
of criminal behavior. J. B. Taylor's review concentrates on newer studies
which have utilized multivariate, multiple equation estimation techniques
to sort out the interaction between criminal behavior and the criminal

justice system. The emphasis is on evaluating the statistical reliability
of these studies both from the viewpoint of policy analysis and for future
empirical work. Rather than summarizing all empirical work in the area,
the author focuses on several papers which are representative of different
types of data and statistical technique.

In Chapter three C. Manski explores the possibilities for inferring
the impact of deterrence policies through observation and analysis of individual criminal behavior. To date almost all empirical analysis of deterrence have been based upon macro models of crime commission using aggregated crime rates, socio-economic and demographic statistics as their data.
Manski argues that the macro approach, as it has been practiced, suffers
from deep logical problems of aggregation and identification which clouds
interpretation of empirical findings.

In Chapter four N. H. Stern presents a partial review of the recent
theoretical literature dealing with public policy towards crime. He argues
that although Becker's (1968) paper has provided the frame work for most
subsequent work in the area, there is a fundamental logical objection to
the Becker model which renders it unacceptable either as a description of
the reasoning behind current policy or as a prescription for policy.

Chapter five begins the empirical portion of the volume. In Chapter
five J. M. Heineke estimates a system of supply equations for the income-
generating activities of burglary, larceny, robbery and "legal work".
Attention is focused upon determining the degree of substitutability or
complementarity which exists between these alternative sources of income
and in assessing the "net" or system-wide response of participation rates
in the several income-generating activities as expected returns and costs
vary.

In Chapter six L. Phillips addresses the question of what it is that police departments produce and how they go about producing it. To answer the latter part of the question Phillips estimates an implicitly additive indirect production function using time series and cross-section data drawn from five big city police departments. One interesting finding is the non-homothetic nature of the production structure. The meaning of such nonhomotheticity in the context of public safety production is explored in some detail.

Chapter seven is another study of the structure of law enforcement production technology, this time from the perspective of a quite general multi-input, multioutput production cost function. The authors, M. Darrough and J. M. Heineke, use a combined cross section and time series drawn from mid-sized U. S. cities to estimate the production structure and then test (i) for the existence of consistent aggregate indices of police output; (ii) for the nonjointness of outputs; and (iii) for the consistency of the estimated cost function with the optimizing behavior of classical theory. In addition, marginal and average costs of solving crimes by type and marginal rates of transformation between solutions of various types are calculated.

Finally, in Chapter eight W. Vandaele develops and estimates an industry supply and demand model for stolen automobiles. The model is analogous in many respects for traditional industry supply and demand models with factor and product markets, although it has been augmented with a crime prevention sector. The estimated model is subjected to forecasting tests both within and outside the sample period. The final section of Vandaele's paper contains a discussion of possible policy uses of the model.

J. M. Heineke

TABLE OF CONTENTS

Economic Models of Criminal Behavior,
J.M. Heineke (ed.)
© *North-Holland Publishing Company, 1978*

CHAPTER ONE

ECONOMIC MODELS OF CRIMINAL BEHAVIOR:
AN OVERVIEW

J.M. Heineke*

Over the past six to eight years, economists have shown increasing
interest in modeling the choice problem confronting individuals engaged
in illegal activities. A number of factors are responsible for this new
found interest, not the least of which are the lack of progress on the part
of criminologists in providing a systematic framework for analyzing criminal
activity, and the belated recognition by economists that the choice theoretic models of microeconomics afford a particularly useful structure for such
an analysis.

Criminologists have approached the task of explaining illegal activity
by attempting to determine those psychological and/or physiological factors
that are unique to criminals. This has led criminologists to study the
social backgrounds and behavior patterns of individual criminals in the
hope of identifying a common set of characteristics which underpin criminal
behavior. Such an essentially inductive approach to model building will
not in general lead to testable models of criminal behavior.

On the other hand, economic models of criminal behavior take as given

*This research was supported under Grant #75-NI-99-0123 from the
National Institute of Law Enforcement and Criminal Justice, L.E.A.A., U.S.
Department of Justice to the Hoover Institution at Stanford University.
Points of view or opinions stated in this document are those of the author
and do not necessarily represent the official position or policies of the
U.S. Department of Justice.

those influences in the personal and social backgrounds of individuals that determine "respect for law," proclivities to violence, preferences for risk and other behavioral characteristics held to be determinants of criminality. These models are based upon characteristics of individuals which are alleged to be common not only to large classes of offenders, but to large classes of economic agents in general. In a sentence, the models of economic choice theory, of which the criminal chioce is a special case, hypothesize that all individuals, criminal and non-criminal alike, respond to incentives; and if the costs and benefits associated with an action change, the agent's choices are also likely to change. More specifically, these models postulate that the decision to commit an illegal act is reached via an egocentric cost-benefit analysis. As is implicit in this statement, the expected benefits and costs associated with an illegal act may contain both monetary and psychic elements. But by treating the individual's "taste for crime" as a datum, one may build a theory of criminal behavior based upon the opportunities confronting the potential offender.

In what follows we construct four rather broad classes of models of criminal behavior and analyze the properties of each class with special emphasis on testable implications. The usefulness of this approach lies in the fact that all models of the economic literature with which we are familiar belong to one of the classes.[1] We find rather dramatic differences in implications across classes with what at first blush may appear to be small differences in model structure.

---

[1] We are referring here to theoretical models based upon the individual as the decision unit, not empirical models. By far the greatest number of papers dealing with criminal behavior have been empirical in focus. These papers usually begin by postulating the existence of aggregate offense functions with certain plausible, but nonetheless ad hoc properties.

A Brief Survey of the Literature

Perusal of the economic literature indicates two distinct approaches to modeling the offense decision. The first approach is essentially a portfolio approach in which the agent makes a decision as to what portion of his wealth to put at risk in a criminal activity. The second approach has been to view the offense decision as a time allocation problem. The papers of Allingham and Sandmo (1972), Kolm (1973), and Singh (1973) have treated the offense decision as portfolio decisions.[2] Such a tack is permissable only in so far as all consequences of the illegal activity in question may be expressed in purely monetary terms. Because each of these papers addresses the question of income tax evasion, there would seem to be little doubt that benefits from the illegal activity are purely monetary in nature. But although the penalty for unsuccessful evasion is almost inevitably a fine, it is doubtful whether the total cost of unsuccessful evasion is the fine, since the convicted evader may experience significant non-monetary costs in the form of loss of respectability, reputation, etc. To the extent that this is the case, it will be inappropriate to employ the portfolio specification.[3] In addition, to the extent that the illegal activity in question is time consuming, it again will be inappropriate to model the decision problem as a choice over wealth orderings. The fact that an illegal activity is time consuming, means that the offense decision problem is formally a labor supply problem with uncertain consequences.[4]

---

[2] In this paper we use the terminology portfolio problem or portfolio decision to designate a decision problem with uncertain consequences in which all "costs" and all "benefits" are pecuniary.

[3] Allingham and Sandmo acknowledge this point and devote a section of their paper to a model which incorporates non-monetary attributes of unsuccessful tax evasion.

[4] See Block and Heineke (1973) for an analysis of the labor supply decision when returns are stochastic.

And given the set of time consuming illegal activities, the more interesting questions, both from the point of view of economic theory and of social
policy, would seem to be those concerned with the factors responsible for
the individual's time allocation between legal and illegal activities and
how responsive the individual is to changes in these factors. The point
is that it will often, but not always, be most appropriate to model the
offense decision as a time allocation problem into which the psychic costs
and benefits associated with criminal activity have been explicitly incor-
porated.

A second group of papers addressing the criminal choice, the papers of
Becker (1968), Block and Heineke (1975a), Ehrlich (1970, 1973), and
Sjoquist (1973), all view the criminal choice problem as a time allocation
problem and to one degree or another acknowledge the role of non-monetary
costs and returns in the offender's decision problem. But although each of
these authors claims to recognize both the time allocative aspects of the
problem and the non-monetary aspects of the penalty if unseccessful, the
qualitative implications of these models differ substantially. The cause
of such variation between models is of considerable interest both theoretically and practically and are examined at some length in what follows.
Briefly, the differences between these models are a result of specialized
assumptions (some explicit, some implicit) concerning either the amount of
time devoted to leisure or the role of non-monetary (psychic) attributes,
or both. We proceed by presenting a series of models into which an
increasing number of characteristics of the criminal choice are incorpor-
ated. Shortcomings of the various specifications and differences in implications are noted at each step. We begin with a simple "portfolio" model.

Model I - The Simple Portfolio Model

Consider an individual with an exogenous income confronted with the problem of deciding what portion of this income to allocate to illegal activity (the risky asset). The following definitions will be used:

W: actual income

W^o: wealth or exogenous income

$U(W)$:   the individual's von Neumann-Morgenstern utility function, $U_W > 0$, $U_{WW} < 0$

x: the proportion of W^o to be allocated to illegal activity, $0 \leq x \leq 1$

$g(x;\alpha)$:   the increase in income if the illegal endeavor is successful; α is a shift parameter

$f(x;\beta)$:   the monetary penalty if the illegal endeavor is unsuccessful; β is a shift parameter

p: the probability that the illegal endeavor is unsuccessful

W_s: the individual's income if the illegal endeavor is successful; $W_s \equiv W^o + g(x;\alpha)$

W_u: the individual's income if the illegal endeavor is unsuccessful; $W_u \equiv W^o + g(x;\alpha) - f(x;\beta)$

If apprehended the individual's income is reduced by the amount $f(x;\beta)$, where $f(x;\beta) \gtrless g(x;\alpha)$. To carry out an analysis of the agent's decision it is necessary to adopt certain conventions concerning the functions $g(\cdot)$ and $f(\cdot)$. These are

$$g(\cdot) > 0, \quad x > 0 \quad ; \quad g(\cdot) = 0, \quad x = 0$$

$$f(\cdot) > 0, \quad x > 0 \quad ; \quad f(\cdot) = 0, \quad x = 0$$

$$g_x > 0 \quad ; \quad g_\alpha > 0 \quad ; \quad g_{x\alpha} > 0$$

$$f_x > 0 \quad ; \quad f_\beta > 0 \quad ; \quad f_{x\beta} > 0$$

These conditions are obvious: Gains and losses from illegal activity (i) are non-negative; (ii) are increasing functions of the amount at risk; and

(iii) are increasing functions of the shift parameters α and β, for given values of x. Finally, increases in the shift parameters α and β are defined to increase not only total gains and total losses, $g_\alpha > 0$, $f_\beta > 0$, but also marginal gains and marginal losses, $g_{x\alpha} > 0$, $f_{x\beta} > 0$.

Adopting this framework, the agent's expected utility is:[5]

(1) $EU(W) = (1 - p)U(W_s) + pU(W_u)$

For the agent to devote some, but not all, of his income to illegal activity there must be an x^o such that

(2) $(1 - p)U'(W_s)g_x + pU'(W_u)(g_x - f_x) = 0$

It is straightforward to interpret these conditions when (2) holds as a strict inequality and either $x^o = 0$ or $x^o = 1$. We leave this to the interested reader and assume $0 < x^o < 1$.

The questions of interest here are the responses of the equilibrium portion of income devoted to illegal activity, x^o, to changes in the several parameters in the model. These are listed next:

(3) $\dfrac{\partial x^o}{\partial W^o} = - ((1 - p)U''(W_s)g_x + pU''(W_u)(g_x - f_x))/J_1^o$

(4) $\dfrac{\partial x^o}{\partial \alpha} = - g_{x\alpha}(\partial EU/\partial W^o)/J_1^o + g_\alpha(\partial x^o/\partial W^o)$

(5) $\dfrac{\partial x^o}{\partial \beta} = (p((g_x - f_x)U''(W_u)f_\beta + U'(W_u)f_{x\beta}))/J_1^o$

---

[5]In what follows we assume that all functions possess continuous derivatives of sufficient order to permit the analysis and that regular, internal maxima exist for each model.

(6) $\dfrac{\partial x^o}{\partial p} = (U'(W_s)g_x - U'(W_u)(g_x - f_x))/J_1^o$

Finally define $\partial x^o/\partial\gamma$ to be the change in x^o due to a shift in the penalty function and a corresponding change in p such that the expected loss remains unchanged. That is, $\partial x^o/\partial\gamma \equiv (\partial x^o/\partial\beta)$, given $d(pf) = 0$. Now $d(pf)$ = $d(f_x dx + f_\beta d\beta) + f dp = 0$, so that $\partial(pf)/\partial\beta = pf_\beta + f(\partial p/\partial\beta) = 0$; which implies $\partial p/\partial\beta = -(pf_\beta/f)$. Therefore,

(7) $\dfrac{\partial x^o}{\partial\gamma} = \dfrac{\partial x^o}{\partial\beta} + \dfrac{\partial x^o}{\partial p}\,\dfrac{\partial p}{\partial\beta}$

   $= \dfrac{\partial x^o}{\partial\beta} - \dfrac{\partial x^o}{\partial p}\,(pf_\beta/f)$

In equations (3) - (7) the symbol J_1^o represents the Jacobian associated with equilibrium condition (2), evaluated at x^o, and is negative by hypothesis. Defining the Arrow-Pratt measure of absolute risk aversion as $R(W) \equiv -U''/U'$ and keeping in mind that we have assumed the potential offender to be risk averse, we adopt the usual assumption that $\partial R/\partial W < 0$. It can be shown (see Appendix) that the model possesses the following qualitative properties:

(3') $\dfrac{\partial x^o}{\partial W^o} > 0$

The individual invests a larger portion of his income in illegal endeavors the wealthier he is.

(4') $\dfrac{\partial x^o}{\partial\alpha} > 0$

Increases in the returns to illegal activity, increase the income allocation to these activities.

(5') $\dfrac{\partial x^o}{\partial \beta} < 0$

Increases in the costs of engaging in illegal activity cause decreases in the allocation to these activities.

(6') $\dfrac{\partial x^o}{\partial p} < 0$

Increases in the probability of "failure" cause decreases in the allocation to illegal activity. And finally, if $f(x;\beta)$ is separable[6]

(7') $\dfrac{\partial x^o}{\partial \gamma} < 0$

Compensated increases in the penalty which leave expected losses unchanged, decrease the allocation to illegal activity. This is equivalent, by equation (7), to saying that proportional increases in punishment (loss) deter illegal activity to a greater extent than do equi-proportional increases in the probability of apprehension. It can also be shown (see Block and Heineke (1975a)), that equation (7) is equivalent to measuring the allocative effect of a mean preserving change in the dispersion of returns. Since mean preserving increases in β increase the dispersion of returns to

---

[6] Here we use "separable" in the sense that $f(x;\beta) = f_1(x)f_2(\beta)$. It does not seem to be possible to establish (7') without restricting $f(\cdot)$. Results of this type reported in the literature are usually obtained under the strong assumption that $f(x;\beta) = \beta x$, i.e., $f_1(x) = x$ and $f_2(\beta) = \beta$. Also note that if we define $\eta = f_x(x/f)$ as the elasticity of the penalty with respect to changes in the income allocation, then $\partial \eta / \partial \beta = 0$ is qualitatively equivalent to the condition $f(x;\beta) = f_1(x)f_2(\beta)$. In fact, as long as shifts in the penalty function do not result in decreases in η, inequality (7') will hold.

illegal endeavors, equation (7') may be interpreted as implying that
increases in the amount of uncertainty surrounding returns to illegal
activity will decrease the income allocated to these activities.

A number of points are of interest here: First, qualitative results
(5'), (6') and (7') depend only upon risk aversion and the fact that the
individual allocates some but not all of his income to illegal activities,
i.e., $0 < x^o < 1.$[7] Results (3') and (4') require in addition the hypothesis of decreasing absolute risk aversion. Second, inequalities (4') –
(7') are the formal underpinning of any unambiguous economic theory of
deterrence. These inequalities tell us that increases in gains always
increase criminal activity, while increases in costs always decrease
criminal activity. In addition, either increases in the probability of
failure or increases in the amount of uncertainty surrounding returns
will assuredly decrease the resources being allocated to criminal activity.
Third, although the return and loss functions of Model I are quite general,
it must be kept in mind that these functions contain only monetary gains
and losses and hence the model will be strictly applicable only when all
returns and all costs from engaging in the illegal activity are monetary
in nature. This implies that there are no non-monetary consequences of
the penalty if a failure occurs and also that the activity in question
does not entail a significant "labor" input, which would introduce elements of a time allocation problem.

One interesting application of this model has been to the problem of
optimal under-reporting of income to the tax authorities. In this case
the labor input tends to be insignificant and the psychic costs associ-

---

[7]In addition to risk aversion, (7') requires the penalty function to
be separable in the sense of footnote 6.

ated with conviction for tax fraud may, in many groups, be relatively
small. As we noted above, this is the problem treated in the Allingham
and Sandmo, Kolm and Singh papers. But, if we are to have a broadly
applicable theory, non-monetary characteristics of illegal activity must
be accounted for.[8]

Model II – Portfolio Models of Time Allocation

The models presented in this section address in a particular manner,
the question of the determinants of the allocation of time between legal
and illegal activity. As we noted at the outset, the term "portfolio
model" is used in this paper to denote that class of models in which all
returns and costs are monetary. So "a portfolio model of time allocation"
is a non-sequitor to the extent that "work," be it legal or illegal, is

---

[8]If the agent prefers risk and the symmetric hypothesis of increasing
risk preference is adopted, $-\partial R/\partial W > 0$, it can be shown (see Appendix)
that

$$(3'') \quad \frac{\partial x^o}{\partial W^o} > 0 \qquad (4'') \quad \frac{\partial x^o}{\partial \alpha} > 0 \qquad (6'') \quad \frac{\partial x^o}{\partial p} < 0$$

as before; and that

$$(7'') \quad \frac{\partial x^o}{\partial \gamma} > 0$$

whenever the penalty function is separable. In fact, under the conditions
of model I, $\partial x^o/\partial \gamma > 0$ iff $U'' > 0$ and $\partial x^o/\partial \gamma < 0$ iff $U'' < 0$. It is interesting to observe that whether the agent is risk averse or risk preferring,
increases in wealth result in an increased portion of that wealth being
devoted to illegal activity. Increased payoffs also result in increased
allocations to illegal endeavors independent of the agent's behavior toward
risk. In addition, increases in the probability of failure results in
decreased illegal allocations independent of risk behavior. The only
result which does not carry over from the risk aversion case is the
response of x^o to changes in the penalty, $\partial x^o/\partial \beta$. The reason is obvious:
Positive shifts in the penalty function decrease mean returns and increase
the dispersion of returns; on the one hand making the agent worse off, and
on the other hand better off. It is not possible to determine the net
effect.

disagreeable, i.e., involves psychic costs. This fact helps explain why
authors who have utilized models of this sort (see Becker (1968), Ehrlich
(1970, 1973) and Sjoquist (1973)), have justified their approach by including in the gain and loss functions of their models both monetary returns
and the "monetary or wealth equivalent" of any psychic gains or losses. It
is shown below that implicit in the models of these authors are rather
strong restrictions on the functional form of the monetary equivalents of
effort and penalties and hence on the preferences of offenders. We first
digress to explore the formal structure of monetary equivalence and then
establish the precise nature of these restrictions. A generalized version
of the Becker-Ehrlich-Sjoquist models is then presented.

A Digression on Monetary Equivalences

Two points are of interest here: (1) Questions concerning the existence of monetary equivalents of the psychic costs of the effort and
penalty attributes of an offense; and (2) questions concerning the form of
"total" (monetary plus psychic) return and "total" cost functions, assuming
the appropriate monetary equivalents exist. The first question has been
discussed in some detail in Block and Heineke (1975a) and in Block and Lind
(1975). For our purposes here it will suffice to merely sketch the
monetary equivalent argument in enough detail to indicate that it is not
generally true that monetary equivalents exist to labor and penalty attributes of an offense.

To begin, it should be noted that there is agreement in the literature
that models of the offense decision must in general account for non-
monetary costs in both the time allocation and penalty aspects of the
decision. In other words, there is agreement that the underlying

von Neumann-Morgenstern utility function is of the form $Z(t_1,t_2,S,W)$ where t_1 and t_2 represent the time allocated to legal and illegal activity, respectively, and S represents a vector of attributes of the penalty (the length of sentence, loss of reputation, and so on).

To proceed, consider an individual with income W, who allocates t_1 "hours" to legal activity, t_2 "hours" to illegal activity and suffers penalty S if unsuccessful. For the individual in question, a monetary equivalent to this effort allocation and penalty exists if and only if there exists an income level sufficiently low, say W*, so that the individual is indifferent between this income with no penalty and no "work" and the given effort allocation, income and penalty. Formally, if there exists an income level, W*, such that

(8) $Z(t_1,t_2,S,W) = Z(0,0,0,W*)$

then $W - W*$ is the monetary equivalent of t_1 "hours" of legal activity, t_2 "hours" of illegal activity, and a penalty of severity S. Clearly, existence of such an equivalence will depend upon the tastes and preferences of the particular offender and there is no reason to expect it to exist in general. If, for example, for a particular effort allocation and penalty the marginal rate of substitution between income and either t_1 or t_2 or S is infinite, then no monetary equivalent exists at that point. Or one could ask whether for any given effort allocation there exists a reduction in income to say $\hat{W}$ such that the agent is indifferent between $(t_1,t_2,0,\hat{W})$ and (t_1,t_2,S,W). If so, $W - \hat{W}$ is the monetary equivalent of the penalty S. Of course this depends upon the given effort allocation, the severity of the penalty and the agent's income. If the penalty is sufficiently severe and/or the discounted value of the agent's lifetime income is sufficiently low, a monetary equivalent to the penalty will not exist. If $\bar{W}$ represents discounted lifetime earnings, then no monetary equivalent to the penalty S exists whenever $W - \hat{W} > \bar{W}$. As the discussion and examples indicate, monetary equivalents to psychic costs may not exist.

From equality (8), if an income level W* exists such that $Z(t_1,t_2,S,W) = Z(0,0,0,W*)$ then $W - W*$ is the monetary equivalent of the "state of the world" (t_1,t_2,S,W) and is a function of t_1, t_2, S and W. Designating this function as $C(\cdot)$, we may write $W* \equiv W - C(t_1,t_2,S,W)$. Defining $Z(0,0,0,W*) \equiv V(W*)$, we have $V(W*) \equiv V(W - C(t_1,t_2,S,W))$ which is the formal justification for collapsing all arguments of the multi-attri-bute utility function $Z(\cdot)$ into one attribute. To summarize, the monetary equivalent approach to modeling the offense decision implies that "return" and "cost" functions into which both monetary and non-monetary returns have been aggregated (via monetary equivalents) will be functions of t_1, t_2, S and W. That is, the function $W - W* \equiv C(\cdot)$ is in general a function of each argument entering the utility function $Z(\cdot)$.

To draw out the implications of this discussion for modeling the criminal choice we define the following functions:

$G(t_2;\alpha)$: the monetary return resulting from t_2 "hours" of illegal activity; $G_2 > 0$, $G_\alpha > 0$ and $G_{2\alpha} > 0$.

$F(t_2;\beta)$: the monetary penalty resulting from t_2 "hours" of illegal activity, if the individual is apprehended and convicted; $F_2 > 0$, $F_\beta > 0$ and $F_{2\beta} > 0$.

$L(t_1;\delta)$: the monetary return resulting from t_1 "hours" of legal activity; $L_1 > 0$, $L_\delta > 0$ and $L_{1\delta} > 0$.

W_s: $W^0 + L(t_1;\delta) + G(t_2;\delta)$

W_u: $W_s - F(t_2;\beta)$

where the symbols α, β and δ represent shift parameters in the respective

functions.[9] It is also helpful to "disaggregate" $C(t_1,t_2,S,W)$ into the

functions $c^1(t_1,t_2,S,W)$, $c^2(t_1,t_2,S,W)$ and $c^3(t_1,t_2,S,W)$, the monetary

equivalents of the psychic costs of legal activity, illegal activity and

the penalty, respectively; and to define $\bar{L}(t_1,t_2,S,W) \equiv L(t_1;\delta) - c^1(\cdot)$,

$\bar{G}(t_1,t_2,S,W) \equiv G(t_2;\alpha) - c^2(\cdot)$ and $\bar{F}(t_1,t_2,S,W) \equiv F(t_2;\beta) + c^3(\cdot)$ as the

as the "total" return functions for legal and illegal activity and the

"total" cost of the penalty, respectively. These are "total" return and

cost functions in the sense that the monetary equivalents of the psychic

costs of "labor" have been netted out of $L(\cdot)$ and $G(\cdot)$ and the monetary

equivalent of psychic costs of the penalty has been added to the monetary

penalty, $F(\cdot)$. Once this has been accomplished the problem

(9) $\max\limits_{t_1,t_2} = \{(1 - p)Z(t_1,t_2,0,W_s) + pZ(t_1,t_2,S,W_u)\}$

is equivalent to the problem[10]

(10) $\max\limits_{t_1,t_2} = \{(1 - p)V(W^o + \bar{L} + \bar{G}) + pV(W^o + \bar{L} + \bar{G} - \bar{F})\}$

---

[9]We should indicate here that the "failure state," W_u, might be characterized either as $\{W^o + L + G - F;p\}$ or as $\{W^o + L - F;p\}$, depending upon
the disposition of G when the individual is captured. A more general failure state can be obtained by defining the random variable Y, $0 \leq y \leq 1$,
with distribution function $K(y)$, to be the portion of G the offender
manages to retain if captured. Then W_u becomes $\{W^o + L + YG - F;p\}$, which
reduces to the above special cases when $y \equiv 1$ and when $y \equiv 0$. See Heineke
(1975) for more detail.

[10]See Block and Heineke (1974, 1975a) for more detail.

Portfolio Models of Time Allocation - Continued

In this section two models are analyzed. Both are special cases of the model given as (10) above and are essentially generalized versions of the models presented by Becker, Ehrlich and Sjoquist. The first case of interest occurs when the monetary equivalent of legal activity is restricted to depend only upon t_1 and the monetary equivalents of illegal activity and the penalty are restricted to depend only upon t_2. Formally, this means that the functions $c^1(\cdot)$, $c^2(\cdot)$ and $c^3(\cdot)$ above reduce to $c^1(t_1)$, $c^2(t_2)$ and $c^3(t_2)$ and hence "total" return and "total" cost functions are $\bar{L}(t_1;\delta)$, $\bar{G}(t_2;\alpha)$ and $\bar{F}(t_2;\beta)$.[11] This will be the case when, for example, the monetary equivalent of t_2 "hours" of illegal activity is independent of (i) the amount of time the agent spends in legal activity, (ii) the attributes of the penalty, S, and (iii) the wealth position of the agent.

Under these conditions the problem is to maximize $(1 - p) V(W_s) + pV(W_u)$ with respect to t_1 and t_2, subject to the constraint $t_1 + t_2 \leq \bar{t}$.[12] Necessary conditions for an internal maximum are

(11)
$$(1 - p)V'(W_s)\bar{L}_1 + pV'(W_u)\bar{L}_1 = 0$$
$$(1 - p)V'(W_s)\bar{G}_2 + pV'(W_u)(\bar{G}_2 - \bar{F}_2) = 0$$

The first equation in (11) provides a hint as to the consequences of the specialized monetary equivalents. In particular, notice that this equation holds only if $\bar{L}_1 = 0$. Therefore if $c^1(\cdot)$ depends only upon t_1 and $c^2(\cdot)$ and $c^3(\cdot)$ depend only upon t_2, the individual's time allocation to legal

___

[11]More precisely, $\bar{L}(t_1;\delta) \equiv L(t_1;\delta) - c^1(t_1)$, $\bar{G}(t_2;\alpha) \equiv G(t_2;\alpha) - c^2(t_2)$, $\bar{F}(t_2;\beta) \equiv F(t_2;\beta) - c^3(t_2)$.

[12]And of course $t_i \geq 0$, $i = 1,2$.

activities will be independent of his wealth and independent of all attributes of the penalty. It is also clear from this equation that the uncertainty surrounding returns to illegal activities has absolutely no effect
on the time allocated to legal endeavors. So no matter what the agent's
wealth may be, no matter how high returns to illegal endeavors, how low is
the penalty or how unlikely is apprehension, model II always yields the
same allocation of time to legal activity. Since these properties of model
II are of a global nature in that, as long as $0 < t_1^o < \bar{t}$, t_1^o remains
unchanged whatever the values of p, W^o, $\bar{G}(\cdot)$ and $\bar{F}(\cdot)$, it follows that the
analagous marginal effects are zero. These results plus other comparative
static properties of the model are presented next. The symbol J_2^o is used
to represent the determinant of the Jacobian associated with system (11)
evaluated at (t_1^o, t_2^o), the equilibrium allocation. The elements of J_2^o
are denoted D_{ij}, i,j = 1,2.

(12) $\partial t_1^o / \partial p = 0$

(12') $\partial t_2^o / \partial p = D_{11}(V'(W_s)\bar{G}_2 - V'(W_u)(\bar{G}_2 - \bar{F}_2))/J_2^o$

(12") $\partial t_2^o / \partial p < 0$

Changes in the probability of apprehension have no effect on the time
allocated to legal activity, while increases in this parameter will deter
participation in illegal activities.

(13) $\partial t_1^o / \partial W^o = 0$

(13') $\partial t_2^o / \partial W^o = -D_{11}((1-p)V''(W_s)\bar{G}_2 + pV''(W_u)(\bar{G}_2 - \bar{F}_2))/J_2^o$

(13") $\partial t_2^o / \partial W^o > 0$

Whether the individual is risk averse, risk neutral or prefers risk, exogenous changes in wealth will have no effect on the time allocated to legal activities. On the other hand, if the individual is risk averse and displays decreasing absolute risk aversion or prefers risk and displays increasing absolute risk preference, $(-\partial R/\partial W > 0)$, participation rates in illegal activities will increase with wealth levels.

(14) $\partial t_1^o/\partial \alpha = 0$

(14') $\partial t_2^o/\partial \alpha = -D_{11}(\partial EV/\partial W^o)G_{2\alpha}/J_2^o + \bar{G}_2(\partial t_2^o/\partial W^o)$

(14") $\partial t_2^o/\partial \alpha > 0$

Changes in the returns to illegal endeavors have no effect on labor force participation rates, although decreasing absolute risk aversion implies the participation rate in illegal endeavors will increase with increases in returns.

(15) $\partial t_1^o/\partial \beta = 0$

(15') $\partial t_2^o/\partial \beta = pD_{11}(V'(W_u)\bar{F}_{2\beta} + \bar{F}_\beta V''(W_u)(\bar{G}_2 - \bar{F}_2))/J_2^o$

(15") $\partial t_2^o/\partial \beta < 0$

Increasing the severity of the penalty for unsuccessful illegal acts will not affect the t_1 decision, but will deter criminal activity. It should be kept in mind here, that the penalty function $\bar{F}(t_2;\beta)$ measures only the level of monetary costs plus those non-monetary costs that depend upon t_2 alone. All other attributes of the punishment, S, are treated as parameters in $F(\cdot)$.

(16) $\partial t_1^o/\partial \gamma = 0$

(16') $\partial t_2^o / \partial \gamma = \partial t_2^o / \partial \beta - (\partial t_2^o / \partial p)(p \bar{F}_\beta / \bar{F})$ [13]

(16'') $\partial t_2^o / \partial \gamma \gtrless 0$ iff $U''(W) \gtrless 0$ [14]

Mean preserving increases in the dispersion of returns to illegal activity will have no affect on the t_1 decision. But if the penalty function is separable, such changes decrease, leave unchanged or increase participation in illegitimate activities if and only if the agent is risk averse, risk neutral or prefers risk, respectively.

(17) $\partial t_1^o / \partial \delta = -D_{22}(\partial EV / \partial W^o) \bar{L}_{1\delta} / J_2^o$

(17') $\partial t_1^o / \partial \delta > 0$

(18) $\partial t_2^o / \partial \delta = \bar{L}_\delta (\partial t_2^o / \partial W^o)$

(18') $\partial t_2^o / \partial \delta > 0$ [15]

Finally, increases in the returns to legal activity increase participation rates in both legal and illegal activity. Legal and illegal activities are gross complements!

To be sure we are not accustomed to finding so many unambiguous qualitative results in the models of economic choice theory. These results stem from the independence of the markets for legal and illegal activities which is implied by the special nature of the monetary equivalences we have used. Of course system (11) is not a system of simultaneous

---

[13]See equation (7) above.

[14]This follows if $\bar{F}(\cdot)$ is separable in the sense of footnote 6 above.

[15]The proofs of these propositions are entirely analogous to those presented for model I once one notes that $\bar{L}_1 = 0$ implies $D_{12} = D_{21} = 0$.

equations, but rather a recursive system in which legal activity decisions

are made and then, given t_1^o, the allocation to illegal activities is

determined. Comparision of (12"), (13"), (14"), (15") and (16") with

inequalities (3')-(7') above indicates that this specification of monetary

equivalence functions has the effect of reducing the time allocation

model given as (10) (or (9)), to an analog of the simple portfolio model.[16]

The question remains as to whether or not it is useful to restrict

the preferences of offenders to such an extent. Only confronting the model

with data can provide the answer. And unlike many of the models of

economic theory, the large number of unambiguous predictions yielded by

model II afford an excellent opportunity for empirical testing. This is

particularly true due to the rather unorthodox predictions that the time

spent in legal opportunities is independent of the structure of returns

to illegal activity and that legal and illegal activity are gross comple-

ments. These results alone provide a strong basis for testing the model.

It is of interest to note that if $\bar{L}_1 < 0$ then $t_1^o = 0$ and again (as

with the "internal" solution) the allocation to legal activities is

invariant to the changes in returns and costs in the market for illegal

activity. So the model predicts that there is no diminution in returns

to illegal activity nor increase in the uncertainty of returns that will

cause "professional criminals" ($t_1^o = 0$) to enter legal occupations. Again,

this is a testable implication of model II. Clearly, the same conclusion

follows if $\bar{L}_1 > 0$. In this case $t_1^o + t_2^o = \bar{t}$ and no time is allocated to

leisure. Moreover, as long as the second equation in (11) holds, all of

---

[16]Notice that the present model does not collapse into an exact
counterpart of the portfolio model represented in equations (1)-(7) above,
since in that model $\partial x^o/\partial \varepsilon > 0$ iff $\partial(1 - x^o)/\partial \varepsilon < 0$, where ε is an arbitrary parameter. Here the signed response of illegal activity to a para-
meter change does not imply the opposite response for legal activity.

the individual's time is allocated to legal endeavors, i.e., $t_1^o = \bar{t}$.[17]

We stated above that the model we have just analyzed is a general version of the Becker, Ehrlich and Sjoquist models.[18] Yet both Ehrlich and Sjoquist report that legal and illegal activities are substitutes in their models, which is clearly inconsistent with model II in its present form.[19] The explanation lies in one additional assumption that was adopted by these authors, viz., that the time allocated to leisure is fixed and independent of the level of returns and costs in the markets for legal and illegal activities. In this case equations (11) above reduce to

$$(19) \qquad (1 - p)V'(W_s)(-\bar{L}_1 + \bar{G}_2) + pV'(W_u)(-\bar{L}_1 + \bar{G}_2 - \bar{F}_2) = 0$$

which will have an internal solution for $\bar{G}_2 > \bar{L}_1$ and $\bar{F}_2 > \bar{G}_2 - \bar{L}_1$. Then

$$(20) \qquad \partial t_2^o/\partial p = ((V'(W_s)(-\bar{L}_1 + \bar{G}_2) - V'(W_u)(-\bar{L}_1 + \bar{G}_2 - \bar{F}_2))/J_3^o$$

$$(20') \qquad \partial t_2^o/\partial p < 0$$

$$(21) \qquad \partial t_2^o/\partial W^o = -(pV''(W_u)(-\bar{L}_1 + \bar{G}_2 - \bar{F}_2) + (1 - p)V''(W_s)(-\bar{L}_1 + \bar{G}_2))/J_3^o$$

---

[17] Although $\bar{L}_1 > 0$ implies no time is allocated to leisure, if the second expression in (12) is strictly positive, other solutions for t_1 and t_2 are possible.

[18] In Ehrlich (1973), $c^1 \equiv W_\ell(t_1)$, $c^2 \equiv W_i(t_2)$, $c^3 \equiv F_i(t_2)$; in Sjoquist (1973) $c^1 \equiv \bar{g}_w t_1$, $c^2 \equiv \bar{g}_c t_2$, $c^3 \equiv \bar{p} t_2$ and in Becker (1968), $c^1 + c^2 = Y_j$, and $c^3 \equiv f_j$. There is a problem in analyzing Becker's model since it is only partially specified and contains no explicit decision variable. The implicit decision variable seems to be the number of offenses, O_j, since Becker states that his approach implies existence of a function relating O_j to the probability of conviction and the punishment among other things (see p. 177). Writing $O_j(t_2)$ transforms the model into the time allocation framework. The Becker model does not include legal alternatives and hence monetary equivalents will be functions of only t_2, S and W.

[19] The Becker model deals only with the market for illegal activities.

(21') $\partial t_2^o / \partial W^o > 0$

(22) $\partial t_2^o / \partial \alpha = -\bar{G}_{2\alpha} (\partial EV / \partial W^o) / J_3^o + \bar{G}_\alpha (\partial t_2^o / \partial W^o)$

(22') $\partial t_2^o / \partial \alpha > 0$

(23) $\partial t_2^o / \partial \beta = p(V''(W_u) F_\beta (-\bar{L}_1 + \bar{G}_2 - \bar{F}_2) + V'(W_u) \bar{F}_{2\beta}) / J_3^o$

(23') $\partial t_2^o / \partial \beta < 0$

and as before

(24) $\partial t_2^o / \partial \gamma \gtrless 0$ iff $V'' \gtrless 0$

where J_3^o is the determinant of the Jacobian associated with equation (19) evaluated at equilibrium.[20]   Comparison of these expressions to equations (12'), (13'), (14'), (15') and (16'') above indicates that fixing the allocation to leisure leaves the predictive consequences of model II unchanged with respect to illegal behavior. Clearly, this will not be the case for the participation rate in legal endeavors. Since if ϵ is an arbitrary parameter, then $\partial t_1^o / \partial \epsilon = -\partial t_2^o / \partial \epsilon$. Therefore

(25) $\partial t_1^o / \partial p > 0$

(26) $\partial t_1^o / \partial W^o < 0$

(27) $\partial t_1^o / \partial \alpha < 0$

(28) $\partial t_1^o / \partial \beta > 0$

(29) $\partial t_1^o / \partial \gamma \gtrless 0$ iff $V'' \lessgtr 0$

---

[20]Again, the proofs of these propositions are virtually identical to those above. Inequality (24) requires $\bar{F}$ be separable as before.

Finally note that

(30) $\partial t_1^o/\partial\delta = -\bar{L}_{1\delta}(\partial EV/\partial w^o)/J_3^o - \bar{L}_\delta(\partial t_1^o/\partial w^o)$

(30') $\partial t_1^o/\partial\delta > 0$

and therefore

(31) $\partial t_2^o/\partial\delta < 0$

Once the leisure margin is fixed, legal and illegal activities become gross substitutes and the model collapses into the simple portfolio model of equations (1)-(7) above.

To summarize the results appearing in this section, notice that if t_3 denotes the time allocated to leisure and θ is any parameter which affects only the distribution of returns and costs to illegal activity, then $\partial t_2^o/\partial\theta = -\partial t_3^o/\partial\theta$ whenever t_3 in free to vary. (Contrast the pairs (12), (12")-(16),(16") with the pair (17'),(18').) Once the leisure margin is fixed, then $\partial t_2^o/\partial\varepsilon = -\partial t_1^o/\partial\varepsilon$, where ε is any parameter in the model.[21] (Contrast expressions (20')-(23') with expressions (25)-(28) and (30') with (31).) So these models are not time allocation models in any usual sense of the word. But the more important question is whether either model describes criminal behavior. Since each model provides a number of unambiguous predictions, testing should be relatively straightforward. For example, one could begin by attempting to discriminate between the fixed and variable leisure margin versions of the model. To test the fixed leisure margin assumption one could test whether $\partial t_1/\partial\varepsilon + \partial t_2/\partial\varepsilon = 0$,

---

[21]The condition $\partial t_2^o/\partial\varepsilon = \partial(\bar{t} - t_1^o)/\partial\varepsilon$ is precisely analogous to $\partial x^o/\partial\varepsilon = \partial(1 - x^o)/\partial\varepsilon$ in the simple portfolio model.

where ε represents any of the parameters entering the model.[22] If this assumption is rejected, one could then proceed to test the twelve restrictions given as (12),(12")-(16),(16") and (17') and (18') above. As we noted previously, special interest lies in testing the independence restrictions, inequalities (12)-(16), and the gross complementarity of legal and illegal activity, (18'), since these properties of model II are associated with a much smaller class of models than are the remaining properties. If both versions of the model are rejected, one has evidence that the preference restrictions utilized in model II are inappropriate. A more general model should be considered.

Model III - The Allocation of Time to Illegal Activity: The Case of Bernoulli Consequences

In this section we present a model which fully accounts for nonmonetary aspects of both the time allocation problem and the penalty. As the title of the section indicates, the model is concerned (as have been the other models in this paper) with the special case where the consequences of illegal activity are Bernoulli distributed. Using the notation developed above, $Z(t_1,t_2,S,W)$ represents the agent's utility indicator with S being a vector of attributes of the penalty. For interpretive convenience we assume here that S is a scalar, the length of the sentence if convicted. It is

---

[22] Notice that this means the rate of substitution between t_1 and t_2 will always be constant and equal to unity. Or alternatively if t_1 and t_2 are interpreted as the time spent by an individual in each of two occupations and $n_{i\varepsilon} \equiv (\partial t_i/\partial\varepsilon)(\varepsilon/t_i)$, $i = 1,2$, then the fixed leisure margin version of model II predicts that $t_1^o/t_2^o = -n_{2\varepsilon}/n_{1\varepsilon}$, where ε is any parameter in the model. In words, the relative sensitivity of the time allocation to occupation two to changes in any parameter is given by the observed proportion of time allocated to the other occupation, t_1^o/t_2^o.

natural to specify $S = S^o + S^1(t_2;\sigma)$, $S^1(0;\sigma) \equiv 0$ and $S_2 > 0.$[23] The term S^o is a constant and represents the minimal prision sentence for the class of activities in question. Analogous to above, we define $S_\sigma > 0$ and $S_{2\sigma} > 0$. The individual's problem is then to

$$(9) \quad \max_{t_1, t_2} \{(1 - p)Z(t_1, t_2, 0, W_s) + pZ(t_1, t_2, S, W_u)\}$$

subject to the condition $t_1 + t_2 + t_3 = \bar{t}$; where $W_s = L(t_1;\delta) + G(t_2;\alpha)$ and $W_u = W_s - F(t_2;\beta)$. Recall that the functions L, G and F contain only monetary aspects of the return to legal and illegal activity and monetary aspects of the penalty, respectively, since here non-monetary aspects of the offense decision enter $Z(\cdot)$ directly.

First order conditions for an internal maximum are

$$(32) \quad \begin{array}{l} (1 - p)(Z_1^s + Z_W^s L_1) + p(Z_1^u + Z_W^u L_1) = 0 \\ \\ (1 - p)(Z_2^s + Z_W^s G_2) + p(Z_2^u + Z_S^u S_2 + Z_W^u(G_2 - F_2)) = 0 \end{array}$$

where $Z^s \equiv Z(t_1, t_2, 0, W_s)$, $Z^u \equiv Z(t_1, t_2, S, W_u)$, $Z_1^s \equiv \partial Z^s/\partial t_1$, etc. It is of considerable interest to calculate the effects on the time allocation to criminal activity of changes in the various parameters and to contrast these with the analogous calculations in models I and II. Straightforward but tedious computations reveal

$$(33) \quad \frac{\partial t_2}{\partial W^o} = \frac{H_{21}\{(1-p)(Z_{1W}^s + Z_{WW}^s L_1) + p(Z_{1W}^u + Z_{WW}^u L_1)\} - H_{11}\{(1-p)(Z_{2W}^s + Z_{WW}^s G_2) +}{J_4^o}$$

$$\frac{p(Z_{2W}^u + Z_{SW}^u S_2 + Z_{WW}^u(G_2 - F_2))\}}{J_4^o}$$

---

[23]Of course it is possible that $S^1(0;\sigma) > 0$, since people do occasionally receive prison sentences for crimes they do not commit.

$$(34) \quad \frac{\partial t_2}{\partial \alpha} = \frac{-H_{11}G_{2\alpha}(\partial EZ/\partial W^o)}{J_4^o} + G_\alpha(\partial t_2/\partial W^o)$$

$$(35) \quad \frac{\partial t_2}{\partial \beta} = \frac{pH_{11}Z_W^u F_{2\beta}}{J_4^o} + \frac{F_\beta\{pH_{11}(Z_{2W}^u S_2 + Z_{WW}^u(G_2 - F_2)) - (1-p)H_{21}(Z_{1W}^u + Z_{WW}^u L_1)\}}{J_4^o}$$

$$(36) \quad \frac{\partial t_2}{\partial p} = \frac{H_{11}(Z_2^s + Z_W^s G_2 - Z_2^u - Z_S^u S_2 + Z_W^u(G_2 - F_2)) + H_{21}(-Z_1^s - Z_W^s L_1 + Z_1^u + Z_W^u L_1)}{J_4^o}$$

$$(37) \quad \frac{\partial t_2}{\partial \delta} = \frac{H_{21}L_{1\delta}(\partial EZ/\partial W^o)}{J_4^o} + L_\delta(\partial t_2/\partial W^o)$$

And finally the effect on the time spent in criminal activity due to changes in the severity of punishment (as measured by the length of the sentence) is given by

$$(38) \quad \frac{\partial t_2}{\partial \sigma} = \frac{-pH_{11}Z_S^u S_{2\sigma}}{J_4^o} + S_\sigma(\partial t_2/\partial S^o)$$

In expressions (33)-(38), $H = EZ$ and J_4^o is the determinant of the Jacobian associated with (32) evaluated at equilibrium. As would be expected, it is not possible to establish the sign of any one of these comparative static derivatives unless one is willing to make much stronger assumptions about the preferences of offenders.

The response of illegal activity to increases in illegal remuneration, $\partial t_2/\partial \alpha$, and legal remuneration, $\partial t_2/\partial \delta$, are composed of stochastic counterparts to neoclassical substitution and income effects. (See Block and Heineke (1973, 1975b).) Even if one is willing to assume that illegal endeavors are inferior activities, it is not possible to sign these terms,

although as usual the direct substitution effect is signed. It is also
interesting to note that the response of criminal activity to changes in
sentence length, $\partial t_2/\partial\sigma$, may be written as in (38) as the sum of two
components: the first measures the response of t_2 to a compensated change
in σ, and is always negative; the latter measures the response of t_2 to a
change in the minimal sentence.

The reader will recall that in both models I and II it was shown that
if the penalty function was separable, increases in the dispersion of
returns to illegal endeavors led to decreases in such activity if and only
if the agent was risk averse and vice versa; i.e., $\partial t_2/\partial\gamma \lessgtr 0$ iff $U'' \lessgtr 0$
in those models. It can be shown that in model III sign[U''] is neither
necessary nor sufficient for determining the allocative effects of changes
in the dispersion of returns.

In other words, if the utility function is left unrestricted vis a
vis specialized assumptions about monetary equivalents, then no conclusions
may be drawn concerning behavior toward risk by observing sign[$\partial t_2/\partial\gamma$].
This point is of interest due to the fact that sign[$\partial t_2/\partial\gamma$] is equivalent
to determination of the responsiveness of offenses due to simultaneous and
offsetting changes in the probability of conviction and in the severity of
punishment. (See the discussion following inequality (7') above.) Therefore Becker's contention that the "common generalization" that a change in
the probability of conviction has a greater effect on the number of
offenses than a change in punishment implies offenders are, on average,
risk takers, is not forthcoming in a more general time allocation model
in which non-monetary aspects the offense decision are left unrestricted.
In fact this "common generalization" is consistent with $U_{WW} \gtrless 0$.

Model IV - The Allocation of Time to Illegal Activity: Generalizations and Problems

Each of the models investigated in this paper have the common attribute that there are but two consequences in the decision problem confronting the offender. At first blush this seems to be an eminently reasonable characterization of the problem. But is it? If the decision problem is viewed as a general time allocation problem, then Bernoulli consequences imply the individual will either succeed on _every_ offense undertaken or fail on _every_ offense undertaken—a hopelessly unrealistic state of affairs.

One suggestion for salvaging the time allocation model was given in Block and Heineke (1975a) and amounts to replacing the Bernoulli density with a more general density function. Then, letting λ be a continuous random variable defined on $[0,1]$ with distribution function $K(\lambda)$, the choice problem posed as model II becomes[24]

$$(39) \quad \max_{t_1, t_2} \{ \int_0^1 Z(t_1, t_2, S, W^0 + L + G - \lambda F) \, dK\lambda \,) \}$$

subject to $S = S^0 + S^1$ and $t_1 + t_2 + t_3 = \bar{t}$. In (39) it is possible for the offender to "fail" on any portion of the total number of offenses committed. Although such a formulation does incorporate "partial success," a ubiquitous feature of the real world, several generalizations are badly needed. First, in model (39) only monetary aspects of the penalty are stochastic. It is clear that in any realistic model of criminal behavior, gains and penalties must be more generally stochastic. But even in such a

---

[24]If λ can assume but two values, say zero and one, and $dK(\lambda)/d\lambda \equiv k(\lambda)$, then $k(1) = p$, $k(0) = 1 - p$ and the function $k(\cdot)$ reduces to the Bernoulli density.

model, a second and more difficult problem remains if prison sentences are
a possible penalty--a problem not usually addressed in labor supply models:
The individual may be apprehended and hence be unable to supply the planned
number of offenses.[25] This predicament arises not from an anomaly unique
to models of criminal choice, but instead is an intrinsic shortcoming of
static models that could be remedied by modeling the decision problem as a
dynamic process in which realized consequences in period t are used to up-
date the model and become the basis for decisions in period t + 1.

Other than a dynamic programming model, an additional possibility for
circumventing the complications introduced by prison sentences is to view
the individual's decision problem as either (i) that of choosing whether
or not to commit any one offense or (ii) that of choosing the time allocation to any one offense. In the first instance the decision variable is
discrete, assuming the values zero and one, while in the latter, $0 \leq t_2 \leq \bar{t}$
as before. The distinction between these approaches is more than merely
pedantic, since the qualitative implications of the two models differ
substantially. If potential offenders view their decision problem as one
of determining the amount of time to allocate to an offense on an offense
by offense basis, then model III, expression (9), is appropriate and no
qualitative implications are forthcoming without imposing strong restrictions on the preferences of offenders.[26] On the other hand, if the decision

---

[25] This is not to say that involuntary exit from the labor market does
not occur in markets for legal skills, e.g., when the individual becomes
too ill to work, but instead that it is an insignificant aspect of the
total problem in these markets.

[26] If this interpretation is adopted, it would be desirable to treat
p as a function of t_2 with $p'(t_2) < 0$. Since for most individuals it seems
likely that the more time spent planning any given offense, the smaller
will be the likelihood of failure.

problem is viewed as a special case of the time allocation problem in which

the potential offender decides to either commit an offense or not on an

offense by offense basis, then strong qualitative implications are forth-

coming.[27] In any event, the discussion points up the fact that further

progress in modeling criminal behavior requires more effort be allocated to

understanding the structure of the underlying decision process and less to

the generation of ad hoc models.

Summary and Conclusions

The purpose of this paper was to provide some perspective on the

problem of modeling the decision problem of a potential offender. The

eight years which have passed since the appearance of Becker's pathbreaking

paper have seen several generalizations of Becker's framework. The papers

of Allingham and Sandmo, Kolm, and Singh have viewed the offense decision

as essentially a portfolio decision. We saw that this specification leads

to a number of testable implications. The papers of Ehrlich and Sjoquist

have adopted Becker's notion of the monetary or wealth equivalent of the

psychic costs of an offense, and if such equivalences exist, there is no

formal objection to this procedure. But if monetary equivalent functions

are generally specified, there seems to be no conceivable advantage to be

gained by the procedure. Next we found that the models of Becker, Ehrlich

and Sjoquist rested upon rather strong, implicit assumptions about the

functional form of monetary equivalences and hence about the nature of the

---

[27]This decision process is a time allocation problem in the sense
that the decision to commit an offense is a decision to allocate a fixed
amount of time to illegal activity. If an offense takes t_2^* "hours," then,
under this interpretation either $t_2^o = 0$ or $t_2^o = t_2^*$, in contrast,
to the models investigated in this paper in which $t_2^o \in [0, \bar{t}]$.

underlying utility function. In effect the assumptions used in these
models transform the offense decision problem into a simple portfolio
problem. This model provides the theoretical underpinnings for the qualitatively unambiguous theories of deterrence which have been reported in
the literature. These results were reported above as model II and a
special case of model II in which the time allocated to leisure is fixed.
Both of these models support the traditional hypothesis concerning the
deterrent effects of changes in the "gains" and "costs" of crime. Not
so traditional results forthcoming from models II include the normality
of illegal activities in each model; the independence of legal labor
market decisions from all parameter shifts in illegal markets and the
complementarity of legal and illegal activity, when the leisure margin
is free to vary; and if the allocation to leisure is fixed, the prediction that changes in labor force participation rates, due to any paramater
shift, will be identical in magnitude but of opposite sign, to changes in
the amount of time allocated to illegal activity.

In the final section we discussed several problems which persist once
psychic costs have been more generally accounted for. For one thing a
time allocation model with Bernoulli distributed consequences implies the
offender either succeeds or fails on every offense undertaken. More
general distributions of consequences eliminate this difficulty. One
fundamental problem remained: It may not be possible for the agent to
carry out his plans if prison sentences constitute punishments. Several
approaches to solving this problem were suggested.

University of Santa Clara

References

Allingham, M. G., and Sandmo, A. "Income Tax Evasion: A Theoretical Analysis," Journal of Public Economics, November, 1972.

Becker, G. "Crime and Punishment: An Economic Approach," Journal of Political Economy, March/April, 1968.

Block, M. K., and Heineke, J. M. "The Allocation of Effort Under Uncertainty: The Case of Risk Averse Behavior," Journal of Political Economy, March/April, 1973.

Block, M. K., and Heineke, J. M. "Multiattributed Preferences and Wealth Equivalents: The Case of Illegitimate Activity," Working Paper No. 16, Graduate School of Business, University of Santa Clara, 1974.

Block, M. K., and Heineke, J. M. "A Labor Theoretic Analysis of the Criminal Choice," American Economic Review, June, 1975.

Block, M. K., and Heineke, J. M. "Factor Allocations Under Uncertainty: An Extension," Southern Economic Journal, 1975.

Block, M. K., and Lind, R. "An Economic Analysis of Crimes Punishable by Imprisonment," Journal of Legal Studies, June, 1975.

Ehrlich, I. "Participation in Illegitimate Activities: A Theoretical Analysis," unpublished Ph.D. dissertation, University of Chicago, 1970.

Ehrlich, I. "Participation in Illegitimate Activities: A Theoretical and Empirical Investigation," Journal of Political Economy, May/June, 1973.

Heineke, J. M. "A Note on Modeling the Criminal Choice Problem," Journal of Economic Theory, February, 1975.

Kolm, S. Ch. "A Note on Optimum Tax Evasion," Journal of Public Economics, July, 1973.

Singh, B. "Making Honesty the Best Policy," Journal of Public Economics, July, 1973.

Sjoquist, D. L. "Property Crime and Economic Behavior: Some Empirical Results," American Economic Review, June, 1973.

Appendix

Model I

By equation (3)

$$(A-1) \quad \partial x^o/\partial W^o = -((1-p)(U''(W_s)g_x + pU''(W_u)(g_x - f_x))/J_1^o$$

$$= (R(W_s)(1-p)U'(W_s)g_x + R(W_u)pU'(W_u)(g_x - f_x))/J_1^o$$

$$= (R(W_s)A + R(W_u)B)/J_1^o$$

where $R(W_s) = -U''(W_s)/U'(W_s)$, etc. Now $A > 0$, $B < 0$ and $A = -B$ by the first order condition for an internal maximum. Since decreasing absolute rish aversion implies $R(W_u) > R(W_s)$ the numerator of (A-1) is negative and $\partial x^o/\partial W^o > 0$. It follows immediately that $\partial x^o/\partial \alpha > 0$. Also, since $(g_x - f_x) < 0$ by the first order conditions, risk aversion alone implies $\partial x^o/\partial \beta < 0$.

To show $\partial x^o/\partial p < 0$ rewrite the first order condition as $U'(W_s)g_x = p(U'(W_s)g_x - U'(W_u)(g_x - f_x))$ and compare with the numerator of equation (6).

Finally, from equation (7) we have

$$(A-2) \quad \partial x^o/\partial \gamma = \partial x^o/\partial \beta - (\partial x^o/\partial p)(pf_\beta/f)$$

Substituting for $\partial x^o/\partial \beta$ and $\partial x^o/\partial p$ and rearranging yields

$$(A-3) \quad \frac{\partial x^o}{\partial \gamma} = \{p(g_x - f_x)U''(W_u)f_\beta - pf_\beta g_x(U'(W_s) - U'(W_u))/f$$

$$+ pU'(W_u)(f_{x\beta}f - f_\beta f_x)/f\}/J_1^o$$

$$= \{pf_\beta(g_x - f_x)U''(W_u) - g_x(U'(W_s) - U'(W_u))/f\}/J_1^o$$

if $f(x;\beta) = f_1(x)f_2(\beta)$. The numerator of this expression is negative iff

$U'' > 0$ and positive iff $U'' < 0$. Therefore if the penalty function is

separable, $\partial x^o/\partial\gamma \gtrless 0$ iff $U'' \gtrless 0$.

Procedures precisely analogous to those used thus far, will verify

the results reported in footnote 6, for the case when $U'' > 0$ and $-\partial R/\partial W > 0$.

Economic Models of Criminal Behavior,
J.M. Heineke (ed.)
© *North-Holland Publishing Company, 1978*

CHAPTER TWO

ECONOMETRIC MODELS OF CRIMINAL BEHAVIOR: A REVIEW

John B. Taylor

Although published studies on the econometric approach to criminal

behavior began to appear only 5 years ago, the field has expanded at such

a rapid rate that, at least in quantitative terms it already appears to have

taken a place beside such old stalwarts of applied econometrics as production

and investment behavior. Most of these recent studies[1] represent a method-

ological advance over earlier empirical research on criminal behavior, in

that they use formal multivariate and multiple equation econometric estimation

techniques to isolate the deterrent effects and to sort out the two-way inter-

action between criminal behavior and the criminal justice system. Whether

this methodological advance has improved our practical knowledge of the

determinants of crime is as yet an open question, however, for a number of

critics[2] have questioned the econometric methodology and the findings of

these studies.

This paper reviews these recent developments in the econometrics of

criminal behavior. Its intention is to outline a consensus of empirical

results which have emerged from the new methodology, and to evaluate their

statistical reliability from the viewpoint of policy analysis and future

empirical work. While the review considers a number of general methodological

questions, its emphasis is on empirical findings. Rather than summarizing

all empirical work in the area, it focuses on several papers which are representative of different types of data and statistical technique.

Section I reviews the theory of criminal behavior which has served as
a framework for much of the empirical work in this field. Section II considers cross-sectional studies which have used aggregate data from different
geographical areas. Section III then examines a number of econometric issues
specific to these models. Finally Section IV discusses the special empirical
problems which have arisen in attempts to measure the deterrent effect of
capital punishment.

I. Theoretical Background

Becker's (1968) utilitarian model of criminal behavior, along with a
number of modifications and extensions[3] has served as the microfoundation"
for most of the econometric work on aggregative crime models. While the
utilitarian appraoch to criminal behavior can be traced back at least to
Bentham, the economic models introduced by Becker improve on earlier work
by making explicit and emphasizing the inherent uncertainty associated with
decisions to engage in criminal activity. Applying the expected utility
approach to criminal decision making, Becker is able to derive a number of
empirically testable propositions about criminal behavior.

To take the simplest case, suppose that criminals maximize the expected
value of a utility function which depends on the net income derived from
criminal activity across two uncertain states: getting caught or getting
away with the crime. If Y is income (monetary as well as psychic) and F
is the penalty if caught, then the value of the utility function U--an increasing function of net income--will be U(Y-F) if the criminal gets caught
and U(Y) if not. If p is the likelihood of getting caught as perceived by
the criminal, then 1-p is the likelihood of getting away, and the expected

utility of engaging in criminal activity is simply

(1) $EU = (1-p) \, U(Y) + pU(Y-F)$.

If this expected utility is high enough relative to the expected utility
from legal pursuits, then it is assumed that criminal behavior will be
undertaken;[4] consequently, any change which increase EU will raise crime
rates.

A number of the propositions implied by this formal analysis are
intuitive--the skeptic might say obvious. For example, equation (1) shows
that increasing the likelihood (p) and/or severity (F) of punishment will
lower the expected utility of criminal activity and hence, according to the
theory, lower crime rates.[5] While an empirical analysis based on such a
theory must consequently incorporate and test for this derived deterrent
effect, even the most theory-deprived elementary empirical study would
entertain the possibility that punishment has an effect on crime. But the
utilitarian model also leads in more substantive directions, and these have
played an important role in guiding the recent empirical work. There are at
least three such directions which are important for the empirical work discussed below.

First, a distinguishing characteristic of the utilitarian approach is
the supposition that criminal behavior can be described in much the same way
as conventional economic behavior, without particular reference to psychological theories. The hypothesis is that criminals act as if they are res-
ponding rationally to incentives and deterrents presented by their socioeconomic environment, including the criminal justice system. According to
this theory, an empirical model of criminal behavior can be specified simply

by obtaining suitable empirical counterparts for the relevant socioeconomic
and deterrent variables--income distribution, age, urbanization, arrest rates,
length of imprisonment, etc. The intermediate and frequently unobservable
psychological process, which describes how these environmental inputs affect
criminal behavior, can be by-passed, enabling one to specify the form of the
empirical model directly. The statistical implication is that regression and
simultaneous equation techniques, based on observable socioeconomic variables,
can be used rather than statistical methods common to psychometrics, such as
factor analysis, which emphasize unobservables. The recent proliferation of
econometric methods in the area of criminal behavior, therefore is not a
coincidence, but is a consequence of the micro-theoretic foundation used.
This is not to say, of course, that econometric techniques are necessarily
the preferred method. If there were doubt about the ability of utilitarian
models to describe criminal behavior, and thereby place restrictions on the
empirical specification, factor analytic methods--which tend to be more agnostic
or symmetric in their use of restrictions--would be the preferred methodology.
Indeed, some recent researchers in one of the traditional fields of economic
analysis--business cycles--have questioned the conventional use of a priori
restrictions and have experimented with factor analytic techniques as an
alternative to the standard econometric methodology.[6]

A second important emphasis of the economic theory of crime, is the
two-way interaction between criminals and the criminal justice system. Equation
(1) is only part of the story. Criminals are not the only expected utility
maximizers; society, in its operation of the criminal justice system, also
maximizes utility by weighing the costs of operating the system against the
costs to society of criminal behavior. The implication of this part of the
theory is that the criminal justice system will respond to changes in criminal

activity by adjusting expenditures on police, courts, or prisons. As a
result, arrest rates, conviction rates, and severity of punishment will tend
to depend on crime rates. Moreover, because the justice system itself is
composed of utility maximizing individuals, there may be an interrelation between arrest rates, conviction rates and severity of punishment; for example,
conviction rates will depend on severity of punishment if anticipation of
potential sentences influences the verdicts of juries. Viewed in conjunction
with the behavior of criminals, therefore, the models suggest that crime and
punishment are jointly determined. Neither can be said to depend on the other,
but together they depend on other variables which are exogenous to both.

This joint determination of the two sides of the law has fairly clear
statistical implications. Care must be taken to insure that the equation of
interest--say the crime rate equation--is _identified_ by the a priori restrictions
of the theory. In particular, the theory must insure that some exogenous
factors influence the criminal justice system, but do not influence crime.
Otherwise we could not hope to disentangle the effect of changes in the criminal
justice system on crime, from the effect of changes in crime rates on the criminal justice system. And given that the equation is identified _simultaneous_
estimation techniques which, at the least, generate consistent parameter estimates should be used rather than inconsistent regression methods such as ordinary least squares.

Finally, among the propositions of the microtheory which have had an
important role in the empirical work is a prediction about the relative magnitude of the effect of certainty versus severity of punishment in deterring
crime. A certain punishment has long been thought by criminal justice experts
to deter criminals more effectively than a severe punishment. Becker's expected utility analysis interprets this conventional wisdom in terms of the potential

criminal's taste for risk. If criminals are not risk averse then, according to the theory, a proportional increase in the severity of punishment cannot be more effective in deterring a criminal act than a proportional increase
in the likelihood of punishment. This result has stimulated empirical research
ers to test for the relative effects of the two deterrents, and consequently
almost all empirical studies have included measures of certainty and severity.
Moreover, these studies have used a functional form--linear in the logarithms--
suitable for comparing proportional impacts (elasticities). As will be discussed later such a specification has had substantive effects on the empirical
findings and, although the proposition has been questioned, it is worth considering its derivation here.

   Using the notation introduced earlier, the statement that the likelihood
of punishment is proportionally more effective than severity can be represented in terms of derivatives as

$$(2) \quad \left| \frac{d(EU)}{U} \middle/ \frac{dp}{p} \right| > \left| \frac{d(EU)}{U} \middle/ \frac{dF}{F} \right| .$$

The left hand side of this inequality is $[U(Y-F) - U(Y)]$ p/U and the right
hand side is pU' (Y-F) F/U, as can be seen by differentiating equation (1).
Hence, inequality (2) will hold if

$$(3) \quad [U(Y) - U(Y-F)]/F > U'(Y-F).$$

But this is simply the condition that the utility function be convex, or
equivalently that the potential criminal prefers risk. Risk preference
therefore implies that certainty of punishment is more effective than
severity in lowering crime rates.

To summarize the discussion of this section, the microtheoretic frame-work appears to have had three important influences on the empirical work on crime: (1) it has enabled empirical researchers to place observable socio-economic and deterrent measures directly into crime rate equations with restrictions on the parameters, and thereby avoid statistical models developed for unobservable variables; (2) it has underlined the need for simultaneous equations methods in order to control for the effect of crime on the criminal justice system, and (3) through its emphasis on relative effectiveness of certainty and severity, it has motivated functional forms which include measures of both deterrents and which are linear in the logarithms.

Assuming that summing data on individual criminal behavior into geo-graphic crime rates causes no aggregation problems, the microtheory therefore suggests that aggregative statistical models of crime should have the following form:[7]

(4) $c = f_1(p,s,x,e_1)$

(5) $p = f_2(c,s,x,e_2)$

(6) $s = f_3(p,c,x,e_3)$

where c,p, and s are the crime rate, perceived probability of punishment, and severity of punishment, respectively, in a geographic area during a given time period. The vector x consists of all relevant explanatory variables, and the e_i are the random disturbances in the model. In principle the theory generates restrictions on which variables enter the functions f_1, f_2, f_3 in order that some or all three equations can be identified. For reasons mentioned above, the functions are usually specified in log-linear form. The following three sections consider various approaches to estimating one or more of the equations in such a model.

II. Studies Based on Aggregative Cross-Section Data

This section reviews six representative empirical studies which have attempted to estimate crime rate relationships of the form of equation (4) using aggregative cross-section data. As can be seen from the summary in Table 1, the papers reviewed represent a fairly wide geographic range of data: states and cities in the U.S., provinces in Canada, police districts in the U.K., counties in California, and police precincts in New York City. The degree of aggregation varies substantially across the different studies. Some examine only the total felony crime rate, while others disaggregate by type of crime. Almost all of the studies utilize some type of simultaneous equation technique (usually two stage least squares), but report ordinary least squares estimates as well.

A. Ehrlich's study of states in the U.S.

Ehrlich (1973) reports crime rate equations in the form of equation (4) based on aggregative state data for three census years 1940, 1950, 1960. The dependent variable in his analysis is the number of reported crimes (C) of a particular type divided by the population of the state (N) in the same year. Seven different types of crime are examined: murder, rape, assault, robbery, burglary, larceny and auto theft. Two deterrent variables are included in the structural equations for each category of crime: the number of imprisonments (I) divided by the number of reported crimes (C), and the average time (T) served by offenders in state prison for that type of crime. In addition, three socioeconomic variables, which do not vary by type of crime, are included in the most frequently reported equations. The median income of families in the

TABLE 1

Summary of Crime Rate Equations based on Cross-Section Data[1]

Authors	Data	Time Period[2]	Level of Crime Aggregation	Deterrent Variables	Estimation Method[3]
Avio and Clark	Provinces in Canada	1970, 71, 72	Robbery, Burglary, Theft, Fraud	Arrest Rate,[4] Conviction Rate, Length of Prison Term	TSLS OLS
Carr-Hill and Stern	Police districts in England and Wales	1961, 62	Felonies	Arrest Rate[4]	FIML
Ehrlich	States in U.S.	1940, 50 60	Murder, Assault, Rape, Robbery, Burglary, Larceny, Auto Theft	Imprisonment, Length of Prison Term	TSLS OLS
Mathieson and Passell	Police precincts in New York City	1970	Murder, Robbery	Arrest Rate[4]	TSLS OLS
Phillips and Votey	Counties in California	1966	Felonies	Conviction Rate Prison-Probation Rate	TSLS OLS
Sjoquist	Cities in U.S.	1963	Aggregate of all Burglaries, Robberies and Larcenies over $50	Arrest Rate,[4] Conviction Rate, Length of Prison Term	OLS

1. These studies are discussed in Section II of the paper.
2. The Avio and Clark study is based entirely on data pooled over the three time periods; the other studies consider separate regressions for each time period.
3. In some of the studies the OLS estimates are based on transformed data, thereby approximating some type of weighted least squares.
4. Arrest rate refers to the reported clearance rate.

state (W), the percent of families below ½ of the median income (X), and
the percent of nonwhite in the population (NW).

The theoretical models of crime suggest that, holding other effects
constant, the two deterrent variables should have a negative effect on crime,
while the three socioeconomic variables should have a positive effect. The
income variables W and X are measures of the relative gain to criminal activity:
in richer states (higher W), potential criminals can expect more loot and in
states with a more skewed income distribution (higher X), that loot will look
relatively more attractive to a larger fraction of the population. Ehrlich
includes the variable NW for similar reasons: legitimate employment opportunities for the nonwhite population may be deficient.

Other explanatory variables are also considered in Ehrlich's analysis,
but his basic empirical results focus on these five. All his results are based
on a log-linear functional form specification which leads to the following
statistical crime rate equation:

$$(7) \quad \ln\left(\frac{C}{N}\right) = b_o + b_1 \ \ln\left(\frac{I}{C}\right) + b_2 \ln T + b_3 \ln W + b_4 \ln X + b_5 \ln NW + e.$$

Equation (7) was fitted over most of the states for all crime categories in
1960, and for a more limited selection in 1940 and 1950.

The results for the deterrent variables are reported in Table 2 and are
in fairly close accord with the forecasts of the theoretical model. In particular b_1 and b_2 are generally negative while b_3, b_4 and b_5 are generally positive and significant. The economic variables X and W tend to have greater
effects on crime against property than on crimes against persons, as one would
expect. In addition, the deterrent variables appear to be more effective in
reducing crimes against persons than against property. Moreover, for all

disaggregated crimes except burglary and sometimes larceny the impact of a more certain punishment (I/C) tends to have a greater impact on crime than a more severe punishment (T)--a finding which is in agreement with the views of most criminal experts, as well as with the theoretical model if potential criminals prefer risk. However, as Ehrlich points outs, the average length of prison term may significantly overstate the expected severity of punishment for a prospective criminal with a high discount rate. If so, the estimated impact of severity on crime rates would be understated. Note also that the differential impact is not evident for the aggregate equation.

The qualitative nature of these results does not appear to depend on the statistical estimation technique. In the 1960 cross section, both ordinary least squares (OLS) and two stage least squares (TSLS) estimation[8] techniques are reported. The direction of impact and statistical significance is generally the same for both estimation techniques. The quantitative effect is quite different, however, with the simultaneous estimation approach (TSLS) yielding estimated elasticities for the deterrent variables which are about twice as large as with OLS. The implicit simultaneous equation model which calls for techniques like TSLS is similar to equations (4) and (5) of Section I. The crime rate (C/N) and the estimated likelihood of punishment (I/C) are assumed to be simultaneously determined for reasons already mentioned. The severity of punishment, however, is not assumed to be jointly determined with the other variables, and consequently an equation like (6) is not considered.

The predetermined variables which are assumed to be excluded from the crime rate equation but not from the probability of punishment equation, and which consequently can be used for identification and for construction of the TSLS estimates are: population, an unemployment variable, the percent of the population of age 14 to 24, the percent of the

population living in SMSA's, the ratio of males to females, average education,
per capita expenditure on police, and dummy variable for southern states. In
addition to these exogenous variable, the crime rate in 1959 was assumed to
be a predetermined variable for estimation of the 1960 cross section. There
does not appear to be much rationale assuming that these variables do not
directly affect crime rates, but do directly affect the criminal justice system. In fact, the classification between included and excluded exogenous
variables differs from other work of Ehrlich[9] and from that of others. Moreover, the use of a one period lag of a dependent variable as a predetermined
variable in a cross-section study is questionable when one expects serial
correlation to be significant relative to the cross-section variation. These
problems have led to criticism of Ehrlich's use of simultaneous equation
methodology;[10] if variables assumed to be excluded from the equation are not
actually excluded then the equation might not be identified and the TSLS
estimate would be meaningless. This issue is discussed in more detail in
Section III.

The OLS and TSLS estimated elasticities for the two deterrent variables
are shown in Table 2 for the various crime types in the 1960 cross section.
For all crimes the estimated elasticity is about $-\frac{1}{2}$ when OLS is used and about
-1 when TSLS is used. If the criminal justice system reacts to higher crime
rates by increasing the likelihood of punishment, then the higher elasticity
for TSLS is in accord with expectations. The simultaneous procedure isolates
the negative deterrent effect from the positive criminal justice effect, and
consequently is able to uncover a larger deterrent effect. This effect of
TSLS is evident for all types of crime.

For analysis of the other cross-section studies it is important to
mention a statistical difficulty which is evident in equation (7). The

Table 2

Estimated Impact of Deterrents on Crime[1]

	TSLS		OLS	
Ehrlich(U.S. - states)[2]	Certainty	Severity	Certainty	Severity
Murder	-.852	-.087*	-.341	-.140*
Rape	-.896	-.399	-.578	-.188*
Assault	-.724	-.979	-.275	-.180*
Robbery	-1.303	-.372*	-.853	-.223*
Burglary	-.724	-1.127	-.534	-.900
Larceny	-.371	-.602*	-.133	-.263
Auto Theft	-.407	-.246*	-.247	-.174*
All Crimes	-.991	-1.123	-.526	-.585
Sjoquist (U.S. - cities)[3]				
Robbery, Burglary				
and Larceny over $50			-.354	-.292
Carr-Hill and Stern (UK)[4]				
All Offences	-.66	-.28		
Avio and Clark (Canada)[5]	Arrest/Conv.		Arrest/Conv.	
Robbery	-.83/-2.8	.04	-.76/-2.9	.48
Break and Enter	-1.52/.67*	.08*	-1.3/.16*	.21
Fraud	-.71/-.59*	-.01*	1.71/-.14*	-.03
Theft B	-.79/-1.6	.24	-.67/-1.7	.08
Theft A	-.74/-1.8	-.50*	-.67/-1.9	.04
Phillips and Votey (Calif.)[6]				
Felonies	-.61	-.34	-.62	-.35
Mathieson and Passell(NYC)[7]				
Murder	-1.96		-.74	
Robbery	-2.95		-1.06	

1. Numbers refer to the estimated coefficient of the logarithm of variables representing certainty and severity of punishment in an equation for logarithm of the crime rate. Certainty is generally measured by arrests, convictions or imprisonment per crime. Sjoquists' study indicates that these measures give similar results (see Table 1, equation (1) and (2) of that study). Severity is measured by the average time served in prison. The numbers marked with an asterisk represent variables with t-ratio less than 2.

2. Ehrlich (1973), Tables 2,3,4, and 5.
3. Sjoquist (1973), Table 1, Equation 2.
4. Carr-Hill and Stern (1973), p. 303; the reported estimates are based on FIML.

5. Avio and Clark (1976), Tables 7 and D1. Reported results give the coefficient of the arrest rate and the conviction rate (given arrest) in the same equation. Both are reported here.

6. Phillips and Votey (1975), Table 1.

7. Mathieson and Passell (1976), Table 2 and 3. This study does not include a severity measure. Hence the estimated elasticity of the arrest rate is likely to be biased upward in absolute value.

number of crimes C in equation (7) is a variable which is generally measured
with considerable error. This problem, which plagues all crime studies and
which is acknowledged by researchers and critics alike, may tend to cause a
negative spurious correlation between C/N and I/C. In principle it is impossible to distinguish this spurious correlation from the deterrent effects
without additional information. Hence, the estimated elasticities in equation
(7) may overstate the true deterrent effect. The TSLS estimates do not circumvent this pitfall, unless the measurement error is eliminated in the reduced
form estimates. Since Ehrlich's reduced form (first stage) contains $(C/N)_{-1}$
on the right hand side of the (I/C) equation, the measurement error would
appear to persist in the TSLS estimates. In order to make practical use of
the estimated elasticities it is necessary, therefore, to assess the quantitative significance of this measurement error. Note that the other deterrent variable in Ehrlich's equation - average time in prison - does not have
the same type of measurement error.[11] This problem is discussed in more
detail in Section III.

B. Sjoquist's study of cities and towns in the U.S.

Sjoquist reports crime rate equations of the form of equation (4) for a
1968 cross section of 53 municipalities in the U.S. with 1960 populations
between 25,000 and 200,000. In order to avoid spillover problems caused by
the tendency for criminals to shift their activity to neighboring cities
when their own law enforcement agencies crack down, only relatively isolated
cities were examined. Municipalities with large neighboring municipalities
were excluded from the sample.

Only one dependent variable was examined: the number of reported robberies
burglaries, and larcenies over \$50 divided by the population. The deterrent

variables included a severity variable - average prison sentence served -
and three alternative variables representing the likelihood of punishment -
arrests per crime, convictions per crime, and convictions per arrest. The
third probability measure is a conditional likelihood and would therefore
be expected to have a smaller effect on crime. The six socioeconomic variables
are population, population density, retail sales, income, education, and the
percent of the population which is nonwhite. A log-linear functional form
was chosen for estimation. Hence, with the exception of the education variable the specification is very similar to that reported by Ehrlich. Note that
Ehrlich excluded education from the crime equation for identification.

Sjoquist only reports OLS estimates for his model and these are reported
for the deterrent variable in Table 2. The results are in agreement with the
theory, with both deterrent variables having a negative effect. The estimated
elasticity of the conviction rate is about -1/3 and is somewhat less than the
average of Ehrlich's estimates, but is not appreciably different, considering
that the focus is cities and towns rather than states. The elasticity of
severity is slightly less than Ehrlich's OLS estimates.

The likelihood of punishment variable reported in Table 2 is the number
of convictions per crime; similar results are reported for arrests per crime,
but the convictions per arrest variable in insignificant. As Sjoquist points
out, this may be due to the absence of the spurious correlation problem for
this variable. The variable may also have less impact because it represents
a probability conditional on an uncertain event (arrest). Alternatively,
multicollinearity may be a problem.

C. Carr-Hill and Stern's study of police districts in the U.K.

Of the studies reviewed here, this is the only one which specifies and estimates a complete model using full information simultaneous equation techniques. Carr-Hill and Stern's data set pertains to urban and rural police districts in 1961 and 1966 in England and Wales. Their statistical tests suggest a significant structural break in the model between these two years, consequently the two samples are considered separately in the main analysis. Focusing on the 1961 results for urban areas, the crime rate, defined as the total number of reported offenses per capita (y) is assumed to depend on two other endogenous variables: the arrest rate (p) and the number of police per capita (c). In addition, two exogenous variables are assumed to influence crime: the proportion (a) of the population between 15 and 24, the value of real estate (t), and the severity of punishment (f). The latter is measured by the proportion of convicted criminals given custodial treatment.[12]   No attempt is made to explain the severity of punishment within the context of the model, so that equation (6) of Section I is implicitly assumed to depend only on the exogenous variables.

The model is completed by specifying equations for the arrest rate and the number of police. In their 1961 model Carr-Hill and Stern assume that the arrest rate equation included police expenditures per capita, total population (n), the working class proportion of the population (s), the proportion of violent crimes (v), and the age variable (a). Finally, the number of police per capita (c) is assumed to depend on the arrest rate (p), the middle class fraction of the population (m), and the proportion of violent offenses (v). The specification for 1966 is similar but includes additional explanatory variables. (The notation corresponds to that of Carr-Hill and Stern, not to Section I above).

As with other research on crimes, all equations are specified in log-linear form. Using the above notation to represent the log of the variables, leads to the following model representation:

(8) $y = \alpha_1 p + \alpha_2 f + \alpha_3 a + \alpha_4 t + \alpha_0 + u_1$

(9) $p = \beta_1 c + \beta_2 a + \beta_3 s + \beta_4 n + \beta_5 v + \beta_0 + u_2$

(10) $c = \gamma_1 p + \gamma_2 m + \gamma_3 v + \gamma_0 + u_3$

The parameters of the above model were estimated using the Full Information Maximum Likelihood (FIML) technique, which gives more efficient estimations than two stage least squares because it incorporates the interaction between the equations. This efficiency advantage, of course, requires that all the equations are specified correctly. If not, then the estimates may not perform as well as two stage least squares or even ordinary least squares. The use of a full information method has an important practical advantage in any case, however, even if one is interested only in the crime rate equation. Such estimates require the investigators to state explicitly the equations which contain variables excluded from the crime rate equation. Hence, the identifiability conditions on the first equation can be evaluated more reliably.

The estimated values of the deterrent variables which result from the FIML techniques are reported in Table 2. The differential between the arrest rate elasticity and the severity elasticity is considerably greater than the estimated values reported by Ehrlich and Sjoquist, but this may be due to the different measures of severity used. Again, the sign of the differential indicates risk preference. The deterrent elasticity of the arrest rate is -2/3, which is between the TSLS estimate of Ehrlich and OLS estimates of Sojquist

and Ehrlich. The estimated deterrent effect of severity is less than that
of the other researchers, but is negative and significant. The "swag" variable t, has a positive effect as does the income variable used in the U.S.
studies. Despite some differences, however, these results are generally
consistent with the results for the U. S. and appear to lend further support
for the theoretical model.

Perhaps the most provocative finding of Carr-Hill and Stern is that the
number of police per capita has significantly negative effect on arrest rates
$(\beta_1 < 0)$. If the arrest rate is viewed as the output of the crime prevention
production function, then this finding would seem to imply negative returns
to additional law enforcement personnel. While negative returns are plausible
over some range of production, it is difficult to believe that police districts
would operate at such a point. Carr-Hill and Stern offer two intriguing explanations for this disturbing finding: first, they argue that with more
police around, more crimes will tend to be reported that are hard to solve
(presumably these would be minor crimes which the police would have less
interest in solving as well); second, a larger police force will have a
large deterrent effect on crimes that are easier to solve, thereby raising
the number of crimes with inherently low arrest rates. The combination of
these two effects is to alter the crime mix by increasing the proportion of
crimes which are hard to solve relative to those that are easier to solve.
Hence, if the magnitudes of the effects are large enough, the number of police
will be negatively related to the arrest rate.

In outlining the policy implications of their empirical model, Carr-Hill
and Stern focus on the reduced form coefficients, which is the correct approach
from a simultaneous equation standpoint. The fact that the arrest rate is
negatively correlated with the crime rate in a simultaneous equation model

offers no immediate policy implications. These two variables are jointly
determined and endogenous; according to the model, therefore, one can only
affect the behavior of arrest rates by altering some exogenous variable.
Moreover, if one is interested in the crime rate, then it is the relationship between the crime rate and the exogenous variables that is important.
The relationships are all captured by the reduced form. Very few of the
studies reviewed here utilize the reduced form for policy, despite the
fact that the exogenous variables used in the first stage of a complete
two stage least squares estimation may be sufficient for estimating an
unrestricted reduced form.

D. Avio and Clark's study of provinces of Canada.

One of the most striking geographic characteristics of crime statistics
in Canada, is the extremely high crime rates in the Yukon and Northwest
Territories compared to the rest of the country. For example in 1966, the
total crime rate in the territories was about 10 times greater than the
average crime rate in the provinces. Such variation would appear to be
invaluable in estimating the determinants of crime. Unfortunately, the
study by Avio and Clark is unable to utilize these extreme variations because of insufficient data on socioeconomic variables. Moreover, the province
with the second highest crime rate--Alberta--must also be eliminated from
the sample. This data loss is especially unfortunate in this study because
of the relatively small number of provinces in Canada. The basic model of
Avio and Clark is estimated with a sample of only 8 cross-sectional observations
corresponding to 8 provinces. Although they do pool this data for three years
1971, 1972, and 1973, the effective information is still small unless there
were unusual fluctuations in crime during those three years. Moreover, pool-

ing the cross-section data over three time periods potentially introduces
serial correlation problems which cannot be adequately handled with such a
small sample.

Despite these data problems Avio and Clark are able to obtain estimates
of a crime rate equation for Canada which are similar to those reported above
for the U.S. and the U.K. The basic equation is estimated in log-linear form
for 5 different types of crime: robbery, break and enter, fraud, and two
types of theft. Included in the equation are the ratio of arrest to crime
(the clearance rate), the ratio of conviction to arrests, the average length
of sentence, the percentage of families with incomes less that ½ of the median
income (the same variable used by Ehrlich for income distribution effects),
and the number of households with record players. The last variable represents
the "victim stock" or the gains from criminal activity. The inclusion of two
different deterrent ratios (the arrest rate and conviction rate) was first
attempted by Sjoquist in the paper discussed above, and has since been used
by other authors.

The estimated deterrent effects are reported in Table 2, and are generally
negative and significant with the important exception of the length of sentence
which is usually insignificant but sometimes perversely positive and significant
The significant differential between the coefficient on the arrest rate and the
conviction rate indicates that the usual aggregation of the two into the ratio
of convictions to crimes may be inappropriate (Sjoquist also finds a similar
differential). Not reported in Table 2 are the elasticities for the income
distribution and the wealth variable which are both positive and significant
as the theory would suggest. The elasticity of the income distribution variable
is greater than one for most crimes, which is also Ehrlich's finding for the
U.S.

The results are very similar for the TSLS and the OLS estimates. However, one must question the advantages of TSLS estimation for such a small sample size. Even with the pooled regressions (where there may be little variability across three adjacent years) there are only 24 observations.

Avio and Clark's discovery that the length of sentence has no deterrent effect and may even increase crime rates is potentially important, for they construct the variable in a way which avoids a potential spurious correlation which may exist in the other studies. The problem is that when crime rates fall and consequently the number of new prisoners also fall, there is a period shortly thereafter during which the average length of sentence for prisoners automatically increases. With the supply of new prisoners down, there are fewer replacements for the recently released short-timers, and the prison population is heavily weighted with long-timers. This raises average sentence lengths. Avio and Clark circumvent the problem by obtaining data directly on sentences handed down by the judicial system with a correction for parole and remissions. Using this alternative data they find that sentence length does not matter. Unfortunately they do not report results using the standard variable on average sentence length. Hence, it is not possible to determine whether the findings of other researchers may be due to this spurious correlation problem.

E. Phillips and Votey's study of counties in California.

The final two studies in this section focus on more limited geographic area within the U.S.—the state of California and the city of New York. Phillips and Votey develop an empirical model for felonies in California in which the crime rate equation is embedded in a model of community operation of the criminal justice system. The three equations of the model include

the crime rate, the conviction rate, and the labor cost for operating the

criminal justice system.

The model is estimated using the standard log-linear functional form

for 50 counties in California using TSLS and OLS. The estimated elasticities

for the deterrent variable appear in Table 2 and are negative and significant

with the usual differential between certainty and severity. Phillips and

Votey use a slightly different measure of severity--the proportion of con-

victed criminals sentenced to state prison, probation with jail, or simply

probation. The result is a much lower elasticity than the average length

of sentence--about the same as the Carr-Hill and Stern estimates. Neverthe-

less the severity effect is negative and significant.

F. Mathieson and Passell's study of precincts in N.Y.C.

This is the smallest geographic area considered in this review. Except

for the problem of overflow of crime from one precinct to another, N.Y.C.

with its single police force would appear to be an excellent region for the

study of criminal deterrents. Mathieson and Passell develop a three equation

crime model and obtain estimates for the crime of robbery and murder in 65

precincts in New York City in 1971. The model consists of equations for the

crime rate, the arrest rate, and the number of police assigned to a precinct.

The crime rate equation includes the arrest rate, median family income, percent

of families with income greater than $25,000, median family income of adjacent

precincts, and a dummy variable for the business districts. It should be

noted that no measure of severity of punishment is included in this model.

Indeed it would be difficult to determine whether severity of punishment is

systematically different across N.Y.C. where the court system overlaps many

precincts. The estimated deterrent effect of the arrest rate is given in
Table 2 for both the OLS and TSLS estimates of the crime equation. The estimated elasticities are negative and significant, but are substantially larger
than those obtained by the other researchers. The TSLS estimate for the
robbery equation yields an elasticity of about -3. One reason for these high
estimated impacts might be the omission of a variable to measure the severity of
punishment. Another might be the overflow problem: it is easy for criminals
to shift their activity to another precinct when the police crack down in their
usual district. This mobility would give a higher elasticity than obtained in
the other empirical work where geographical distances are greater (recall that
Sjoquist discarded cities and towns from his sample if they were adjacent in
order to avoid this problem). If this overflow problem is substantial then
one must be cautious when applying these elasticities to a region when mobility
is more restricted. For example, one would expect a much smaller reduction
in crime if arrest rates rose in all of New York City, than if they rose in a
single precinct as in the estimated equation.

    An interesting feature of the Mathieson and Passell study is the arrest
rate equation. Arrest rates are assumed to depend on police manpower per
reported crime and a measure of neighborhood stability--the percentage of
families who have lived in the same neighborhood for more than 5 years. The
neighborhood stability variable appears to have little effect, but police
manpower per crime is usually positive and very significant. This finding
seems reasonable but is at odds with that of Carr-Hill and Stern who found
a _negative_ relation between police and arrests. Is the NYC police system
that much different than that of England or Wales? Aside from the different
countries and type of data, there is an important difference between the two
studies. Mathieson and Passell divide police by reported crimes, while

Carr-Hill and Stern divide by the population of the police district. Since
the dependent variable is the ratio of arrests to reported crimes, a potential
spurious correlation problem is introduced to the Mathieson and Passell equation
which cannot exist for Carr-Hill and Stern. This spurious correlation may
be caused by measurement error in crime rates and would generate a positive
relation between arrest rates and police per crime. It is certainly possible
that such measurement error accounts for the difference between the two studies.
One might want to examine the rationale for deflating police expenditures by
crimes rather than population, and whether an alternative deflator would alter
the Mathieson and Passell results.

The Mathieson and Passell paper is alone among the papers considered here
in its application of the estimated elasticities to a cost-benefit analysis of
police expenditure increases. However tentative, the estimates such an analysis
is instructive and is a check on the plausibility of the estimated results.
The cost-benefit analysis is based on a quasi-reduced form (the arrest rate,
but not police manpower, is treated as an exogenous variable) which as argued
above is the correct approach in a simultaneous equation framework. Their
finding is that a one percent increase in police, which would cost $4.2 million
in 1971, would save New Yorkers $2.85 million. Further savings or greater
actual deterrent effects would be necessary to have the estimated benefit cover
the cost.

III. Problems of Econometric Methodology

Like most applied econometric work, a number of recurrent statistical
problems are evident in the above studies. And also like most applied econometric work, these problems have been examined closely by both critics and
proponents of the econometric approach to empirical work on crime. In this

Section, two econometric problems--measurement error and identification--
are selected for further discussion from the longer list of problems that
were only touched on in Section II. These two methodological problems have
generated considerable debate in the criminal deterrence literature.

A. The Identification Problem.

In the above discussion of Ehrlich's model I noted the lack of a formal
theory for excluding some variables from the crime rate equation--age, for
example--while including such variables in the other equation in the simultaneous model. The lack of theory is evident in most of the empirical work
reviewed above, especially when the models are compared. Some studies include
variables that other studies exclude, and visa versa. In some case this inconsistency is evident in different studies by the same author. Since the proper
exclusion of predetermined variables is crucial for identifying structural
equations, the lack of formal theory has led some critics to the conclusion that
the models of crime are not adequately identified and consequently that the
statistical results are unreliable: if the crime equation is not identified
then the resulting estimate may reflect the behavior of the criminal justice
system rather than of criminals. For example, in their examination of the
identification problem in models of crime, Franklin Fisher and Daniel Nagin
conclude that "... it appears very doubtful that work using aggregate cross-
sectional data can _ever_ succeed in identifying and consistently estimating
the deterrent effect of punishment on crime."

While one cannot deny the apparent inconsistency in the choice of zero
restrictions for identification, a reasonable argument can be made that the
crime models are identified when one takes a broader view of the identification
problem. For the sake of illustration consider a two observation sample of

crime rate (c) arrest rate (a) pairs. Suppose that one observation is taken

from a region--the Wild West of the 1880's, say--with very high crime rates

and low arrest rates, and that the other observation is taken from a region--

the Established East--with very low crime rates and high arrest rates. These

hypothetical observations are represented by the points WW and EE in Figure 1

and 2, for two alternative crime rate functions.

In Figure 1 the two observations lie on a negatively sloped crime rate

function, at the intersection of this function and two levels of the criminal

justice function. The criminal justice function has the same slope but its

level in the Wild West is much lower than in the Established East--perhaps

because of different tastes or more likely because of the high cost of law

enforcement in an area with low population density. (The slope is shown to

be positive, but the same argument would hold if it were negative.) As the

figure is drawn, the crime rate function is clearly identifiable. Moreover,

even if one could not find observable exogenous variables to explain the

different levels of the criminal justice system (tastes, for example), the

crime equation could still be identified. In fact OLS would give a fairly

accurate estimate of the deterrent effect. The important qualitative char-

acteristic of Figure 1 is that the criminal justice function is shifting much

more than the crime rate function. The difference in shifts may be entirely

due to unobservable factors and may therefore merely reflect that the variance

of the disturbance term in the criminal justice function is much greater than

the variance of the disturbance term in the crime rate function. In effect,

the crime rate function can be approximately identified by a priori restriction

on the variance-covariance matrix of the residuals of the strucural equation.[13]

The a priori assumption is that all shifts in the crime rate function occur

within a very narrow band, while shifts in the criminal justice system are

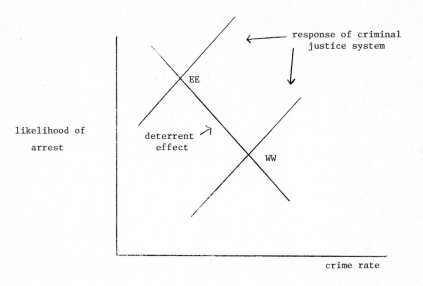

Figure 1

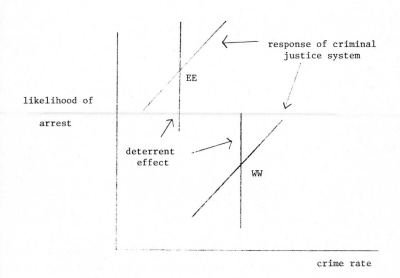

Figure 2

spread out. Drawing such bands around the lines in Figure 1 would illustrate the approximate nature of the identification.

A much different picture is represented in Figure 2, where the same two observations on arrest rates and crime rates are assumed to be caused by shifts in both the crime rate function and the arrest rate function. The crime rate function in Figure 2 has no real deterrent effect, yet an OLS estimate, or a TSLS estimate based on improperly excluded exogenous variables, would generate a negative deterrent. Those who criticize the econometrics of crime for lack of identification, are likely to have Figure 2 in mind. Note that the observations in Figure 2 could be the result of roughly equal variability of the unobservable disturbances in the crime rate function and arrest rate functions. The a priori condition on the relative variability, which could be used for approximate identification in Figure 1 cannot be used in Figure 2.

Whether one can practically identify a crime rate equation using cross-section data, therefore, seems to depend on whether a priori variance conditions of the kind illustrated in Figure 1 are plausible. However, a satisfactory answer to this question would require further research, for example, one might attempt to show that the variance of the unobservable shifts in the criminal justice system are substantially larger than the corresponding variance of the crime rate equation. In the Wild West versus Established East example, the "wide open spaces" would make law enforcement costly, and the high crime rates are likely to be due to the resulting low level of law-enforcement (the migration of illegal activity across geographical regions should be included here). The more recent high crime rates in the Yukon and Northwest Territories of Canada are likely to be the result of similar conditions. In general one might argue that human response to deterrents is more homogenous over cross-sections, than is the criminal justice system. If so, the identification problem associated with models of crime is not nearly as severe as an inspection of zero restrictions would suggest.

B. Measurement Error and Spurious Correlation

A second major econometric difficulty with models of crime is evident in all the studies reviewed above. With the dependent variable defined as the ratio of reported crimes (C) to population (N), and with the major explanatory variable defined as the ratio of arrests (A) to reported crimes, any measurement error in the number of reported crimes will generate a spurious correlation between the crime rate and the arrest rate. The problem is easiest to illustrate in the context of a crime rate equation which depends only on the arrest rate:

$$(11)\quad \ln\left(\frac{C}{N}\right) = \beta\ln\left(\frac{A}{C}\right) + u$$

where u is a random disturbance. Letting lower case letters represent the logarithms of the variables and subscripts to indicate observations, equation (11) becomes

$$(12)\quad c_i - n_i = \beta(a_i - c_i) + u_i$$

If c is measured with error ε, then the OLS estimate of β is given by

$$(13)\quad \hat{\beta} = \frac{\sum_i (a_i - c_i - \varepsilon_i)\,(c_i + \varepsilon_i - n_i)}{\sum_i (a_i - c_i - \varepsilon_i)^2}$$

which, after substitution of $c_i - n_i$ from (12) can be shown to converge stochastically to

(14) $\dfrac{\beta M - \sigma^2}{M + \sigma^2}$

where M is the average of $(a_i - c_i)^2$ in the limit, and σ^2 is the variance of ε.
(The measurement error and the disturbance term u are assumed to be uncorrelate
Except for the special case where the true values of the elasticity β is equal
to -1, (14) will not be equal to $\hat{\beta}$ when there is measurement error. Hence, $\hat{\beta}$
will not be a consistent estimator of β.

Expression (14) illustrates two things about the impact of measurement
error. First, the measurement error will create bias only if it is large
relative to the variability of the true arrest rate. Even if measurement
error is great (σ^2 is large), substantial variability in the arrest rate
(large M) will prevent the measurement error from generating faulty results.
Second, the measurement error has two types of impact; a multiplicative
effect $M/(M + \sigma^2)$ which is less than one and therefore tends to bias β
towards zero, and an additive effect $-\sigma^2/(M + \sigma^2)$ which will reduce the
estimated value of β. If the true value of β is negative (as the deterrent
theory would suggest), then these two effects work in opposite directions.
The multiplicative effect reduces the estimated elasticity in absolute value
and the additive effect raises its absolute value and the additive effect
raises its absolute value. Since the multiplicative effect is more powerful
the larger is β while the additive effect remains constant, the total effect
can generate either positive or negative effects. If $0 > \beta > -1$ the total
effect raises the estimated impact, if $\beta = -1$ the effects cancel each other
out. In sum, the measurement error drives the estimate of β towards -1.

Even in this simple case, the measurement error can cut both ways. Howeve
if the estimated elasticities are any guide, the error seems to exaggerate
the estimated deterrent effect. Only in a few cases are the estimated elasticities much greater than one, though such large estimates are the rule in the

Mathieson/Passell study. But even these results are no guarantee that the true values are greater or less than -1.

In the multiple regression model the situation is more complicated, and one cannot obtain simple conditions such as (14) to estimate the extent of inconsistency. Hence, what is generally thought to be spurious negative correlation could turn out to be spurious positive correlation. In a recent paper Forst, Filatov, and Klein performed some experiments on a multivariate murder equation (which is discussed in more detail in Section IV), and found that the spurious correlation tends to be negative in such a model. More detailed Monte Carlo experiments would be useful in order to establish whether this finding is true of the cross-section models discussed here. Without such a study it is difficult to estimate the extent of the measurement error effects.

Finally, in evaluating the relevance of such econometric problems for the reliability of the estimates in crime models, it is useful to examine their impact in other areas of applied econometrics work. A reasonable reliability criterion in the econometrics of crime is the state of the art of applied econometrics in general. With regard to measurement error, situations analogous to equation (11) arise in many econometric studies, and completely satisfactory solutions to the problem are yet to be found. Perhaps the best example is in labor economics where labor supply equations are estimated by a regression of hours of work on the wage rate. In most cases the wage rate is determined by dividing individual weekly earnings by the number of hours worked per week. The resulting regression thus takes the form:

$$(15) \qquad \ln H = \alpha + \beta \ln \left(\frac{E}{H}\right) + u$$

Clearly if there is measurement error in H this will generate a spurious
correlation which is analogous to that of equation (11). Note an important
theoretical difference, however. Microeconomic theory[14] suggests that β will
be _positive_ in equation (15) and _negative_ in equation (11). Thus, as long as
$|\beta| < 1$ the measurement error works against the economic theory of labor supply
and in favor of the economic theory of criminal behavior. It is interesting
in this regard that very few empirical researchers have been able to confirm
the economic theory of labor supply--hence the fame of the backward bending
supply curve. In contrast, very few empirical researchers have been able to
disconfirm the economic theory of criminal deterrents.

IV. Special Problems in Measuring the Deterrent Effect of Capital Punishment

The preceding review of cross-sectional empirical work on criminal behavior indicates a striking similarity of results, despite widely different
data sets. Moreover, the statistical and econometric problems evident in most
of this work do not seem to be substantially more serious in many other areas
of applied econometrics. In sum, the general statistical finding that punishment deters crime appears to be reasonably robust across geographical regions
and statistical technique. This is not to say, however, that all specific
statistical findings about particular types of crimes and punishments are
equally robust. On the contrary, a number of statistical results in this
area have been shown to be particularly sensitive to the chosen data set and
the way the data set is employed to obtain statistical estimates. An important
example concerns the deterrent effect of capital punishment. Statistical
results about the use of the death penalty have generated considerable controversy in a number of scholarly journals, and have been submitted as evidence
before the Supreme Court of the United States.[15] This Section of the paper
discusses some special problems in the econometrics of capital punishment.

A. Time Series Evidence

Ehrlich (1975) attempted to measure the deterrent effect of capital
punishment by estimating a murder rate equation for the United States--
analogous to the various crime rate equations discussed earlier--in which one
of the explanatory variables was the ratio of the number of executions for
murder to the number of convictions for murder. Two other deterrent variables--
measures of the clearance rate for murder and the conviction rate for murder--
were also included in the regression, a procedure very similar to that employed
by Sjoquist for property crimes in the U.S. Because of data limitations, however, Ehrlich was not able to include the length of prison sentence as an
explanatory variable. Five socioeconomic variables were also included in the
equation: the labor force participation rate, the fraction of the population
between 14 and 24 years of age, an estimate of real per capita income, the
unemployment rate, and a time trend. As with the studies reviewed earlier,
the equation was specified in log-linear form.

The equation is estimated using an annual time series for the U.S. from
1935-1967 and consequently involves econometric problems and techniques different from those which arose in the cross-section models described earlier. A
two-stage estimation procedure proposed by Fair (1970) was used to deal both
with the simultaneous equations problem and serial correlation of the residual,
the latter being frequently troublesome in time series work. The first stage
involves a regression of the deterrent variables (those which are assumed to
be endogenous) on current and lagged values of the predetermined variables,
lagged values of all the endogenous variables, and a number of exogenous
variables excluded from the murder equation (police and total government
expenditures per capita, and the fraction of non-whites[16] in the population).
The second stage uses an iterative technique to estimate the first order

serial correlation coefficient. Ehrlich reports several versions of this
equation most of which show significant deterrent effects for the clearance
rate and the conviction rate. But contrary to earlier[17] empirical work
Ehrlich was also able to report a significant deterrent effect from the
execution rate. The estimated coefficient of the execution rate in this
murder equation was used by Ehrlich to estimate a trade-off between execution
and lives of potential victims of the order of magnitude of 1 to 8.

Passell and Taylor (1977)[18] disputed Ehrlich's estimated trade-off on a
number of grounds. First they showed that Ehrlich's model does not remain
stable over the sample period, and thereby violates an essential assumption
for time series analysis. Observing that murder rates appear to behave
differently after the early 1960's, they tested and rejected the hypothesis
that the murder equation had the same structure from 1935 to 1962 as from
1963 to 1969. This in itself casts doubt on the estimated coefficients of
such a model. Moreover, they found that the model's structure appeared to
differ in a very important way: when estimated from 1935 to 1962, no deterrent effect of capital punishment appeared. The elasticity was -.008 and
insignificant for the earlier period as compared to -.062 and significant
for the whole sample period. And when the sample period was extended to
1964, the coefficient was still insignificant. Hence, Ehrlich's estimated
deterrent effect appears to be based soley on the observations from the
late 1960's. This dependence of the results on the last few observations is
disturbing, because one suspects that a number of factors other than the
diminished use of the death penalty may have been causing murder rates to
rise. Crime rates in general rose in the late 1960's even though the death
penalty was not a factor in the decision to commit most of these crimes.[19]

As an illustration of the importance of this general increase in crime rates, Forst, Filatov, and Klein (1977) included an index of other crime in Ehrlich's equation and found that the deterrent effect of capital punishment becomes insignificant. The magnitude and significance drops even further when an index of violent crime is added to the equation. In addition, one of the many possible explanations for this rise in crime is the increased proportion of youth in the 1960's as a result of the post World War II baby boom. While Ehrlich attempted to control for the age effect, Passell and Taylor (1977) used a narrower age group (18-24) rather than (14-24) and excluded members of the armed forces overseas. They found that the inclusion of this age variable re-duced the estimated impact of the capital punishment variable and made it statistically insignificant. Hence, the deterrent effect estimated by Ehrlich is not robust to modifications of the other independent (control) variables which were known to behave differently in the late 1960's. This calls into question his heavy reliance on these years to obtain the deterrent effect. Ehrlich has responded to this criticism by stressing the importance of using all available information: when observations from the late '60's are "thrown away" it is not surprising that the estimated variances of the estimates rise. His critics argue that these observations cannot be added to the earlier period for statistical inference if the model has changed its structure.

A second element of Passell and Taylor's criticism of Ehrlich is the dependence of his results on the log-linear specification. Though there is little a priori reason to prefer the log-linear to the linear functional form, most models of crime have been specified to be log-linear in order to interpret the coefficients as elasticities. Becker's (1986) derivation of the relative importance of severity versus certainty may be one reason for the interest in proportional effects, as mentioned above, but this does not

justify the use of this log-linear form. However, the choice of log-linear

form appears to be very important in the use of capital punishment. Passell

and Taylor have shown that if the murder equation is estimated using the

linear form, then the deterrent effect become insignificantly different from

zero, while the other variables in the equation remain significant. Forst,

Filtov and Klein have replicated this finding.

Of course, there is a wide range of possible transformations of the

dependent and independent variables which also might be considered; the

linear and log-linear represent only two possibilities. Passell and Taylor

(1977) experimented with the Box-Cox (1964) transformation of the form

$y_t = (x_t^\alpha - 1)/\alpha$ of all the variables in the murder equation. They found

that the deterrent effect was significant for some values of α and insignifi-

cant for others. They also noted that the value of α which gave the largest

correlation between the fitted and actual murder rate was .19, and that this

value resulted in a significant deterrent effect of capital punishment

(t - ratio = -3.89). Ehrlich has used this later finding as support for his

results. However, the important aspect of an examination of alternative

functional forms is to show that the statistical significance of the deterrent

effect is not robust to arbitrary changes in structure. In fact, the finding

that the value of α which gives the best fit, also gives a significant deterrent

effect is not surprising from a curve-fitting point of view. Only the execution

variable is sensitive in a substantial way to the functional form in this model.

Hence, if any value of α gives a significant effect for the execution variable,

so also will the one which gives the best fit. With the other variables in-

sensitive to the functional form, the value of α is chosen, in effect, so that

the execution variable will be significant.[20] The finding that the "best" α also gives a significant deterrent effect does not therefore invalidate a sensitivity analysis which shows how the deterrent effect is very sensitive to the value of α which is chosen.

The third point made by Passell-Taylor concerns the use of coefficients of a structural equation for policy analysis, as implicit in the trade-off calculated$^\wedge$ by Ehrlich between executions and the lives of potential victims. As was discussed in Section II of this paper, an important contribution of the economic analysis of crime is the emphasis on the joint determination of crime and punishment. The structural equations of the model represent this joint determination while the reduced form shows how each of the dependent variables are functions of the exogenous variables. The policy implication of this simultaneous determination is that the reduced form rather than the structural form should be used to calculate trade-offs. To illustrate the importance of this result in a simple example, Passell and Taylor (1976) show how the trade-off between executions and murders depends crucially on what is assumed to happen to another endogenous variable: the arrest rate. If the arrest rate is held constant then Ehrlich's 1 to 8 trade-off is obtained; but if the number of crimes cleared through arrest is held constant then the estimated coefficients imply that the trade-off reverses: more executions will increase the number of murders.

In a separate paper, Ehrlich and Gibbons (1977) have discussed this example in great detail. They argue that it is illogical to assume that arrests will be held constant, and just as illogical to use such an assumption to derive a positive trade-off between executions and murders. But the point of this simple example is not to show that more executions will cause more murders. Rather, it illustrates that policy analysis through a structural

equation is misleading: the results are highly sensitive to what happens
to other dependent variables in the model.

In sum, the time series evidence does not permit one to accept the
hypothesis that capital punishment has a significant effect on murder.
Statistical findings that the death penalty acts as a significant deterrent
are not robust to changes in functional form or period of observation; and
the reported trade-offs between executions and murders make arbitrary assumptions about the behavior of other endogenous variables in the model.

B. Cross-Section Evidence

In addition to these time series analyses of capital punishment, a
number of cross-section studies of states in the U.S. have recently attempted
to measure the deterrent effect of the death penalty using econometric techniques. The equations estimated in these studies are very similar in form
to the crime rate equations discussed in Section II, except that a measure
of the perceived likelihood of punishment by death is included in the equation.
A major advantage of the cross-sectional analysis is that a measure of the
length of prison term for murder is available and can therefore be entered
into the equation. This Section briefly reviews three of these studies--
Passell (1975), Ehrlich (1977) and Forst (1977).

Each of the studies is based on a cross-section for one or more recent
Census years: 1940 and 1950 for Ehrlich, 1950 and 1960 for Passell, and
1960 and 1970 for Forst.[21] Ehrlich's and Passell's estimates are based on
regressions for each year, while Forst's are based on regressions for the
difference between the 1970 and 1960 observations. The results from the
cross-section do not show[22] as much sensitivity to the functional form as
the time series estimates, though "statistical significance" is usually

greater with a nonlinear specification. Forst considers only the linear
form while Passell and Ehrlich consider various values of the Box-Cox
transformation discussed in the preceding section. The log-linear form is
not practical because of the large fraction of states with zero executions.

The central results of the three studies are not consistent. In particular Forst and Passell find no evidence of a deterrent effect of capital
punishment while Ehrlich does find evidence of a significant deterrent effect.
Because of a basic similarity among the econometric specifications of the
three studies, however, it is fairly easy to trace down the source of this
major discrepancy: Ehrlich includes in his full sample regressions a dummy
variable which distinguishes executing states from nonexecuting states as
well as the ratio of executions to convictions in that state. Passell also
considers this dummy for nonexecuting states, but only as an alternative to
the ratio of executions to convictions. Ehrlich's results tend to confirm
that the simultaneous inclusion of this dummy and the execution variable is
responsible for the discrepancy between the various studies, for he reports
that the deterrent effect vanishes when this dummy is excluded from the nonlinear regressions. Hence, Ehrlich's estimated deterrent effect appears to
require that both variables be in the regression.

The reasons for this requirement are intuitively clear. In the U.S. sample,
states which used the death penalty during the sample years tended to have high
murder rates, even after one controls for other deterrents and socioeconomic
factors. Hence a regression which includes either a dummy for executing states
or the ratio of executions to convictions, but not both, will be unable to uncover a negative deterrent effect. The estimated coefficient will be positive
or at least insignificantly different from zero. The only way to obtain a
strong negative effect is to place both variables in the regression. Consequently if one is to place any confidence in the estimated deterrent effect,

one must have a good theory as to why both variables should be in the model.

Ehrlich offers two possible explanations: (1) potential murderers in
nonexecuting states believe that the probability is greater than zero that
they will receive the death penalty (and greater than the probability would
be in executing states should executions suddenly drop very close to zero in
those states) and (2) certain variables are missing from the equation which
would explain the higher murder rate in executing states. It is, of course,
very difficult if not impossible to determine whether either of these possible explanations is true. Hence, the theoretical grounds for placing both
variables in the regression are not strong.

As with the time series analysis, the results from the cross section,
therefore, are inconclusive. Arguments can be made in support of including
both variables or of including only one. Hence, unlike other deterrent
variables, such as arrest rates, conviction rates, and prison terms, which
show strong effect in reducing crime, this research suggests that one cannot
reject or accept the claim that capital punishment is a deterrent.

V. Concluding Remarks

A central theme of this review is that in general the econometric problems associated with recent studies of crime are not noticeably more serious
than in other areas of applied econometrics--especially when one "seasonally
adjusts" for its relatively late development--and, moreover, that the findings
are in agreement with a priori theoretical expectations and are robust across
widely different geographical cross-sections.[23] However, this general statement
must be qualified in particular cases, especially if the results are to be
used seriously in policy analysis. The most important qualification concerns

the death penalty, where a significant deterrent effect is not usually found.

Such a conclusion does not, of course, imply that the important econometric and measurement problems in this area have been solved. Indeed much additional research is required to clarify a number of important issues before the results can be used with any confidence. To mention a few: the theoretical rationale for including or excluding variables and for using a particular functional form, the estimation of efficient trade-offs using complete models, the quality of the data and the quantitative importance of measurement error, and a reconciliation of time-series and cross-section results.

Columbia University

FOOTNOTES

1. I refer here to the group of studies which began to appear in pub-
    lished form in 1973; for example, Carr-Hill and Stern (1973), Ehrlich
    (1973) and Sjoquist (1973). Research had begun in the 1960's, however,
    as evidenced by Ehrlich's 1970 Columbia dissertation and other unpub-
    lished work. This paper is a selective review in the sense that it
    focuses on a number of studies which are representative of different
    facets of the literature; it does not provide an exhaustive summary or
    bibliography of all empirical work on criminal behavior. See Nagin
    (1977), Cook (1977) or Palmer (1977) for additional references. It
    should be noted that in selecting cross-section studies for review, I
    have chosen one paper to represent each data source examined, even
    though several papers may have analyzed the same data. For example,
    Ehrlich's (1973) study of states in the U.S. is discussed in Section II,
    while Forst's (1977) study which has somewhat different findings is not.
    Anyone interested in pursuing empirical work on a given body of data
    should, of course, consult these other studies as well.

2. See Fisher and Nagin (1976), Cook (1977), and Nagin (1977), for example.

3. See Ehrlich (1973), Block and Lind (1975) and Block and Heineke (1975).
    A similar analysis is also found in Fleisher (1966). The modifications
    and extensions of Becker's theoretical model have, in some cases, qual-
    ified his results; see especially Block and Heineke (1975). Since our
    main interest is with empirical issues, we only consider the rudimentary
    theoretical model here.

4. The analysis can formally incorporate the allocation of time to criminal
    activity. Corner solutions can then represent legal activity.

5. We are assuming here that any wealth or income effects are dominated by substitution effects.

6. See Sargent and Sims (1977).

7. Aggregation analysis does not appear to be any different than in other areas of applied econometrics and consequently is not discussed here. Note that some of the studies discussed below also consider the endo-geniety of expenditures in police.

8. Ehrlich also reports results from a modification of the TSLS estimate to take account of the correlation between different crime types. These seemingly unrelated regression (SUR) estimates are very similar to the TSLS results and are not discussed separately here.

9. Ehrlich (1975) excluded NW from the crime rate equation and uses it as an instrument for TSLS, exactly opposite to the assumption of his 1973 paper.

10. Fisher and Nagin (1976).

11. Avio and Clark argue that another type of measurement error may exist with length of sentence variables.

12. Note that there is some problem in distinguishing between severity and certainty. Ehrlich's measure of certainty is the ratio of imprisonments to crimes, which except for the denominator, is similar to the measures used by Carr-Hill and Stern for severity.

13. Fisher (1966, Chapter 3) examines the possibility of approximate identi-fication using restrictions on the variances, and establishes some general criterion for what he defines as a "nearly identified" equation. In their study of identification in crime models, Fisher and Nagin (1977) do not utilize the concept, however.

14. In both cases we are assuming that substitution effects dominate income and wealth effects.

15. The paper by Ehrlich (1975) and the critique by Passell and Taylor (1975) were submitted as evidence for Fowler vs. North Carolina in a Brief for the United States as Amicus Curiae and in a Reply Brief for the Petitione respectively.

16. Note that this treatment of the nonwhite fraction is different from Ehrlich (1973); see footnote 9 above.

17. Sellin (1959).

18. The first version of the Passell and Taylor critique appeared as a Columbia Economics Workshop Discussion Paper in February 1975. The less technical aspects of this critique are published in Passell and Taylor (1976). A revised version using alternative data was published in the American Economic Review in 1977 and is discussed here. A number of other authors have reported similar results; in particular Bowers and Pierce (1975) and Baldus and Cole (1975). See also the discussion in Forst, Filatov and Klein (1977).

19. Care must be used in determining which crimes are not influenced by the death penalty. For example, while burglary was not punishable by death during the sample period, the prospective burglar might consider the chance of a murder during the act and the chance that this would be treated as a capital offense.

20. This statement is strictly true in a simple regression with only one explanatory variable. It is approximate in a multivariate regression model if the estimated coefficients of all variables except the one of interest are insensitive to functional form.

21. Forst's cross section included only 32 states because of the lack of conviction data in 1970; Ehrlich's samples are 43 and 44 for the two years respectively, while Passell's are 47 and 44 for his two years.

22. An exception to this generalization is one of Ehrlich's regressions in 1950 where the linear form yields a very insignificant deterrent effect.

23. It should be noted that some researchers have not found significant deterrent effects. See Forst (1977), for example.

REFERENCES

Avio, K. L. and C. S. Clark (1976), "Property Crime in Canada: An Econometric Study," Ontario Council Economic Research Studies, Ontario Canada.

Baldus, D. C. and J. W. Cole, (1975),"A Comparison of the Work of Thorsten
Sellin and Isaac Ehrlich on the Deterrent Effect of Capital Punishment,"
Yale Law Journal, 85, 187.

Becker, G. S. (1986), "Crime and Punishment: An Economic Approach" Journal
of Political Economy, 78, 2 (March/April), 526-36.

Block, M. K. and J. M. Heineke (1975), "A Labor Theoretic Analysis of the
Criminal Choice," American Economic Review, 65, 3 (June), 314-325.

Block, M. K. and R. C. Lind (1975), "Crime and Punishment Reconsidered,"
Journal of Legal Studies, 4, January, 241-47.

Bowers, W. J. and G. L. Pierce (1975),"The Illusion of Deterrence in Isaac
Ehrlich's Research on Capital Punishment," Yale Law Journal, 85, 170.

Box, G. and D. Cox, (1964),"An Analysis of Transformations," Journal of the
Royal Statistical Society, Series B, 26, January, 211-43.

Carr-Hill, R. A. and N. H. Stern (1973), "An Econometric Model of the
Supply and Control of Recorded Offense in England and Wales," Journal
of Public Economics, 2, 289-318.

Cook, P. J. (1977), "Punishment and Crime: A Critique of Current Findings
Concerning the Preventative Effects of Punishment," Law and Contemporary
Problems, 41, 164-204 (Winter).

Ehrlich, I. (1973), "Participation in Illegitimate Activities: A Theoretical
and Empirical Investigation," Journal of Political Economy, 81, (May/June)
521-65.

_____.(1975),"The Deterrent Effect of Capital Punishment: A Question of
Life and Death," American Economic Review, 65, 3 (June), 397-417.

_____.(1977), "Capital Punishment and Deterrence: Some Further Thoughts
and Additional Evidence," Journal of Political Economy, 85, 4, 741-788.

Ehrlich, I. and J. C. Gibbons, (1977), "On the Measurement of the Deterrent
Effect of Capital Punishment and the Theory of Deterrence," Journal
of Legal Studies, 6, (January), 35-50.

Fair, R. C. (1970), "The Estimation of Simultaneous Equation Models with
Lagged Endogenous Variables and First Order Serially Correlated Errors,"
Econometrica, 38, May, 507-16.

Fisher, F. M. (1966), The Identification Problem in Econometrics, McGraw-
Hill (New York).

Fisher, F. M. and D. Nagin (1976), "On the Feasibility of Identifying the Crime Function in a Simultaneous Model of Crime Rates and Sanction Levels," in Deterrence and Incapacitation: Estimating the Effects of Criminal Sanctions on Crime, National Academy of Sciences.

Fleisher, B. (1966), The Economics of Delinquency, Quadrangle, Chicago.

Forst, B., Filatov, V. and L. R. Klein (1976), "The Deterrent Effect of Capital Punishment: An Assessment of the Estimates," in Deterrence and Incapacitation: Estimating the Effects of Criminal Sanctions on Crime, National Academy of Sciences.

Forst, B. (1977), "The Deterrent Effect of Capital Punishment: A Cross-State Analysis of the 1960's," Minnesota Law Review, 61, 5(May),743-767.

_____.(1977), "Participation in Illegitimate Activities: Further Empirical Findings," Forthcoming in Policy Analysis.

Mathieson, D. and P. Passell (1976), "Homicide and Robbery in New York City: An Economic Model," Journal of Legal Studies, 6, 83-98.

Nagin, D. (1977), "General Deterrence: A Review of the Empirical Evidence," Forthcoming in Management Science.

Palmer, J. (1977), "Economic Analysis of the Deterrent Effect of Punishment: A Review," Journal of Research in Crime and Delinquency, 14, (January) 4-21.

Passell, P. (1975), "The Deterrent Effect of the Death Penalty: A Statistical Test," Stanford Law Review, 28, 1(November), 61-80.

Passell, P. and J. Taylor (1976), "The Deterrence Controversy: A Reconsideration of the Time Series Evidence," in Capital Punishment in the United States, H. A. Bedau and C. M. Pierce (eds.) AMS Press, 359-371.

_____. (1977), "The Deterrent Effect of Capital Punishment: Another View," American Economic Review, 67, 3 (June), 445-51.

Phillips, L. and H. L. Votey (1975), "Crime Control in California", Journal of Legal Studies, 4, 2(June), 327-350.

Sargent, T. J. and C. A. Sims (1977), "Business Cycle Modeling Without Pretending to Have Too Much A Priori Economic Theory," in New Methods in Business Cycle Researc: Proceedings from a Conference, Federal Reserve Bank of Minneapolis.

Schuessler, K. F. (1952), "The Deterrent Influence of the Death Penalty," Annals of American Academy of Political and Social Science, November 54-62.

Sellin, T. (1959) The Death Penalty, Philadelphia.

Sjoquist, D. L. (1973), "Property Crime and Economic Behavior: Some Empirical Results," American Economic Review, 63, 3 (June), 439-446.

Economic Models of Criminal Behavior,
J.M. Heineke (ed.)
© *North-Holland Publishing Company, 1978*

CHAPTER THREE

PROSPECTS FOR INFERENCE ON DETERRENCE THROUGH EMPIRICAL
ANALYSIS OF INDIVIDUAL CRIMINAL BEHAVIOR

Charles F. Manski*

This paper explores the possibilities for inferring the impact of

deterrence policies through observation and analysis of individual crimi-

nal behavior.

While society's ultimate interest in deterrence policies may be in

their impact on aggregate crime rates, such policies directly act by

influencing individual criminal behavior. To study deterrence at the

level of individual decision making is therefore natural. To date almost

all empirical analyses of deterrence have been based on macro models of

crime commission and have used aggregated crime rate, socio-economic and

demographic statistics as their data. As currently practiced, the macro

approach suffers from deep logical problems of aggregation and model

identification which make clear interpretation of empirical findings

difficult to achieve. Empirical analysis of individual criminal behavior

avoids these problems, hence the practical interest in this approach.

---

*Associate Professor of Economics, School of Urban and Public Affairs,
Carnegie-Mellon University. An earlier version of this paper was prepared
for the Panel on Research on Deterrent and Incapacitative Effects,
National Academy of Sciences and is being published by the Academy. I
have benefited from discussions with Alfred Blumstein and Daniel Nagin and
from the opportunity to discuss the ideas contained herein at a conference
convened by the National Academy Panel and at a seminar at the Hoover
Institution. All opinions and conclusions expressed in this paper are
those of the author alone.

Unfortunately, individual level analysis of criminal decision making has its own difficulties, these being basically operational rather than conceptual.

In what follows, Section I overviews the issues which make empirical analysis of individual criminal behavior appealing in the abstract but troublesome in practice. The primary problem hindering individual level analysis is data availability. A secondary problem exists with respect to the structuring of realistic and tractable behavioral models. These two concerns are examined in some detail in Sections II and III respectively. Section IV summarizes the prospects for obtaining useful evidence on deterrence from studies of individual criminal behavior.

I. An Overview of the Issues

A. Deterrence and Crime Rates

Deterrence policy might be characterized as an attempt to balance society's desire for lower crime rates with the resource costs of so doing and with the constitutional requirements of due process and a punishment suited to the crime. By lowering the attractiveness of criminal activities, deterrence policies seek to channel individual decisions away from such activities, thus lowering the aggregate rate of crime commission. The actual impact of any policy on crime rates can, however, be difficult to assess. Two distinct forces create this problem.

First, an individual's reaction to shifts in deterrence policies can be quite complex. For example, an increase in efforts to deter a particular type of crime may induce the individual not to stop his criminal activities but to shift them to other crime types. That is, deterrence policies can have crime substitution effects as well as crime rate effects.[1] As another example, an increase in severity of sentences may lead persons committing crimes to more strongly resist apprehension, thus inducing further crimes. In particular, a person facing capital punishment if caught can be expected to resist capture by whatever means he can. A comprehensive analysis of deterrence policies requires one to cope with behavioral complexities such as the above.

Second, determination of the impact of a deterrence policy on aggregate crime commission is not simply a matter of adding up isolated effects across individuals. While the individual may view his environment as exogenous, the aggregate crime rates for crimes of different types are endogeneous variables in a system in which criminals seek opportunities of the various crime types and potential victims seek through collective and private action to dissuade the criminals. To determine the ultimate effect of a deterrence policy on crime rates one should model the behavior of all the actors in the system and appropriately characterize their interactions. In particular, crime rate determination might be treated as an equilibration process.

The present paper concerns itself with issues that arise in empirically modelling the possibly complex manner in which deterrence policies may influence individual criminal behavior. It does not address the larger question of empirically modelling the ultimate, equilibrium impact of deterrence policies on aggregate crime rates.

B. The Attempt to Infer Deterrent Effects from Macro Crime Models

To date, almost all empirical analyses of deterrence have been based

---

[1]This phenomenon has been studied by Heineke. See Chapter 5 of the present volume

on macro models of crime commission and aggregated crime data. In particular, see Carr-Hill and Stern (1973), Ehrlich (1973, 1975) and Forst
(1976) among others. A fairly complete listing of macro studies is given
in Blumstein, et. al., (1978). Both the logical foundations and operational aspects of the macro studies have recently been subjected to
intense scrutiny by the profession. See Fisher and Nagin (1978), Klein,
Forst and Filatov (1978), Nagin (1978), Passell and Taylor (1976), Peck
(1976) and Vandaele (1978) for reviews of portions of the literature and
see Blumstein, et. al., (1978) for a comprehensive overview. Given the
extensive critiques available, it is necessary here only to state the two
fundamental problems with macro studies that particularly motivate
interest in individual level analysis of deterrence. These are as follows.

First, as alluded to earlier, aggregate crime rates are determined
within a system whose actors include criminals, victims, and the various
organs of the criminal justice complex--the police, courts, prisons, etc.
Attempts to realistically model the interplay of these actors at the macro
level inevitably conclude that the decisions of the actors are so directly
interdependent and share so many common exogeneous determinants that the
effects of deterrence policies on aggregate crime rates cannot easily, if
at all, be isolated within a macro model. That is, within such a model,
realistic prior assumptions sufficient to identify a deterrent effect are
often not available.[2]

Second, in the absence of considerable homogeneity in the circumstances of individual criminals, the aggregation of individual criminal

---

[2]See Fisher and Nagin (1978) for a thorough discussion of the
identification issue in the crime modelling context.

behavior over the population may yield no simple macro function adequately
capturing the behavior of that population. Whether individual criminals
are homogeneous enough in the criminal opportunities they have available,
the sanctions they face and the decision rules they apply to justify the
existence of macro crime supply functions of the type assumed to date in
the literature seems unlikely. Whether macro crime functions which allow
a reasonable amount of heterogeneity in the population yet still are
tractable might be developed remains to be seen.[3]

Before proceeding to discuss individual level crime analysis, it
should be noted that the identification and aggregation problems that
arise in the macro modelling of criminal behavior are not qualitatively
different from similar issues that appear in the macro modelling of other
economic decisions. Yet macro level empirical analysis remains accepted,
indeed the norm, in many areas of study even though the identification
and aggregation concerns have long been recognized. One may speculate as
to why macro-crime analysis has been more thoroughly scrutinized than
other macro analyses and whether the relatively harsh judgement the
profession has made of the existing macro crime literature is deserved.
Conversely, it might be asked how well macro analyses is other areas
would stand up if subject to the same scrutiny given the crime literature.
These matters need not be decided here. To motivate the present paper it

---

[3]In the context of linear models, conditions for consistent aggregation are well known. For a textbook discussion, see Theil (1971). In
non-linear models, the necessary conditions (say for existence of a
representative consumer) are much more stringent. It should be pointed
out that intermediate between the individual level and macro approaches
is that in which individuals are divided into groups and a separate
macro crime function is assumed for each group. If the population can
in fact be divided into a small number of relatively homogeneous groups,
the realism of individual level analysis and simplicity of macro analysis
may both be preserved.

is necessary only to observe that legitimate questions regarding macro
level analysis exist and that an alternative approach surmounting these
problems has been identified. This approach, individual level analysis,
should therefore be explored.

C. Empirical Analysis of Individual Criminal Behavior:
    The Conceptual Advantages

The advantages of individual level analysis of criminal behavior for
the study of deterrence stand in counterpoint to the problems inherent in
the macro approach.

First, because any individual can generally only negligibly influence
the level of aggregate criminal opportunities and the operation of the
criminal justice system, it is realistic to model the individual criminal
as acting within a recursive system where the aggregated decisions of
other actors influence his own behavior but not vice versa. Given such a
recursive structure, deterrent effects are in principle identifiable
through examination of individual criminal behavior.

Second, in contrast to the ad hoc reasoning on which direct specifications of macro crime functions have been based, there exists substantial,
if conflicting behavioral theory and observation to guide model selection
when the individual is the unit of analysis. Moreover, given a model of
individual criminal behavior, the appropriate function characterizing
population behavior, both in and out of equilibrium, can be ex post
derived by explicitly aggregating the individual decisions predicted by
that model.

The above conceptual advantages of individual level analysis are, of
course, not specific to the context of criminal behavior. They are rather
expressions of general arguments in favor of empirically modelling

behavior at the level it occurs.

D. Empirical Analysis of Individual Criminal Behavior:
    The Operational Problems

Beginning with Becker (1968) and continuing through Ehrlich (1973)

and Block and Heineke (1975) among others, economists have produced a

succession of theoretical models of individual criminal behavior. In the

decade since Becker awoke the profession's interest in the economics of

crime, almost no attention has been given to the empirical analysis of

such behavior.[4] This contrast between the theoretical and empirical

literatures is striking, particularly since theoretical models, by their

nature, may suggest the existence of a deterrent effect but can provide

no evidence as to its magnitude. The question of existence, it seems

fair to say, is relatively uncontroversial. The crucial policy matter

of magnitude is inherently an empirical issue.

The absence of empirical work on individual criminal behavior derives

primarily from the lack of suitable data. However the criminal's decision

problem is theoretically structured and whatever form of decision rule the

criminal is assumed to use, empirical analsis of criminal choice requires

that one be able to characterize the alternatives available to each of an

appropriate sample of individuals and specify what choices each one makes.

The only readily available data on individual criminal behavior have

been contained in the "rap sheets," that is individual criminal histories,

---

[4]Attempts at individual level empirical analysis within limited
contexts have been made by Weimer and Stonebraker (1975) and Witte
(1976). The empirical analysis performed in Ehrlich (1973) is at the
macro level and is only marginally related to the theoretical individual choice model he develops in the same paper. This point concerning Ehrlich's work is discussed by Heineke in Chapter One of the
present volume.

maintained by the criminal justice system for individuals with an existing
criminal record.[5] These files, which record arrests, dispositions of
cases, and limited individual demographic data, are of very limited use in
behavioral modelling. In particular, because rap sheets can only report
those crimes resulting in an arrest, these files provide a systematically
biased sample of crimes actually committed and no data at all characterizing the opportunities, both criminal and legitimate, that an individual
has available but does not select. If empirical analysis of criminal
behavior is to be pursued, alternative data sources, less accessible than
rap sheets, will have to be developed.

A secondary problem hindering empirical research has been the absence
of satisfactory econometric models of criminal behavior. Perhaps because
lack of data has made empirical behavioral modelling seem impractical,
the existing theoretical models of criminal choice have not been developed
with empirical application in mind. These models, while insightful, are
too idealized and abstract from too much of the criminal decision problem
to serve as useful bases for empirical work. If empirical criminal choice
analysis is to be pursued, appropriate econometric choice models must be
developed, not only for their direct application but also to guide the
process of data collection.

The prospects for remedying the data and modelling problems confronting empirical analysis of criminal behavior are not clear. Section II
below explores some potentially useful but as yet untested data sources

---

[5]While public use data files are not generally maintained, rap sheet
data in various forms have been made available by the FBI and some state
agencies to a number of researchers for studies of crime commission.
Some of the sources used are described in Cohen (1978).

and elaborates on the uses and limitations of rap sheet data. Section
III then discusses the features econometric models of criminal behavior
should have and introduces a new modelling approach which may prove useful in practice.

II. Data Needs and Sources

A. Data Requirements for Behavioral Modelling

The data requirements for empirical behavioral modelling can be
described only in the context of a specified behavioral model and inferential procedure. If we adopt the usual economic approach in which
behavior is manifested by choice from a given choice set or, more
generally, a time path of choices from a sequence of such sets, and where
inference is predicated on the observation of revealed preferences, two
general if fairly obvious principles for data collection can be asserted,
as follow.

First, as stated earlier, the data should, for each decision maker
in an appropriate sample, be sufficient to suitably characterize the
decision maker, his available alternatives and his actual decisions. It
should be emphasized that for empirical choice analysis it is as important to know what alternatives are available but not chosen as to identify
the chosen alternatives. In attempting to use for choice analysis data
sets originally collected for other purposes, researchers often find that
such data sets specify in great detail what people do but give no information about what they could have done. To perform his analysis, the
researcher must then deal with a sometimes difficult missing data

problem.[6]

Second, I have referred to the need for an "appropriate sample" of

decision makers. Part of the specification of a behavioral model must

be a definition of the population of decision makers to which the model

applies. Given a specified population, data may be collected using any

sampling process as long as two conditions are met. First, the sampling

process should be informative. In particular, if inferences are to be

based on the distribution of point estimates of parameters, the relevant

parameters should be estimable under the sampling process used. Second,

the analyst should have enough prior knowledge of the sampling process

to be able to specify a proper inferential procedure. It is too often

forgotten in econometric work that the statistical properties of an

estimator depend on the sampling process by which observations are drawn

from the population as well as on the economic process governing the

population.[7]

---

[6]In a neo-classical choice context where the choice set is fully
determined by knowledge of commodity prices and consumer income, the
missing data problem is easily handled. In discrete choice contexts,
where choice sets usually differ in complex ways among decision makers,
the problem can be quite serious. The prevailing "fix" is for the
analyst to make a point prediction of the available alternatives, thus
imputing a choice set to the decision maker. Kohn, Manski and Mundel
(1976) provide an example of choice set imputation in a study of
students' educational choices. Lerman and Ben-Akiva (1975) use a
different imputation procedure in a study of transportation choices.
A theoretically more satisfactory but considerably less practical
solution to the missing data problem would be for the analyst to
predict a probability distribution of choice sets and, integrating over
this distribution, make unconditional inferences on behavior.

[7]In the context of linear models, the literature on "limited dependent variables" has made the dependency of estimator properties on the
sampling process clear. See for example Tobin (1958) and Hausman and
Wise (1977) where it is shown that ordinary least squares estimation is
inconsistent if the sampling process draws observations based on the
value of the dependent variable. In the context of discrete choice

Within the context of the modelling of criminal behavior, some additional guidance for data collection beyond the above general principles can be offered.

First, anyone can commit a crime. Hence, the relevant decision making population for a study of criminal behavior should be the entire population of an area and not some a priori specified "criminal element." To effectively analyze criminal behavior it will usually be essential to sample from the full population rather than only the sub-population known to have previously committed a crime.[8]

Second, the decision to engage in criminal activities is a temporarily recurrent one, not a single irrevocable act. Over time, people can move in and out of criminal activities or among criminal activities of different types. It follows that in modelling criminal behavior, longitudinal data will be useful for some purposes and crucial for others.

Finally, the criminal's decision problem may be structured in a variety of distinct ways. For example, some of the existing theoretical

-----

models, the literature on "choice based sampling" demonstrates this same dependency. In particular, see Manski and Lerman(1977) where it is proved that a familiar maximum likelihood estimator is inconsistent if the sampling process draws observations based on the identities of chosen alternatives.

[8] I say "usually" rather than "always" because there do exist circumstances, rarely achieved in practice, in which prior information about the characteristics of the decision making population allows the analyst to draw inferences about population behavior given a sample of known criminals only. A sample consisting only of known criminals is a "choice based sample" in that decision makers are drawn into the sample based on their past choice of a criminal career. Estimation in choice based samples is possible under realistic informational conditions is at least some individuals selecting each available alternative are included in the sample. Thus, we need to include non-criminals as well as criminals in the sample. A random sample of the population is not required to make estimation feasible. See Manski and McFadden (1977) for a detailed examination of estimation in choice based samples.

models of criminal behavior regard the decision problem as one of time

allocation without reference to the actual commission of criminal acts.

Other studies view the criminal as instantaneously deciding whether or

not to commit a given crime and make no reference to a time allocation

decision. Clearly, the data one wishes to collect will depend on the

way one wishes to model the criminal decision problem.[9]

In the remainder of this section, three alternative data sources on

criminal behavior will be examined in light of the above discussion.

These sources are, in order of consideration, self-reports, criminal

justice system records and victimization surveys.

B. Data Sources: Self-Reports of Criminal Behavior

In principle, self-reports of criminal behavior, obtained through

surveys instruments, provide by far the most comprehensive source of data

on individual criminal behavior. In particular, self-report surveys can

give direct data on committed crimes not resulting in an arrest and

information about the criminal and legitimative alternatives available to

but not chosen by individuals. They can provide perceptual data such as

subjective probabilities of arrest and conviction for crimes of different

types as well as individual background data in great detail. The poten-

tial comprehensiveness of the self-report data obtainable for each

sampled individual is complemented by the flexibility the analyst in

principle has in selecting a sample. In particular, self-reports may

provide the only viable mechanism for sampling individuals not engaged

in criminal activities and for whom, consequently, criminal justice

---

[9]For further discussion of this point see Chapter One of the present
volume.

system records can provide no data.

If trained as an economist, one's temptation may be to dismiss analyses based on criminal self-reports out of hand. The incentives to mis-report criminal activity plus the frailty of human memories, it will be said, make self-report data too inaccurate to be useful. Such a judgement should, I think, at least temporarily be withheld, for the following reasons.

First, substantial experience with self-report surveys in the sociological literature has produced numerous instructive failures and some apparent successes. Certainly a considerable amount has been learned. See Reiss (1973) for an interesting overview of this literature.

Second, it should be recognized that self-report data need not be objectively correct in order to be useable. What is necessary is that responses be systematically related to the "truth" and that it is possible to determine the nature of this relation. For example, if it were known that respondents tend to under-estimate frequency of crime commission in a systematic way, then reported frequencies could be blown up to their true values expost.

The third and most compelling reason for interest in self-reports are the inherent limitations in alternative data sources. It will be seen in Sections C and D below that criminal justice system records and victimization survey results, the only other data sources apparent to me, are both fairly restricted in the sampling processes possible and in the information obtainable for each sampled individual. Given this, self-reports may provide the only vehicle for the study of many aspects of criminal behavior.

Because there presently exists considerable uncertainty about the

meaningfulness of self-reported crime data, it is premature to recommend
acceptance of self-reports as a data strategy for studying criminal
behavior. We note that if self-report surveys are eventually to be used
in empirical deterrence analysis, some modifications to existing survey
practices will be required.

A good example of current practice is a recent Rand Corporation
survey of repetitively violent offenders. This study consists of in-depth
interviews with a small number (fifty) of persons convicted on robbery
charges and subsequently imprisoned. The Rand survey asks for extensive
personal background data and a history of crimes committed, arrests and
convictions by crime type. It also seeks subjective arrest expectations
and asks the respondent to make some hypothetical choices. See Petersilia,
et. al., (1977) for a description of the survey and analysis of the
results.

Ignoring problems with the way some questions are worded, the Rand
survey, like others before it, is inadequate for deterrence analysis on
two grounds, both remediable. First, the survey seeks no information on
the environments in which crimes were and were not committed. In particular, alternative criminal and legitimate alternatives available to the
individual but not selected are not identified. Second, limitation of
the respondents to convicted felons makes it impossible to use the
study to ask why some people pursue criminal careers and others do not.
For that purpose, administration of the survey to a broader cross-section
of the population would be necessary.

C. Data Sources: Criminal Justice System Records

The data available from the criminal justice system regarding

individual criminal behavior takes two forms. First there are the individual criminal histories or rap-sheets mentioned earlier. Second, there
are some less accessible but possibly more useful data on plea and
sentence bargaining decisions. The two data forms are different enough
to warrant separate discussions.

1. Individual Criminal Histories

Rap-sheets, it will be recalled, record arrests, disposition of
cases, and limited demographic data for individuals with a known criminal history. The use of such data to analyze criminal behavior is
problematic for a number of distinct reasons.

First, while the behavioral modeller's concern is with crimes
committed, rap-sheet record arrests, not crimes. The use of arrest
records as a proxy for crimes committed is possible only if the arrest
process is a priori known or otherwise can be disentangled from the crime
commission process. To see why, consider a person with attributes s
arrested for a crime of type γ during some time period. Let Q denote the
deterrence policies in effect at the time of the crime and arrest. The
probability of observing such an arrest can be written as

$$P(\gamma \text{ arrest}/s,Q) = P(\gamma \text{ crime}/s,Q) \ P(\gamma \text{ arrest}/\gamma \text{ crime}, s,Q)$$

where it is assumed for simplicity that false arrests do not occur and
where determinants of the probabilities other than s and Q have been
suppressed.

The problem is that the crime commission probability $P(\gamma \text{ crime}/s,Q)$,
reflecting criminal behavior, and the conditional arrest probability
$P(\gamma \text{ arrest}/\gamma \text{ crime},s,Q)$, reflecting police action, may both depend non-
trivially on the same variables s and Q. For example, a person's

criminal skill can be expected to affect his crime commission probability
positively and his conditional arrest probability negatively. The density
of police patrols should negatively influence crime commission and positively influence the arrest rate on committed crimes.[10]

Clearly, without further information, any attempt to analyze observed
arrests as a function of personal characteristics s and deterrence
policies Q will confound criminal behavior with police action. In other
words, in the absence of prior assumptions, the two structural processes
jointly determining arrests cannot be identified relative to one another.

The only way to use rap-sheets to study deterrence is to make enough
prior assumptions about the arrest process to render the crime commission
process identifiable. For a few crime types, such as draft evasion and
bail jumping, almost all offenses result in the issuance of an arrest
warrant, if not actual capture, so crime commission can be properly
inferred from criminal justice system records. See for example the study
of draft evasion by Blumstein and Nagin (1977). More generally, however,
little is known about the arrest process so that realistic identifying
assumptions cannot be made. In the operations research literature
modelling crime commission as a stochastic process, it is conventionally
assumed that conditional arrest probabilities given crime commission are
not affected by deterrence policies, and do not vary systematically across
individuals. See for example Shinnar and Shinnar (1975) and the review by

---

[10]The statement that increased density of policy patrols will increase
the arrest rate on committed crimes must be interpreted in a ceteris paribus
sense only. If crimes differ in the ease with which arrests are made and if
police vigilance dissuades the commission of easily arrestable crimes more
than it does other crimes, then an increase in police patrols may move the
mix of crimes committed toward those where arrests are difficult. Hence,
we may observe a negative relation between police efforts and arrest rates.

Cohen (1978). These assumptions are not substantiated in this literature and seem quite unrealistic.

If the identification problem in arrest records can be suitably resolved, other difficulties still confront the use of such data to study criminal behavior. For one thing, rap-sheets can provide no information about criminal and legitimate opportunities available to but not selected by the sampled individuals. Another problem, referred to earlier, is that the sampling process generating observations excludes non-criminals.[11] Finally, the personal attributes recorded for sampled individuals are generally limited to demographic characteristics.

The above problems severely restrict the potential usefulness of rap sheet data for deterrence analysis. Such data may find application in circumstances where the arrest process can be a priori specified, the criminal's choice set can be successfully imputed by the analyst, data on the behavior of non-criminals is available from other sources and the personal characteristics relevant to decision-making are basically demographic ones. These circumstances should be expected to be only rarely found.

2. Plea and Sentence Bargaining Decisions

An important issue in deterrence policy concerns the relative deterrent effects of high arrest and convictions probabilities on the one hand and long sentences given conviction on the other.[12] Interestingly, data on plea and sentence bargaining decisions may be able to shed light on this question.

---

[11]This statement ignores the possibility of false arrests.

[12]See Becker (1968), Ehrlich (1973), Block and Heineke (1975), Brown and Reynolds (1973) and Heineke (1975).

Consider the arrested person offered a plea bargain by the district
attorney. His choice between a guilty plea to a reduced charge and an
innocent plea to a higher charge is essentially a choice between a certain
conviction with a relatively low sentence and an uncertain conviction
carrying a longer sentence. A similar trade-off between probability of
conviction and sentence length is faced in a sentence bargaining situation.
What this suggests is the use of observations on plea and sentence bargain
decisions to infer the relative weights criminals give to conviction
probabilities and sentences and hence, the relative effectiveness of each
in determining crime.

Fortunately, criminal justice system data on plea and sentence bargain decisions can be quite good. As a concrete example, in Alameda
County, California, the District Attorney's Office routinely records all
offers of plea bargains, defendants' responses, ultimate case dispositions,
and defendant criminal background data. These records also include
prosecutors' subjective probabilities of conviction if the case goes to
trial. Assuming that defendants' subjective probabilities coincide with
the prosecutors', these data provide a solid base for analysis of plea
bargaining and ultimately, for inferrence on deterrence.[13] A paper by
Weimer and Stonebraker (1975) has already opened up this fertile source.
Most district attorney's offices do not keep as organized or extensive a
set of records as does the Alameda County office. There would, however,
appear to be no fundamental reason preventing analogous, or even more
sophisticated systems from being instituted elsewhere.

----

[13]When the defendant has an experienced lawyer, it is plausible to
assume that defense and prosecution subjective probabilities will coincide. In other situations, however, such coincidence of opinions seems
harder to justify.

Obviously, analysis of plea and sentence bargaining decisions cannot illuminate all aspects of criminal behavior. Even where such analysis appears useful in principle, operational problems may make inference difficult. In particular, if the interaction of the arrested person and the district attorney is really one of bargaining, that is gaming, behavior analysis will be complicated by the absence of a pre-specified choice set and by the presence of strategic elements in decisions. Another potential problem regards the transfer of inferences based on plea bargains decisions to forecast aspects of crime commission decisions. Conceivably, although I think unlikely, criminals weigh conviction probabilities against sentence differently in the two contexts. In exploring the use of plea and sentence bargaining data for deterrence analysis, one should keep these possible difficulties in mind. Nevertheless, such exploration seems quite worthwhile.

D. Data Sources: Victimization Surveys

Self-reports of criminal activity and criminal justice system records would appear to be the only data sources allowing direct investigation of individual criminal behavior. In this section, I would like to suggest a somewhat indirect approach, but one which may be useful in deterrence analysis. This involves the use of victimization surveys.

Consider for concreteness the set of gasoline stations in a given metropolitan area. A victimization survey of these stations would indicate the frequency with which each was robbed or burglarized in a given interval of time and the conditions under which each incident took place.

If we imagine a population of potential gas station robbers and burglars living in the area, it is reasonable to assume that each such

criminal could conceivably "hit" any of the area's stations. In general,

the number and locations of the attempts each criminal does make will

depend on personal characteristics and on the characteristics of the

available alternatives. In particular, we might expect that the criminal's

decisions are determined in part by the "take" at each station, by the

quality of the private protective system each station possesses, by the

extent of local police surveillance, and by the sanctions administered in

the local court.

The above suggests that a gasoline station victimization survey can

reveal aspects of the structure of criminal behavior. Specifically,

observation of the relative frequencies of crimes at stations character-

ized by different takes and different protective systems should indicate

something about the reward-risk trade-offs criminals make and about the

deterrent value of alternative protective systems.[14] Because victimi-

zation surveys cannot usually provide the attributes of individual

offenders, it should not be expected that individual criminal decision

functions will be estimable from such data. Determination of exactly

how victimization surveys can be fruitfully used in deterrence analysis

will require considerable further thought. Beyond the above gas station

example, such surveys would appear useful in studying the determinants

of bank robberies, home burglaries and muggings, among other crime types.

---

[14]Note that the take and the security of a given station can vary
over the day and week. Hence, reports of the timing of different
incidents at a single station can also provide useful information on
criminal behavior.

III. Modelling Concerns and Approaches

Successful empirical analysis of criminal behavior requires the
development of econometric models that are at the same time behaviorally
realistic and operationally practical. In selecting a model specification
the analyst must appropriately structure the decision problems individuals
face over time and specify the decision rules they use. In Section A
below we discuss some important concerns in specifying an econometric
model of criminal behavior. In Section B, a behaviorally appealing and
potentially practical modelling approach is introduced.

A. The Dimensions of Model Specification

1. Structuring the Criminal Decision Problem

Within the theoretical economic literature on criminal behavior, the
criminal decision problem has been posed in two distinct ways.[15] Some
authors, including Becker (1968), Ehrlich (1973) and Block and Heineke
(1975) view the individual as facing a time allocation decision in which
some available activities are legitimate and others criminal. Essentially
these authors simply extend the conventional labor-leisure model so as to
distinguish among different forms of labor, some of which society labels
criminal.

In the second approach, typified by Allingham and Sandmo (1972),
Kolm (1973) and Singh (1973), it is assumed that at some moment the
individual faces a set of criminal opportunities, one of which is the
"null option" of not committing a crime. Crime commission in these
models is an instantaneous event, separate from any time allocation the

---

[15]In preparing this section, I have benefitted from an insightful
review of the literature by Heineke (1976).

individual may make.[16]

Both conceptualizations capture important aspects of criminal behavior but neither by itself suffices. The time allocation models recognize the search and planning activities that precede the commission of premeditated crimes and characterize the professional criminal. These models do not however provide any description of how time spent in such activities relates to the number of crimes actually committed. The criminal opportunities models recognize that the actual commission of most crimes consumes very little time and hence that crime commission may realistically be often treated as a timeless event.[17] Such models do not, however, describe how the individual's criminal opportunity set arises. In particular the role of past planning and search activities in creating present criminal opportunities is ignored.

Clearly, realistic modelling of criminal behavior requires a synthesis of the time allocation and crime commission approaches. The individual's allocation of time among criminal and non-criminal activities will naturally depend in part on the kinds of opportunities he expects criminal activity will yield. Conversely, the actual criminal opportunities the individual has available at any moment will depend in part on the past effort he has expanded in seeking out and planning crimes. A

---

[16]The models in the literature make the restrictive assumption that all consequences associated with a criminal act are monetary, so that the criminal decision problem falls formally within portfolio theory. This aspect of the literature is irrelevant here.

[17]Actually most crimes are legally _defined_ as timeless events. In some cases, such as murder, robbery, forgery and theft such a definition is natural. In other cases, such as speeding, price fixing, and operation of a brothel, crime commission has an inherent time dimension. Here it might be preferable to make part of the definition of an offense its duration.

model of criminal behavior should therefore explain both time allocation
and crime commission decisions and appropriately incorporate the linkages
between them.[18]

2. Specifying the Individual's Decision Rule

With the criminal decision problem structured, the substance of a
behavioral model is the decision rule assumed to govern choice. Because
the analyst's specification of a rule must be context specific, I shall
limit myself to a brief remark about the "economic" model of criminal
behavior and its empirical representation.

An economic model of crime is simply one in which criminal decisions
are consistent with a preference ordering. Usually it is assumed that
this ordering can be described through a utility function.[19] In empirical

---

[18]In some contexts it may be reasonable to simply assume that the
number of crimes committed is proportional to the time allocated to
criminal activity, thus effectively condensing the two decisions into
one. Unfortunately such an assumption will often be unrealistic because
individuals may vary in their search and planning skill and because the
time devoted to planning per crime may vary with deterrence policies.
While the time allocation decision often constitutes the aspect of
criminal behavior most closely tied to crime commission itself, other
dimensions of behavior certainly exist. For example, there are decision
problems involving choice of accomplices, choice of weapons and amount
of monetary expenditure for crime related purposes. Moreover, where
crimes are not premeditated, the time allocation aspect of behavior will
itself be irrelevant. Because the legal system defines so many different
forms of crime and because criminal behavior has so many dimensions, to
attempt to capture all crime related decisions within a single model
seems hopeless. One might as easily try to capture all of human behavior.
Inevitably, empirical modelling will require the development of models
confining their domains to restricted classes of crime types and
dimensions of criminal behavior.

[19]Much of the theoretical economic literature on criminal behavior
imposes the very stringent requirement that all consequences of criminal
actions are desirable in monetary terms and that utility is a function
of money alone. This restriction is of course in no way necessary to an
economic model of crime. For further discussion see Chapter One of the
present volume.

applications, where not all factors influencing behavior can generally be observed, a natural representation of maximizing behavior is a random utility model, that is a model in which utilities are treated as random variables and behavior is expressed in choice probabilities. Random utility models of aspects of criminal behavior will be developed in Section B below.

3. Modelling Criminal Behavior Over Time

Earlier we noted that over time the individual faces a succession of criminal decision problems and that a decision to engage in criminal activities is not an irrevokable act. Given this, it is clear that an empirical model of criminal behavior should aim to describe the time path of criminal choices, not simply behavior at one instant.

Modelling the dynamics of criminal decision making poses two distinct issues, one behavioral and the other observational. First, there is the behavioral matter of how the individual actually deals with decision making over time. Does he, at each decision moment, formulate a hypo-thetical optimal time path of future behavior based on his present knowledge and circumstances or does he act more myopically?[20] How do realizations of uncertain events modify the individual's circumstances, particularly his expectations? These questions must be addressed by the analyst in specifying the decision rule the individual is assumed to use each moment.

If for every decision moment the analyst could specify the individual's

---

[20] If the individual does, in the manner of dynamic programming, select an optimal behavioral path at a given decision moment, this path is only hypothetical because realizations of presently uncertain events may lead him to modify the path over time. The hypothetical and actual behavioral paths should be expected to coincide only in a world of perfect information.

decision rule and choice set with certainty, the analyst could perfectly predict the time path of individual behavior simply by applying the posited choice model recursively over the succession of decision moments.[21] Unfortunately, as pointed out earlier, some factors influencing behavior will generally be unobserved in empirical applications. This fact produces the second issue in dynamic modelling, namely how unobserved factors should be represented.

In a static context, unobserved factors may be treated as random variables. In a dynamic model, with entire time paths of relevant factors unobserved, it is necessary to treat such factors as random functions of time. The analyst's problem is to specify these random functions in a concurrently realistic and tractable manner.

Historically, empirical analyses of individual behavior over time have usually handled this specification problem in unacceptable ways. One approach has been to assume that the unobserved factors are drawn once and thereafter remain fixed over time while a second has been to assume independent drawings each decision moment. If, as seems realistic, unobserved factors generally are positively but not perfectly correlated over time, then the former approach will tend to underpredict and the latter overpredict the extent to which behavior fluctuates over time. Recently,some authors have developed more palatable stochastic specifications, but at some cost in behavioral interpretability. See in particular Bass, Jeuland and Wright (1976), Ginsberg (1971), Heckman and Willis (1975), Hausman and Wise (1976) and Levy (1976). The model

----

[21]This presumes that the sequence of decision moments is specified exogeneously. See Section B below for discussion of alternative approaches in specifying this sequence.

introduced below attempts to achieve an acceptable stochastic specifications while retaining an explicit behavioral derivation.

B. A Dynamic Random Utility Approach to Modelling Criminal Behavior

The issues to be faced in specifying an empirical model of criminal
behavior become sharpened when one actually attempts to frame such a
model. Existing modelling approaches, we have noted, do not adequately
recognize the linkage between time allocation and crime commission
decisoins nor the essential dynamic character of criminal behavior. I
have therefore sought to develop a more satisfactory approach. The basic
elements of this approach are described presently.

The econometric choice model introduced here is a dynamic generalization of the static random utility models which have increasingly been
found useful in empirical choice analysis. After laying out the mdoel
in abstract terms, I indicate how it may be applied to analyze time
allocation and crime commission decisions. The section concludes with
some remarks on the stochastic process models of crime commission preva-
lent in the operations research literature.

1. Dynamic Random Utility Models

The conventional static random utility model presumes a population
of decision makers T each member of which must select an alternative from
a finite choice set C. With each decision maker $t \in T$ and alternative
$i \in C$ there are associated attribute vectors s_t and x_i respectively. It
is assumed that for each decision maker $t \in T$, choice from the set C is
consistent with maximization of a utility function $U_{ti} = U(s_t, x_i)$ over
$i \in C$.

Some components of the attribute vectors x and s are observed by the analyst, the rest unobserved. Hence utilities are themselves not directly observable and so perfect predictions of choice are not possible. However, if the unobserved attributes are considered a drawing from some probability distribution, then utilities, being functions of those attributes, are random variables. Therefore probabilistic predictions of choice are possible. In particular, the probability that t chooses i is, assuming indifference among alternatives occurs with probability zero, simply $P_r(U_{ti} \geq U_{tj}$, all $j \in C)$. As expressed above, the random utility model has been studied and applied by numerous authors. See Luce and Suppes (1965) and McFadden (1976) for reviews of parts of the literature.

Conceptually, generalization of the static random utility model to one of choice over time is quite straightforward. Let each decision maker in T be required to select an alternative from C at every moment in an ordered set of decision moments M.[22] Let s_{tm} and x_{im} now be dated attribute vectors for $m \in M$ and let $U_{tim} = U(s_{tm}, x_{im})$. Assume that the time paths of some components of x and s are observed by the analyst, the rest unobserved. If the time path of the unobserved components is considered a drawing from a probability distribution of paths, then utilities are random functions of time. The probability that t chooses i during some set of decision moments $M_o \subset M$ is, ignoring indifference, $P_r(U_{tim} \geq U_{tjm}$, all $j \in C$, $m \in M_o)$. More generally, if c_{tm} designates the alternative selected by t at moment m, the probability distribution of choice paths $(c_{tm}, m \in M)$ can be derived from the distribution of utility paths.

---

[22]The set M may be countable, in which case we have a discrete time model or a continuum, in which case a continuous time model results. However M is specified, it is important that it be exogenous rather than determined within the decision process itself.

In empirical applications of the static random utility model, it is
usually assumed that for each $t \in T$, the utilities U_{ti}, $i \in C$ have the
form $U_{ti} = z_{ti} \cdot \theta + \varepsilon_{ti}$ where $z_{ti} = z(s_t, x_i)$ is a vector of functions
of observed attributes, $(\varepsilon_{ti}, i \in C)$ is a drawing from a multivariate
distribution $F_t(\phi)$, and θ and ϕ are parameter vectors to be estimated
from the simple data.[23] The obvious dynamic generalization of this speci-
fication is to let $U_{tim} = z_{tim} \cdot \theta + \varepsilon_{tim}$ where $z_{tim} = z(s_{tm}, x_{im})$ and
where $(\varepsilon_{tim}, i \in C, m \in M)$ is a drawing from a multivariate stochastic
process. Just as in the static literature an important concern has been
to find realistic yet tractable distributional specifications for the
disturbances, in the dynamic context it will be important to find
appropriate stochastic process specifications. Work on this problem is
now in its early stages.[24]

2. Application to the Time Allocation and Crime Commission Decisions

The dynamic random utility approach offers an appealing vehicle for
modelling both the time allocation and crime commission aspects of criminal behavior.

Consider first the time allocation problem. Let C be a set of
activities, or uses of time, including criminal search and planning
activities, legitimate employment and leisure activities. For concrete-

---

[23]For example, the assumption that the disturbances are i.i.d.
Weibull leads to the conditional logit model of McFadden (1973). If the
disturbances are specified multivariate normal, a multinomial probit
model results. See Albright, Lerman and Manski (1977) among other
sources.

[24]Certainly, two specifications which should usually be avoided are
the one in which ε_{tim} is fixed over $m \in M$ and the one in which each
decision moment brings a temporally independent drawing. Historically,
attempts to apply static random utility models to analyze inherently
temporal behavior have of necessity made one or the other of these
extreme assumptions.

ness, let M, the set of decision moments, be an interval on the real line
so that decisions are updated continuously. At each moment m $\in$ M, the
individual must, we assume, select exactly one activity from C. Decision
making, we assume, does not itself consume time. The individual's
selected activity path determines his time allocation over the interval
M. In particular, his allocation of time to criminal activities is
simply that subset of M on which he selects a criminal activity. If
choice of an activity at every moment is consistent with utility maximization and if, in the manner described earlier, utilities are treated as
observationally random functions of time, then the individual's time
allocation process is described by a dynamic random utility model.

Figure 1 illustrates how an individual's realized time path of
utilities determines his activity path and hence his time allocation.
The figure depicts a situation in which the individual must, at every
moment, select among three activities, criminal (c), work (w) and leisure
(1). His time allocation, determined by the identity of the activity
maximizing utility at each moment, gives the intervals $[m_0, m_1)$ and $[m_3, m_4)$
to leisure, $[m_1, m_2)$ to work and $[m_2, m_3)$ to criminal activity.[25] Note that
as drawn the utility time paths are everywhere continuous functions of
time. In practice it will often be desirable to allow discontinuities at
certain decision moments. For example if there exist transitional costs
in switching among activities, discontinuities can be expected at the
switch points. A different source of discontinuities appears in modelling
crime commission decisions, to which subject we now turn.

---

[25]The intervals are made half open to resolve the ambiguity in choice
that occurs at points of transition among activities.

utilities

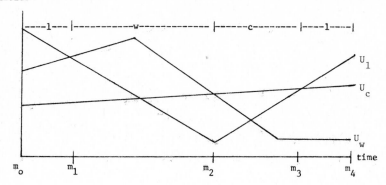

Figure 1: Activity Utilities and Choices

Suppose that the generation of criminal opportunities can be described by a birth and death process. That is, every so often a new criminal opportunity appears and has some life span over which its characteristics may vary. An opportunity may go out of existence in one of two ways. Either it is "used up" by the individual as he commits the relevant crime or, unused by him, it ends in some other manner at some time.

Given the above process the individual will at every moment have available some population of opportunities. While the size and character of this population will generally vary with time, we shall suppose that one alternative is always available. This is the "null option" of committing no crime. Assume now that at every moment the individual must select exactly one opportunity. If, as before, his choices over time are consistent with utility maximization and if utilities are again treated as random functions of time, then a dynamic random utility model describes crime commission behavior.

The crime commission process is illustrated in Figure 2. In the

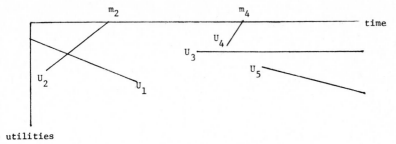

Figure 2:   Crime Commission Utilities and Choices

figure, the null option's utility is normalized to equal zero always.
Opportunity 1 is born before the beginning of the time period M and dies
unused. Opportunity 2 is born and eventually is used, the crime being
committed at moment m_2. There exists a time interval between the death
of opportunity 1 and emergence of opportunities 3, 4 and 5 in which only
the null option is available. Opportunity 4 is used at moment m_4 and
opportunities 3 and 5 still exist as the time period of observation ends.

It remains to specify how our models of time allocation and crime
commission relate to each other. Consider the crime commission model.
It should be expected that both the birth rate of criminal opportunities
and the evolution of their characteristics over time will in part depend
on the amount of time the individual has allocated to criminal search and
planning activities. Thus, past time allocation decisions help determine
the criminal opportunity sets faced and hence, may influence crime
commission decisions. Note that present crime commission decisions may
also be influenced by past crimes committed. In particular, the outcome
of past attempted crimes may affect the individual's wealth, criminal
record and perceived probabilities of arrest and conviction. And these
factors may in turn affect present crime commission decisions. Similar
forces will in general make present time allocation decisions a function

of both past crime commission and time allocation choices.

3. Some Remarks on Stochastic Process Models of Crime Commissions

In the econometric model of crime commission described above, the
temporal nature of the criminal decision problem and the analyst's limited
information make crime commission appear to follow a stochastic process.
At present, the manner in which different structural assumptions translate
into stochastic process properties for crime commission is unknown.   In
particular, it is not known whether realistic structural assumptions
yielding convenient stochastic processes exist.

A number of authors, working in the operations research tradition,
have directly formulated stochastic process models of crime commission.
For example, Blumstein and Greene (1976) construct a career length--crime
rate model in which the length of a criminal career is Gamma distributed
in the population and the crime rate for an active criminal is Poisson
distributed, independent of his career length.   Other models describe
transitions among crime types.   For example, an estimated "crime switch"
matrix may form the basis for a Markov model of crime commission.   See
Blumstein and Larson (1969), Avi-Itzhak and Shinnar (1973), and Shinnar
and Shinnar (1975) for further examples of stochastic process models of
crime.   Cohen (1978) reviews the relevant literature.

The existing stochastic process models offer a variety of analytically
convenient forms for the description of crime commission.   Unfortunately,
these models are, in their present form, decidely non-behavioral.   Not only
are they derived from no behavioral model but their parameters are treated
as physical constants.   Criminals, it is assumed, behave essentially like
light bulbs.[26]

---

[26]In fairness to the authors working in this literature, it should be

From the perspective of deterrence analysis, the above suggests two things. First, it would be of interest to ask what structural assumptions, if any, would yield stochastic process models of the forms found in the operations research literature. Where a match can be made, the given stochastic process model will be interpretable as a reduced form for the underlying behavioral model. Moreover, the parameters of the stochastic process model will be functionally determined by parameters of the relevant behavioral model. Hence, study of the stochastic process model may be useful in recovering the behavioral model.

Second, ignoring any formal behavioral-stochastic process model relations, the convenient analytical forms of the stochastic process models can be exploited by directly specifying the parameters of these models to be functions of behaviorally relevant variables. For example, the crime rate for decision maker t at moment m might be assumed Poisson with parameter

$$\lambda_{tm} = \lambda(Q_m, s_{tm}, \rho)$$

where Q_m is a vector characterizing deterrence policies, economic conditions and the like and ρ is a parameter vector. The empirical problem would then be to estimate the pseudo-behavioral parameters ρ. In non-crime contexts, ad hoc approaches to behavioral analysis like the one suggested here have been used by Ginsberg (1972) and Heckman and Willis (1975).

---

noted that they do not claim that stochastic process models are relevant to deterrence analysis. Rather, their interest has centered on the impact of incapacitation policies on the crime rate, holding deterrent policies constant. For this purpose, only a descriptive model of criminal action is necessary.

IV. Conclusions

Overall, the prospects for useful inference on deterrence through empirical analysis of individual criminal behavior seem decidedly mixed. Because the data likely to be available for such analysis has limitations and because criminal behavior can be so complex, the emergence of a definitive behavioral study laying to rest all controversy about the behavioral effects of deterrence policies should not be expected. On the other hand, data capable of illuminating important aspects of criminal behavior is obtainable and realistic, tractable behavorial models can be developed. The propsects for a piecemeal accumulation of useful evidence on deterrence are therefore good.

In thinking about modelling criminal behavior, it is natural to ask whether the paradigm of economic, that is rational, man can in fact successfully be applied in this context. I obviously believe so. There do however exist two respects in which modelling criminal behavior differs in degree from the typical economic modelling problem. First acquiring suitable data for modelling criminal behavior seems a more difficult task than is usually the case. Second, because the deterrence issue is so sensitive and because empirical evidence may play a role in judicial decisions as well as legislative policy formation, the desired standard of proof sought in empirical analyses of crime is higher than that found acceptable in most other contexts.[27]

---

[27] The most notable recent example of a role played by empirical analysis in judicial deliberation is the advancement by the U.S. Solicitor General in the case Fowler vs. North Carolina of Ehrlich's (1975) results as an argument in favor of finding capital punishment constitutional. In their opinions, the U.S. Supreme Court, wisely I think, declared that this evidence was too uncertain to influence their decision on the capital punishment issue. See U.S. Solicitor General (1975) and U.S. Supreme Court (1975).

For this reason, researchers should be quite cautious in the performance and interpretation of empirical work on criminal behavior.

REFERENCES

Albright, R., S. Lerman and C. Manski, "The Multinomial Probit Estimation
    Package: Features and Operational Tests," Cambridge Systematics, Inc.,
    1977.

Allingham, M., and A. Sandmo, "Income Tax Evasion: A Theoretical Analysis,"
    Journal of Public Economics, Volume 1, November, 1972.

Avi-Itzhak, B., and R. Shinnar, "Quantitative Models in Crime Control,"
    Journal of Criminal Justice, Volume 1, January, 1973.

Bass, F., A. Jeuland and G. Wright, "Equilibrium Stochastic Choice and
    Market Penetration Theories: Derivations and Comparisons," Management
    Science, Volume 22, June, 1976, pp. 1051-1063.

Becker, G., "Crime and Punishment: An Economic Approach," Journal of
    Political Economy, Volume 78, pp. 189-217, 1968.

Block, M., and J. Heineke, "The Allocation of Effort Under Uncertainty:
    The Case of Risk Averse Behavior," Journal of Political Economy,
    Volume 81, March/April, 1973.

Block, M., and J. Heineke, "A Labor Theoretic Analysis of the Criminal
    Choice," American Economic Review, Volume 65, pp. 314-325, 1975.

Blumstein, A., D. Nagin and J. Cohen (eds.), Deterrence and Incapacitation:
    The Effects of Criminal Sanctions on Crime Rates, National Academy of
    Sciences, 1978.

Blumstein, A., and D. Nagin, "The Deterrent Effect of Legal Sanctions on
    Draft Evasion," Stanford Law Review, Volume 28, No. 2, January, 1977.

Blumstein, A., and M. Greene, "The Distribution of the Length of Criminal
    Careers," School of Urban and Public Affairs, Carnegie-Mellon
    University, unpublished, 1976.

Blumstein, A., and R. Larson, "Models of a Total Criminal Justice System,"
    Operations Research, March/April, 1969.

Brown, W., and M. Reynolds, "Crime and Punishment: Risk Implications,"
    Journal of Economic Theory, Volume 6, pp. 508-514, 1973.

Carr-Hill, R., and N. Stern, "An Econometric Model of the Supply and
    Control of Recorded Offenses in England and Wales," Journal of
    Public Economics, Volume 2, 1973.

Cohen, J., "The Incapacitative Effect of Imprisonment: A Critical Review
    of the Literature," in Blumstein, et. al., (eds.), Deterrence and
    Incapactiation: The Effects of Criminal Sanctions on Crime Rates,
    National Academcy of Sciences, 1978.

Ehrlich, I., "Participation in Illegitimate Activities: A Theoretical and Empirical Investigation," Journal of Political Economy, Volume 81, pp. 521-567, 1973.

Ehrlich, I., "The Deterrent Effect of Capital Punishment: A Question of Life and Death," American Economic Review, Volume 65, pp. 397-417.

Fisher, F., and D. Nagin, "On the Feasibility of Identifying the Crime Function in a Simultaneous Model of Crime Rates and Sanction Levels," in Blumstein, et. al., (eds.), Deterrence and Incapacitation: The Effects of Criminal Sanctions on Crime Rates, National Academy of Sciences, 1978.

Forst, B., "Participation in Illegitimate Activities: Further Empirical Findings," Policy Analysis, 1976.

Ginsberg, R., "Semi-Markov Processes and Mobility," Journal of Mathematical Sociology, Volume 1, 1971, pp. 233-262.

Hausman, J., and D. Wise, "The Evaluation of Results from Truncated Samples: The New Jersey Income Maintenance Experiment," Annals of Economic and Social Measurement, Volume 5, no. 4, 1976, pp. 421-446.

Hausman, J., and D. Wise, "Social Experimentation, Truncated Distribution, and Efficient Estimation," Econometrica, Volume 45, no. 4, May, 1977, pp. 919-938.

Heckman, J., and R. Willis, "A Beta-Logistic Model for the Analysis of Sequential Labor Force Participation by Married Women," NBER Working Paper No. 112, August, 1975.

Heineke, J., "Economic Models of Criminal Behavior: Implications and Shortcomings," Technical Report EMCRD-1-76, Center for the Econometric Studies of Crime and the Criminal Justice System, Hoover Institution, Stanford University, April, 1976.

Heineke, J., "A Note on Modelling the Criminal Choice Problem," Journal of Economic Theory, Volume 10, pp. 113-116, 1975.

Klein, L., B. Forst and V. Filatov, "The Deterrent Effect of Capital Punishment," in Blumstein, et. al., (eds.), Deterrence and Incapacitation: The Effects of Criminal Sanctions on Crime Rates, National Academy of Sciences, 1978.

Kohn, M., C. Manski and D. Mundel, "An Empirical Investigation of Factors Influencing College Going Behavior," Annals of Economic and Social Measurement, Volume 5, No. 4, pp. 391-420.

Koln, S., "A Note on Optimum Income Tax Evasion," Journal of Public Economics, Volume 2, 1973.

Lerman, S., and M. Ben-Akiva, "A Disaggregate Behavioral Model of Auto Ownership," Transportation Research Record, 1975.

Levy, F., "How Big is the American Underclass?", Graduate School of Public
Policy, University of California, Berkeley, unpublished, 1976.

Luce, R., and P. Suppes, "Preference, Utility and Subjective Probability,"
in R. Luce, R. Bush and E. Galanter, eds., Handbook of Mathematical
Psychology, Volume III, Wiley, 1965.

Manski, C., and D. McFadden, "Alternative Estimators and Sample Designs
for Discrete Choice Analysis," Department of Economics, University
of California, Berkeley, unpublished, April, 1977.

Manski, C., and S. Lerman, "The Estimation of Choice Probabilities from
Choice Based Samples," Econometrica, Volume 45, pp. 1977-1988, 1977.

McFadden, D., "Conditional Logit Analysis of Qualitative Choice Behavior,"
in Zarembka, eds., Frontiers in Econometrics, Academic Press, 1973.

McFadden, D., "Quantal Choice Analysis: A Survey," Annals of Economic
and Social Measurement, Volume 5, No. 4, pp. 363-390, 1976.

Nagin, D., "General Deterrence: A Review of the Empirical Evidence" in
Blumstein, et. al., (ed.), Deterrence and Incapacitation: The
Effects of Criminal Sanctions on Crime Rates, National Academy of
Sciences, 1978.

Passell, P., and J. Taylor, "The Deterrence Controversy: Reconsideration
of the Time Series Evidence," in H. Bedauand, C. Pierce, eds.,
Capital Punishment, AMS Press, 1976.

Peck, J., "The Deterrent Effect of Capital Punishment: A Comment," Yale
Law Journal, Volume 86, pp. 354-367, 1976.

Petersilia, J., P. Greenwood and M. Lavin, "Criminal Careers of
Repetitively Violent Offenders," Rand Corporation Report R-2144-DOJ,
March, 1977.

Reiss, Jr., A., "Survey of Self-Reported Delict," Department of Sociology,
Yale University, unpublished, 1973.

Shinnar, R., and S. Shinnar, "The Effects of the Criminal Justice System
on the Control of Crime: A Quantitative Approach," Law and Society
Review, Volume 9, No. 4, Summer, 1975.

Singh, B., "Making Honesty the Best Policy," Journal of Public Economics,
Volume 2, 1973.

Theil, H., Principles of Econometrics, Wiley, 1971.

Tobin, J., "Estimation of Relationships for Limited Dependent Variables,"
Econometrica, Volume 26, pp. 24-36, 1958.

U.S. Solicitor General, Amicus Curiae Brief on Fowler vs. North Caroline,
Case no. 73-7031, U.S. Supreme Court, 1975.

U.S. Supreme Court, Opinion on Fowler vs. North Carolina, Case no.
    73-7031, U.S. Supreme Court, 1975.

Vandaele, W., "Sentitivity Analysis of Simultaneous Econometric Models,"
    in Blumstein, et. al., (ed.), Deterrence and Incapacitation: The
    Effects of Criminal Sanctions on Crime Rates, National Academy of
    Sciences, 1978.

Weimer, D., and M. Stonebraker, "Sentencing Patterns, DA Policy and the
    Decision to Go to Trial," Graduate School of Public Policy,
    University of California, Berkeley, unpublished, October, 1975.

Witte, A., "Testing the Economic Model of Crime on Individual Data,"
    Department of Economics, University of North Carolina, Chapel
    Hill, unpublished, April, 1976.

Economic Models of Criminal Behavior,
J.M. Heineke (ed.)
© *North-Holland Publishing Company, 1978*

CHAPTER FOUR

ON THE ECONOMIC THEORY OF POLICY TOWARDS CRIME*

Nicholas Stern

§ 1. Introduction

The theory of punishment was a major concern of the great utilitarian

Jeremy Bentham.[1] However, the first formal economic analysis of policy towards

crime, in terms of the costs and benefits of offences and their deterrence did

not appear until 1968. The article in question[2], Becker (1968), has set the

framework for most of the subsequent theoretical work on the economics of crime

and punishment. In his model the government chooses the level of punishment for

offences and the expenditure on the police, and thus the probability of appre-

hension, to minimise a social loss function. Losses include damage from offences,

expenditure on police and costs of punishment. Central to the model is a deter-

rence function which relates the number of offences to the probability and severity

of punishment through the theory of individual choice in the presence of uncertainty.

We shall concentrate in this paper on the model proposed by Becker. An

explanation of his model and the main results is provided in the next section. We

examine first Becker's result that crime, at the optimum, should not pay together

with comments on this result by certain authors. Secondly, we discuss the proposi-

tion that fines should be related the damage done by the offence and be independent

of the circumstances of the offender.

We shall argue in § 3 that there is a fundamental logical objection to

the Becker model which renders it unacceptable as either a description of the reasoning behind current policy or as a prescription for a desirable

policy. In the fourth section we examine modifications and criticisms of

the Becker framework as presented by a number of authors and relate them

to the objection registered in § 3. Becker's model bears, as he himself

pointed out, a striking resemblance to the standard economic theory of

externality and these similarities are discussed in § 5. In the sixth

section we argue that any notion of the "just" punishment is absent from

the cost-benefit approach. The final section is devoted to concluding

remarks.

The purpose of this paper is then twofold. We shall be providing

a partial review of the recent theoretical literature on policy towards

crime. It should be stressed that there is no claim to comprehensive

coverage. We have omitted, for example, discussion of the related liter-

ature on tax evasion (see, for example, Allingham and Sandmo (1972), Kolm

(1973) and Srinivasan (1973)). Secondly, we shall be presenting and explain-

ing a basic objection to the Becker model and examining its implications

for that model and the related theory of externalities.

§ 2.   Becker's Framework

2.1   The Model

The government chooses the severity of punishment measured by f and

the probability of apprehension measured by p to minimise a social loss

function L(p, f), the components of which are defined below. We make no

distinction here between apprehension and conviction and assume that all

punishment can be reduced to a common denominator and expressed in money

terms. Faced with the p and f set by the government individuals decide

how many offences to commit; thus if we denote the number of offences by

Y we have the offence or deterrence function Y(p, f). We are supposing here that there is just one type of offence. [We follow Becker's notation here except that we avoid using O for offences. The use of O can cause confusion with zero]. The offence function has been discussed in other papers[3] in this volume, particularly in relation to individual utility maximisation and we shall therefore return to it only briefly below.

There are three components to the social loss function: the damage from offences, the cost of apprehension and the cost of punishment. The first is a function of the number of offences Y, the second of the number of offences, Y, and the proportion solved or p, and the third of the number of punishments pY and the severity of each punishment f. We write D(Y) for the damages from offences, C(Y,p) for the cost of apprehension and bpfY for the cost of punishment. This last expression requires explanation. Becker multiplies the total number of punishments by the severity per punishment to obtain the overall quantity of punishment pfY expressed in money terms. The factor b translates this total quantity into social loss.

The government desires to choose p and f to minimise

(1) $L(p, f) = D(Y) + C(Y, p) + bpfY.$

We suppose that p, being a probability, lies between zero and one and that punishment cannot be negative. The maximisation of (1) is therefore subject to the constraints

(2) $0 \leq p \leq 1$

(3) $0 \leq f$

The first order conditions for an interior solution, $0 < p < 1$ and $0 < f$, are that the first derivatives with respect to p and f, L_p and L_f respectively should vanish. Thus

(4) $L_p = (D' + C_Y + bpf)Y_p + bfY + C_p = 0$

(5) $L_f = (D' + C_Y + bpf)Y_f + bpY = 0.$

D' is the derivative of D with respect to Y, C_Y and C_p the partial derivatives of C with respect to Y and p, and Y_p and Y_f the partial derivatives of Y with respect to p and f. We suppose that D' is positive (damages increase with the number of offences) and that C_Y is positive (an increase in offences implies an increase in costs of apprehension if p is to be maintained). We suppose also that Y_p and Y_f are negative (an increase in the probability of apprehension or the level of punishment reduces offences). We assume that the signs of these partial derivatives are strict.

2.2   Individual Behaviour

Becker bases his analysis throughout his paper on these two first order conditions. In this subsection we follow him in examining results concerning individual behaviour. From (4) and (5) we have:

(6) $\dfrac{bfY}{Y_p} + \dfrac{C_p}{Y_p} = \dfrac{bpY}{Y_f}$

Note that if $b = 0$ equation (6) contradicts the assumptions that have just been made about the signs of the partial derivatives. This leads to a reconsideration of the formulation of the problem for this case and is

the subject matter of § 2.3 and § 3. For this subsection we assume that
b ≠ 0. From (6) using the definitions (7) of the elasticities of offences
with respect to p and f, respectively

(7) $\varepsilon_p = - \frac{p}{Y} Y_p$ and $\varepsilon_f = - \frac{f}{Y} Y_f$

we have

(8) $\frac{1}{\varepsilon_p} - \frac{1}{\varepsilon_f} = \frac{C_p}{bfpY_p}$

If the cost of punishment is positive (b > 0) then the right hand side of
(8) is negative and we have, assuming $C_p > 0$ and $Y_p < 0$,

(9) $\varepsilon_p > \varepsilon_f$.

Becker drew particular attention to this result. It accords, he suggests,
with a common supposition that potential offenders are more responsive to
the probability of detection than the level of punishment and, he claimed,
that empirical studies supported this view.

By relating (9) to individual decisions and the maximisation of
expected utility Becker concluded that, if (9) holds, offenders will be
"on balance" drawn from those who have a convex utility function, and
hence who are risk-preferrers, (see Becker (1968) p. 178 and 183). Thus
offenders would be accepting unfair gambles and would eventually become
poor and hence, he said, at the optimum "crime does not pay". The argument
is as follows.

Let W be the wealth of an individual contemplating an offence.
Becker includes in W the gains from the offence if committed and where
there is no apprehension or punishment. The individual if apprehended
loses f. Thus f includes confiscation, if any, of the proceeds from the

offence. The expected utility from committing the offence becomes

(10) $EU = (1 - p) U(W) + pU(W - f)$.

It is easy to show (and see Becker (1968) footnote 19 on p. 178) that the
change in EU with respect to a (proportional) change in p is greater than
that with respect to f only if the function U is convex.

Brown and Reynolds (1973) objected to the Becker analysis on the
grounds that it is peculiar to include in W the proceeds from an offence
if it is unpunished. And it must be agreed that one does not usually
count in one's wealth the proceeds from all offences that can be contemplated.
Heineke (1975) argued that the acceptability of the Becker formulation
would depend on whether proceeds from an offence were actually recovered
and confiscated. Both Brown and Reynolds (1973) and Heineke (1975) agree
that if one replaces the measures of wealth, and consequently, punishment,
with the measures that they respectively suggest (see below) then one
cannot conclude from a comparison of the elasticities with respect to the
probability and level of punishment, such as (9), that U is convex. Brown
and Reynolds (1973), for example, replace W by W' + G, where G is the
potential gain, and W-f by W'-L where L is the new measure of punishment
and W' a more usual measure of wealth. By differentiating the reformulated
equation (10) with respect to p and L the reader can easily check that
$\varepsilon_p > \varepsilon_L$ (where Y is now a function of p and L and ε_p and ε_L are the
elasticities) does not imply that U is convex.

The change just made, however, replaces one convention by another
and assumes nothing about confiscation. It is not necessarily a criticism
of Becker that his convention does not accord with common parlance. In
order to evaluate his measure one has to look at the use which Becker
makes of his convention. And here Becker is vulnerable in two ways.

First, his variable f appears elsewhere in his social loss function, in
the third term measuring cost of punishment, and his model of individual
behaviour should be consistent with this further usage. Secondly he
appeals to empirical work and common supposition in support of the notion
that offenders are more responsive to the probability than to the level of
punishment.   If this empirical work is admissible as evidence relevant
to Becker's argument it should use measures of punishment similar to those
chosen by Becker. Whilst it is rare indeed that an empirical measure
reflects precisely its theoretical counterpart an important interpretation
("crime does not pay") turns in this case on the measure used; thus we
must examine the nature of measures available for empirical work.

The use of the variable f in the measurement of the cost of punishment
does not seem to be consistent with its use in the analysis of individual
behaviour. In the latter f measures everything foregone by an individual
who has committed an offence.[4] These losses as perceived by individuals
include such confiscation as takes place, and costs and shame of court
appearance in addition to the punishment imposed by the court. But one
cannot then multiply this f by some constant b to calculate the social
cost of the punishment. One would want to treat the elements of punishment just described as relevant for the individual differently from
each other in the translation to social cost. For example the individual's
costs of court appearance are direct resource costs in terms of time of
lawyers and so on but any confiscation would involve a transfer from the
individual to the victim. The individual simply adds these together to
find their contribution to his f. One would certainly not want to take
a simple unweighted addition in calculating social cost of punishment.

The empirical work cited by Becker in 1968 in support of his
observation concerning ε_p and ε_f had not then been published (although
some work by Ehrlich has now appeared - Ehrlich (1973)).   But it would

be most surprising if such work could be based on the f as used by Becker

in his model of individual behaviour. For published statistics on punish-

ment would not in general include any measure of confiscation or costs and

shame incurred by the punished offender. Indeed the difficulties which

would be associated with collecting such data are obvious.

We shall not press the analysis of results about individual behaviour

any further here, but we must draw attention to the particular nature of

the model of individual behaviour presented. It should be noted that we

have here followed Becker in presenting the model as one of simple choice

under uncertainty where utility depends only on wealth. There is no

question, in the model, of allocation of time. The individual simply

accepts or refuses a gamble. We can thus invoke the standard discussion

of increasing or decreasing risk aversion (see, for example, Arrow (1970)).

It is commonly argued (again see Arrow (1970)) that there is decreasing

absolute risk aversion. In this case the rich would be more likely, in

this model, to commit any given offence than the poor. We shall return

to this conclusion in § 5. It should be noted that models which involve

the allocation of time do not necessarily yield this result. For further

discussion of models of individual behaviour see Chapter 1 (Heineke) of

this volume.

The model would appear to refer better to minor offences where an

individual acts in response to an opportunity which appears rather than to

substantial offences which may take time to commit and involve major planning.

Such minor offences form, for example, the vast majority of indictable

offences in England and Wales. In 1966 for example 44% of all recorded

indictable offences in England and Wales were thefts of articles value less

than ten pounds, and 70% less than one hundred pounds and involving no

violence against the person.[5] Indictable offences correspond roughly with

U.S. felonies except that there is no monetary cut-off for the former.
A theft of an item, however small in value is an indictable offence. Note
that the type of offences being considered is important for a judgement of
which model is appropriate -- thus we are suggesting that, for the majority
of indictable offences and offenders in the U.K., the allocation of time may
not be an important consideration.

And one must take into account in making inferences about individual
behaviour that some data involve monetary cut-offs. In that case individuals
may commit felonies "by mistake". If I steal an item which I think is worth
$50 (where we suppose the cut-off is $100) and it turns out that the item
is worth $101 then I have committed a felony when I intended to commit some-
thing more minor. And similarly some may not commit felonies whilst
intending to do so. The commission of offences by mistake is something
which has received insufficient attention in both the empirical and
theoretical literature.

In this and the previous subsection we have presented Becker's model
of optimum policy towards crime and have examined some of his conclusions
from that model concerning individual behaviour. We have seen that the
model involved an odd and inconsistent approach to the measurement of
punishment. We turn now to a case on which Becker laid special emphasis;
that where punishment is by fine.

2.3   The "Optimum" Fine

Becker argued that the social cost of punishment by fine is zero
since a fine is a transfer payment. Let us, for the most part, accept that
in this case the cost of punishment is zero (we return to the point in
§ 5). Let us accept too, for the sake of argument, a second assumption
that was important for Becker's argument, namely that punishment is
certain -- that is $p = 1$. The fixing of p like this is crucial to what

follows and will play a   central role in our basic criticism of the model
in the next section.

We then have, following Becker, from (5)

(11) $D' + C_Y = 0.$

We now examine the damages from offences in a little more detail. Becker
splits these damages into the harm to the victim, H, and the gain to the
offender, G; thus D is H - G, where both H and G are functions of Y.
Substituting for D' in (11) and rearranging we have, where a prime denotes
derivative,

(12) $G' = H' + C_Y .$

Now, Becker continues, since the punishment is certain the value of the
marginal gain to the individual, G', will be, when he has chosen his optimum
number of offences, equated to the value of the punishment f. We then have

(13) $f = H' + C_Y.$

Equation (13) (Becker (1968) equation (29)) is the basis of his
discussion of the optimum fine. We can interpret (13) to say that the
optimum fine is equal to the   harm inflicted on the victim plus cost of
apprehension. Thus it would appear we have an argument that the punishment should be equal to the damage and that this argument is independent
of the notion of retribution. It also follows that the fine should be
independent of the circumstance of the offender.

We shall be arguing that the conclusions just drawn are unacceptable.
Our objections center on the assumption that p is fixed. An examination
of the consequences of relaxing that assumption will lead to some basic
questions concerning the use of the cost-benefit framework in the analysis
of policy towards crime. It is to this we now turn.

§ 3.   A Fundamental Objection

We have so far followed Becker in basing our analysis on the first
order conditions (4) and (5). In other words we have supposed the optimum
probability to be between zero and one, the optimum fine to be finite and
greater than zero and that, at the optimum there is some corresponding
finite non-zero level of offences. But what if the government announced
punishment so large, together with some non-zero probability of apprehension
p that no offences were committed? There would be zero social loss -- no
offences, no cost of apprehension, no punishments (and no evidence to
contradict the announced p). This, in the model, would surely be optimum.
The point is unanswerable in the model (Becker's model) of the previous
section. We shall demonstrate this formally for the case of costless
punishment, which Becker made central. The argument in favour of zero
offences is yet stronger where punishment is costly.

Becker's analysis is immediately seen to be futile. There is no
point in supposing we have an interior solution and examining, and interpreting associated first order conditions, when one can show that the
model cannot have this solution.

In the next section (§ 4) we shall examine certain modifications
to the Becker model some of which might appear to save it from the extreme
conclusion. We shall be arguing, although it will be a question of judgement rather than formal proof, that they cannot.

Suppose we have the model of § 2.3 with b = 0 (costless punishment)
except that we now suppose, as we did in § 2.1 and 2.2 that the probability
of apprehension is also to be chosen. We retain the assumption on the
signs of the derivative of the functions in the model which were presented
in § 2.1. If we are to have an optimum with probability of apprehension,
p, between zero and one and severity of punishment, f, greater than zero
(and finite) then the selected p and f must satisfy (4) and (5). We shall

see immediately that this is impossible and hence that our supposition
that we have an interior optimum is false. Putting b = 0 in (4) and (5)
we have

(14) $(D' + C_Y)Y_p + C_p = 0$

(15) $(D' + C_Y)Y_f = 0$.

If extra punishment deters Y_f is not zero. Then $D' + C_Y$ is zero from (15).
But we then have a contradiction in (14) because, we suppose, C_p is strictly
positive.

     The intuition is clear. If we have set punishment so that the marginal
net loss from an extra offence is zero then we save on apprehension costs
by reducing the probability of apprehension, with, on the margin, no offsetting costs from the increase in offences. Or, if deterrence is costless
through f we should avoid using the costly p.

     We have seen that if extra punishment deters ($Y_f < 0$) and punishment
is costless (b = 0) then an interior solution is impossible. We must
ask whether there are optima which are not interior, and if the answer is
negative we must conclude that the problem as formulated has no solution.
The argument just given in our demonstration that (14) and (15) are
contradictory shows also that the corner solution p = 1 is not optimum.
For if it were we should require $L_p < 0$ (or the left-hand side of (14)
less than or equal to zero) and we have shown that (15) implies (if $Y_f < 0$)
that $L_p > 0$. The other possible corner solutions are either p = 0 or
f = 0 (or both). Thus both remaining candidates for the optimum involve
no punishment, either because individuals are not caught, or they are not
punished if caught. Let us assume directly that the absence of punishment
is not optimum.

We are left with the possibilities of allowing $Y_f = 0$ (it was supposed < 0 in § 2.1) or that there is no solution. The interpretation of these last two possibilities is similar. In the former case we have punishment levels set so high that there is no further deterrence from increasing punishment -- for example because there are no offences. In the latter no solution exists because the problem as formulated dictates infinite punishment f. One can make this last statement precise as follows. Suppose we impose an upper bound on f, call it F. The problem becomes then the minimisation of a (we suppose) continuous function $L(p, f)$ over a compact set $\{0 \leq p \leq 1 ; \ 0 \leq f \leq F\}$, and thus has a solution. We have seen that, if Y_f is strictly less than zero the solution can only be at F with $L_f < 0$. Thus one could reduce social loss by increasing punishment but the upper bound prevents us from doing so.[6]

The analysis presented in § 2.3 with p fixed (at one) would appear to avoid the problem since we deal with only one first order condition -- that for f. However, first it is still possible that the model with fixed p would dictate zero offences[7] -- whether it does or not depends on whether there can exist a residual of offences which are beneficial. For zero offences involves zero social loss and negative social loss can only be achieved (see (1)) by negative damages (D) from offences (for further discussion see § 4). An example of a beneficial offence might be breaking the speed limit to get an injured person to the hospital quickly. It is natural to suppose such examples are rare (see § 4). Secondly, it is odd to fix the probability of apprehension in a model which is to a large extent designed to explain it.

We have shown formally, in the sense just described, that the Becker model with costless punishment has no interior solution, satisfying (15). But Becker's discussion of the optimum fine was based entirely on (15) (or its equivalent here (13)). That discussion is therefore unacceptable unless one makes the peculiar assumption that p is fixed. In the cost-benefit

framework the arguments in favour of very large punishment and thus zero

offences are stronger when punishment is costly (b > 0) than when it is

costless. Thus we suppose Becker's analysis of (4) and (5) is open to the

same basic objection as that just described -- the first order conditions

described do not give an optimum since the optimum either does not exist

(f indefinitely large) or involves announced punishment so severe that

there are zero offences.   Conclusions draw from those first order conditions,

such as the responsiveness to the probability of conviction should be

greater than that to the severity of punishment are therefore invalid.

We examine possible modifications to the Becker model in the next

section. We record here that at various points in his article Becker

appeared to be aware of the problem we have been discussing. See for

example Becker (1968) pp. 183-4, footnote 26, p. 189 (his case b = 0

and Fig. 4) and p. 193. Nowhere however does he acknowledge that the

model he has written down must have the extreme solution that we have noted.

§ 4.   Modifications to the Becker Model

We have discussed, in § 2.2, contributions associated with the

conclusion that offenders are risk preferrers and that therefore crime

should not pay. We examine here some modifications to the social loss

function and to its constituent cost elements which have been suggested

in the literature. We examine in particular the work of Carr-Hill and

Stern (1976), Harris (1970), and Stigler (1970).

Harris argued that the problem as specified in (1) here seemed to

imply that any measure which reduced costs of obtaining convictions

(reduced the C function) was justified. This he feared might be used to

justify increased police powers or lower legal safeguards. The costs of

decreases in legal safeguards are, he suggests, in terms of increased

punishment of the innocent. He therefore proposes another choice variable
and another term in the maximand. The choice variable is intended to measure
legal safeguards and the additional term, costs of punishing the innocent.
He shows for example that an increase in concern over punishing the innocent
will lead, at the optimum, to higher legal safeguards.

Stigler attempts to extend the Becker framework into the wider area of
enforcement of rules and contracts. He suggests that the decisive reason
why enforcement is not complete is that it is costly. He notes however
(1970) p. 527 that deterrence is available through increases in punishment
and that one seems to be led to the conclusion that punishment should always
be increased. It appears that he has understood the objection to the Becker
model set out in the previous section.

Stigler goes on to say, however, that Becker provides an upper limit
to punishment by introducing the social value of the gain to an offender.
Stigler doubts the usefulness of the last concept and suggests that an
upper limit to punishment can be derived from the absence of a marginal
deterrent for large punishment levels ($Y_f = 0$ in the above). His suggestion
is important and we shall examine it in detail when we come to possible
modifications to the Becker model which might save it from the peculiar
conclusions we have noted. First, however, we must record that Stigler is
in error in claiming that the introduction of a social value to offences
provides a sensible solution in the Becker framework.[8] The point is
important and we shall explain it in a little detail.

The condition that the net marginal cost of an offence is zero
($D' + C_Y = 0$) does indeed imply that there is marginal benefit from an
offence ($D' < 0$) counterbalanced by a marginal cost of maintaining the
probability of apprehension at p ($C_Y > 0$). But we saw[9] that it was
precisely this condition which led to the contradiction explained in § 3

since $D' + C_Y = 0$ implies that savings in social costs are available from
reducing the probability of apprehension, p. Thus allowing the possibility
that D' can be negative does not, by itself, provide an upper limit for the
case of costless punishment (b = 0).

If we have marginal social benefits from an offence together with
marginal social benefits from punishment (negative b above) one can
conclude that we are likely to have an optimum with finite f and positive
offences. We shall explain this claim in detail in § 5 when we examine
analogies with the theory of externalities. Briefly the benefits from
punishment will be tax revenue so that an increase in punishment involves
a trade-off between discouraging the (beneficial) offences and increasing
the tax revenue. We shall argue that the story is better applied to productive activities with undesirable externalities rather than to offences.
We note here merely that beneficial offences by themselves are no escape.

How then can we avoid the implication from models of the Becker-type
that punishment should be pushed to the point where deterrence is no
longer effective ($Y_f = 0$) or where there are zero offences? We have,
up to now, approached the Becker model rather formally and have asked,
and have tried to answer, questions inside the framework of the model.
We shall examine possible answers to the question just posed less
formally and more speculatively, for two reasons. First, the extreme
solutions of the model if translated into the real world can embroil
one in arguments about, for example, the humanitarian aspects of extreme
punishment. Whilst important, that would sidetrack us from our main
issue which is whether the utilitarian approach provides a useful model
of punishment for the main bulk of offences (in the U.K. minor thefts).
Secondly, most possible answers involve complications to the model. We
shall discuss the likely consequences of these complications but shall not
offer the detailed workings of the formal model for each case of the extra
consideration which are being examined.

We shall proceed then by reformulating the question as follows: If
extra punishment deters why is punishment not raised? We are following
here the approach of Carr-Hill and Stern (1976). To keep matters simple
and concrete let us consider a particular type of offence -- say a minor
act of vandalism such as breaking a window in a train. The fine for
such an offence in the U.K. might be of the order of fifty pounds. Supposing
the fine is at that level, what are the arguments, if any, against making
it one hundred pounds?

We shall suppose that the offences in question are seen to be damaging.
This is perhaps obvious in the example quoted but seems a reasonable
assumption generally for, as Stigler (1970) has argued, one must expect
society having declared certain acts criminal to ask its policy makers to
view the commission of such acts as harmful.

We shall mention several possible "economic" answers and comment on
their acceptability. We leave the reader to think of others and to form
his own judgement as to their adequacy. [Carr-Hill and Stern (1976) set
out the discussion in some detail and the reader who wishes to pursue the
matter further may wish to consult that paper and some of the references
mentioned there.] We shall come to the judgement that the arguments,
singly or collectively, cannot provide a satisfactory answer and conclude
that we have to search outside the economic models, simple or complicated.
We shall suggest that punishments are in general thought to be "just" in
relation to the damage involved in the offence. This will involve the
notion of retribution.

It must be emphasised here that we are not arguing that the economic
approach is irrelevant, but that it cannot be the whole story. It is clear
that an examination of the effectiveness of deterrence, damages from offences
and the costs of apprehension and punishment is very important to the

formulation of policy towards crime, and we take these considerations
as defining the economic approach. But the sense in which they fail to
provide the whole story is also important and, it seems, crucial to an
understanding of the system of punishments as we find them in say, the
U.K. or the U.S.A.

We shall be using the terms economic, utilitarian and cost-benefit
approach interchangeably in what follows and we have given a definition of
what we mean by the terms. It is clear that they involve a class of models
much wider than the particular one used by Becker. Indeed, the modifications
to be discussed are designed to look further afield than the Becker model.
We should, however, note that further complications of the individual choice
problem (see, for example, Chapter 1, Heineke) will not be particularly
relevant to what follows provided they do not overturn the conclusion that
extra punishment deters.

We have seen in the simple Becker model where the probability of
apprehension and the level of punishment are to be chosen, and increase
in the former are costly and the latter are not, that one cannot, in general,
explain why extra punishment if it deters is not imposed. Let us examine
five possible economic modifications to the model which might be thought to
answer the question.

First, one might argue that the government attaches a cost to a transfer
from a poor finee to its own coffers and thus that the transfer payment
involved in the fine is associated with $b > 0$. But this would require the
dubious assumption that the government sees a unit of income in its own
hands as less valuable than to the criminal being punished. And we have
seen (§ 3) that a model where $b > 0$ can also lead to the result that potential
punishment is so high that there are neither offences nor punishment.

One can include in this first argument the existence of a constraint
on the level of the fine which is imposed by the wealth of the offender.
It emerges as a special case by making the assumption that the social
marginal cost of a fine tends to infinity as the (post-fine) wealth of
the offender tends to zero. But it is unlikely in the examples that we
have in mind that the social costs of immiseration of the finee prevent
the fine from being increased, if only because the increase under consideration
would not, in general, result in the confiscation of the entire wealth of
the finee.

Secondly, the government might attach a premium to its own revenue
(so that b < 0) and worry that extra punishment may cause a serious drop in
its fine income. It is hard, however, to imagine a government suggesting
that it does not want to over-discourage vandalism because it cannot afford
to lose the fine revenue (but see § 5).

Thirdly, one might object to the assumption that extra punishment deters.
This may be because the individuals in question might be so embittered by
(their view of) the injustice of the punishment that they have a desire to
wound. Alternatively they may substitute in favour other, possibly more
harmful activities. Substitution amongst offences has been discussed elsewhere in this volume (see Chapter 6, Heineke) and has been stressed by
Stigler (1970). It is encapsulated in the dictum that "you may as well be
hung for a sheep as a lamb". If it is indeed true that extra punishment
does not deter then our starting point (for the sake of the argument here
a fine of fifty pounds) is consistent with the utilitarian or cost-benefit
solution, $Y_f = 0$ and this framework "has no case to answer". We should
suggest however that for the example under discussion it is fair to presume
that extra punishment would deter and that substitution towards other
offences would be negligible. And many empirical studies (reviewed

elsewhere in this book, see Chapter 2, Taylor) have indeed found significant
deterrent effects around current punishment levels. It is hard to believe
that the whole structure of offences is so delicately balanced that no
further deterrence of minor acts of vandalism is possible without causing
an increase in more serious offences.

It must be acknowledged, of course, that a model with several offence
types would considerably complicate the notion of deterrence. But the
question with which we started remains unanswered provided only that there
exists just one offence type, extra punishment for which deters that offence,
yet this extra punishment has negligible interaction with other offence types.

Fourthly, the level of punishment might directly affect the cost of
apprehension, in the sense that individuals have a greater incentive to
take evading action, and hire better lawyers where caught, if penalties
are high. The argument has some plausibility but we know of no empirical
evidence in favour of the view that the effects indicated are substantial
for the kind of offences we have in mind. It may be a consideration of
greater importance for more serious offences.

Fifthly, there may be a cost associated with punishing the innocent,
as argued by Harris (1970). It is doubtful, however, whether this is a
serious worry for decision-makers for the example we have in mind. There
would, in general, be substantial confidence that the individual was guilty.
Further any wrong would be seen to be related more to the act of conviction
than the precise level of the fine, and the money involved in punishment
by fine can be repaid.

We have suggested that this fifth argument does not provide sufficient
reason for refraining from raising punishment where that deters. There
are, in any case, good grounds for objecting to its classification as
"economic" in the sense in which we have been using the term. The principle

that we should punish only those who have done wrong is essentially

retributive. Hart (1968) refers to this principle as "Distributive

Retribution".[10]

We do not so far seem to have found a satisfactory economic answer

to the question as to why punishment, if it deters, is not increased. The

suggestions examined above leave unperturbed the conclusion that utilitarian

models will lead to the prescription that punishment should be pushed so

far that no further deterrence is possible. Stigler (1970) recognises the

point (see his p. 527). But if those who make the social decisions collect-

ively refuse to raise punishment levels, in the light of the knowledge or

assumption that such increases would deter, what should we conclude? The

answer appears to be that they reject the cost-benefit framework and retain

some notion of the "just" punishment which lies outside that framework.

We return to the point in § 6.

§ 5.   The Theory of Externalities

The Becker presentation of the optimum fine was described in § 2.3

and we argued in § 3 that the model was mistaken. Becker's model, however,

is a simple generalisation, to include enforcement costs, of the standard

economic theory of externalities (see for example Buchanan and Stubblebine

(1962)). In that standard representation the optimum is where D' is

zero and $G'(Y) = H'(Y)$ --the marginal gain from an activity is equal

to the marginal harm. Just as in § 2.3 we argue that individual utility

maximisation leads to $f = G'$ and hence at the optimum we have $f = H'$, the

fine is equal to the marginal harm.

If Becker's model as a generalisation is mistaken must we conclude

that the standard theory of externalities is also mistaken? We shall argue

that this standard theory can be rescued from any problems which arise

in a generalisation to include enforcement costs in a way which is not open

to the Becker model. We shall argue that there is an optimum where
marginal benefits from the externality producing activity are traded off
against the benefits of extra tax revenue.

The introduction of enforcement costs is welcome in that it adds an
element of reality into the first-best world of standard welfare economics.
The problems of the Becker model do not arise if we abandon a second of the
assumptions of standard first-best welfare economics. That is the assumption
which says that lump-sum taxes are possible. Under this assumption the
government can manipulate the distribution of income costlessly and without
problems of incentives. If we drop this assumption we can no longer make
the claim that views about income distribution can be embodied in, and
confined to, a redistributive tax system and so can be ignored in our
analysis of externalities. Neither are we justified in arguing that a
fine, as a transfer payment from individual to government, is of zero
cost or benefit. If different individuals or groups have different
social weights on increases in their incomes then our analysis of policy
towards externalities should take that into account.

We can proceed formally as follows. We write the minimand

(16) $L(p, f) = D(Y) + C(Y, p) - \alpha R(p, f)$

where R is net government revenue from administering the probabilities and
taxes at levels (p, f) for the externality producing activity (net of all
costs not included in $C(Y, p)$). The parameter α denotes the premium on
tax revenue, or uncommitted public income, relative to private income.
We subtract αR from the minimand since extra revenue is a gain not a loss.
In the terms of the previous loss function (1) α is -b and R is pfY. The
use of such a premium is now standard in the literature on cost-benefit

analysis -- see Little and Mirrlees (1974), Sen (1968) -- and arises from
the recognition that since public revenue can be raised only with some cost
on the margin it will be more valuable than private income. We consider here,
using α, the value of increments in public income relative to increments
for a representative individual. The relative values for different individuals
are considered below.

The first order condition for the optimum tax f becomes

(17) $(D + C_Y)Y_f - \alpha R_f = 0.$

If we suppose R_f is positive (raising taxes raises more revenue) and
Y_f is negative (the taxes decrease the level of the activity) we have that,
at the optimum

(18) $D' + C_Y < 0.$

Given that $C_Y > 0$ we must have $D' < 0$. Hence at the optimum there must
be a marginal benefit from the externality producing activity. It is easy
to check that we cannot deduce from (17) that there is a cost reducing
change in p available as we did when α is zero or the last term is absent.
There is no reason to suppose that an optimum fails to exist in this model.
Tax revenue will fall if taxes are pushed too high and high taxes will
also discourage activity which is of value on the margin. Hence there is
a presumption that infinitely high tax rates will not be "optimum".

We can now see why this route is not really open to the Becker
analysis of crime. We can argue that at the optimum there should be a net
benefit from a factory producing a valuable commodity as well as damaging
smoke (where the calculation is made before allowing the costs of collection
or the revenue raised) but it is much more difficult to conceive of

beneficial offences, or at least offences which governments would want to
count as beneficial given that the activity has already been made illegal.

In his interpretation of the condition that fines should be set equal
to marginal damage (here (13)) Becker laid great stress on the implication
that fines should therefore be independent of the circumstance of the
offender, in particular whether he is rich or poor. We have seen that
one cannot base conclusions on (13) since the model does not have this
solution where p is also open to choice, but let us examine the proposition
that fines should be independent of the position of the offender in an
analogous model where we do have a solution.

We saw that the problem (16) would in general have a solution. Let
us consider the problem (16) as applied to two groups of individuals.
Incomes are equal within the groups and in all respects other than income
the groups are identical, but one group is richer than the other. If one
assumes diminishing social marginal utility of income then the fines or
taxes for the poorer group should be lower. The reasons are as follows.
First, the value of α the premium on incremental income to the government
relative to that to the individual would be lower for the poorer group.
It is intuitively obvious and each to check that a fall in α will imply a
lower optimum f.

Secondly the net damage D(Y) from activity level Y will be seen as
lower for a poorer individual since such gains as accrue in money terms
(and we are supposing that the activities are identical for the two groups)
to the poorer individual have higher value by the assumption made for the
previous argument. Again it is easy to check that a downward shift in the
D $(\cdot)$ function implies lower optimum punishment.

Finally, we saw, for the model discussed in § 2.2, that the propensity
to indulge in the (risky) activity (the level of the function Y(p, f)) will
be lower for the poor group since given diminishing absolute risk aversion

poorer individuals will be less likely to accept a given gamble. And one
can also check that a downward shift in the Y function will involve smaller
optimum punishment.

Hence the Becker proposition that fines should be independent of the
circumstances of the offender which cannot be examined in his model (since
it has no solution) turns out not to hold in this more general framework
when one assumes diminishing social marginal utility of income. In this
case we can give a definite answer--ceteris paribus fines or taxes on
externality producing activities carried out by the poor should be lower
than for the rich.

§ 6. Justice and the Cost-Benefit Approach

We concluded our discussion of modifications to the Becker approach
with the suggestion that one requires a notion of justice to explain punishment levels as observed, for example, in the U.K. We argued that cost-
benefit or utilitarian models whether simple or elaborate would in general
yield the conclusion that punishment, at least in the case where punishment
is by fine, should be pressed to the point where there is no longer further
deterrence from increases. Since we assume, and here we are supported by
many empirical studies, (see Chapter 2, Taylor) that at current levels
extra punishment does deter, the cost-benefit framework does not provide
an explanation of the decision concerning current punishment levels.

The introduction here of the notion of retribution as providing
limit to the "just" punishment does provide us with an answer to the
question why penalties are not raised. Reaction to a punishment that is
seen as particularly harsh is often expressed by saying that it bears no
relation to the crime. Retribution is often viewed as a severe criterion.
Those who take this view generally think of retribution as stipulating a
lower limit to acceptable punishment. But the other side of the coin is

that retribution provides an upper limit and it is this upper limit which, we presume, leads decision makers to reject increases in punishment which would deter.

We are not concerned here to press the virtues or vices of retribution. We record merely that we seem to require this notion of justice to explain punishment levels as we see them. Doubtless punishments selected are a curious amalgam of notions of deterrence and cost-benefit approaches, retribution, rehabilitation, humanitarianism and so on (for further discussion of the philosophy of punishment see Hart (1968) and Walker (1972)).

Retribution could be introduced into a social function by a term which expressed the loss associated with departures from the "retributionist target" punishment. The humanitarian argument that certain treatments of criminals are in themselves wrong could also be included in social loss function. One can always amalgamate different criteria on modes of conduct into a grand social loss function. This author, at least, would not find such an amalgamation particularly helpful.

§ 7.   Concluding Remarks

We shall not attempt to summarise here the contents of this paper. A brief description of the subject matter section-by-section was given in our introduction. We shall confine ourselves to a brief judgement of the contribution of the literature we have been discussing.

Our main concern in this review has been to show the limitations of economic analysis in policy towards crime and to argue that we appear to need the concept of retribution to explain punishment levels as we see them. This is partly in resonse to the impression one can carry away from previous authors (particulary Becker (1968) and Stigler (1970)) that the sole rational approach to policy towards crime resides in an extension of the economist's usual analysis of resource allocation in terms of costs and benefits. We must not, however, in turn minimise the contribution of the economic approach. We explained (in § 4) that we wished to indicate that something important had been omitted from the economic models and had no desire to argue that those considerations which were included were unimportant. At the same time, we should emphasise that the omission of the concept of retribution or the "just" punishment cannot be dismissed with the claim that all models neglect something. This particular omission implied that the simple economic approach to policy towards crime, in terms of damages of offences and costs of apprehension and punishment, could not provide a satisfactory explanation of punishment levels as we see them. But bearing in mind the limitations we have described let us point to some of the lessons provided by the economic approach to policy towards crime.

We have seen that discussions of attitudes towards risk can lead to interesting remarks on the propensity to offend of different groups. The result of the cost-benefit framework that punishment by fine should be pushed to the limit of effective deterrence is striking, if unattractive. We saw that the extension of the theory of externalities to include enforcement costs produced useful results provided we recognised that we should at the same time take account of the social value of income transfers. Under the assumption of diminishing social marginal utility of income we found that such models would lead to lower taxes on externality producing activities for those who are less wealthy. And Stigler's (1970) discussion for example of the allocation of resources to different types of enforcement is both useful and interesting, although it is not examined in detail here. That there are important criteria outside the simple cost-benefit approach does not imply that any arbitrary use of resources can be justified.

University of Warwick

Footnotes

* The paper was written whilst visiting the Laboratoire d'Econométrie of the
  Ecole Polytechnique in Paris. I am very grateful for their hospitality.
  My thinking on the economics of crime has been greatly influenced by R.A.
  Carr-Hill, a criminologist, with whom I have been collaborating for several
  years. Some of the ideas in this paper, particularly our basic criticism
  of the Becker model, see below, were first presented in Carr-Hill and
  Stern (1976), and some of them are elaborated in our forthcoming book,
  <u>Crime, the Police and Criminal Statistics</u> to be published by Academic
  Press. The editor and referees for this volume made many helpful comments
  and I am grateful to them.

1. See Bentham (1789) and (1830).

2. There may be earlier work on tax evasion. See, for example, the unpublished
   work quoted by Srinivasan (1973).

3. See, in particular Chapters 1, 3 and 5 by Heineke, Manski and Heineke
   respectively.

4. Note, however, that Block and Lind (1975) have shown that it is not always
   possible to reduce all such consequences to a "fine-equivalent" f.

5. The values involved in thefts are given for 904,182 out of the 1,199,859
   indictable offences. The percentages in the text are in relation to the
   latter figure (most of the remaining 295,677 would not be offences for
   which a value of property stolen would be directly relevant). For
   further details see HMSO, <u>Criminal Statistics</u>, 1966.

6. One might imagine F being given by the wealth of the offender. We return
   to this and other modifications of the Becker model in the next section.

7. We are supposing at this point that, given p, there is some level of
   punishment that yields zero offences. See Block and Lind (1975) for a
   discussion of this and related issues. They concentrate however on
   whether there exists a punishment level which could eliminate offences
   for all $p > 0$ rather than for a given $p > 0$.

8. It must be admitted that the same error is implict in the discussion in
   Carr-Hill and Stern (1976), § 1.5.

9. It is clear from the context (p. 527) that Stigler was not referring
   to the case where p is fixed. Thus the objection raised in § 3 applies,
   as is explained in the text.

10. The notion cannot be justified by an appeal to horizontal equity or
    incentives to commit offences - see Carr-Hill and Stern (1976).

References

Allingham, M. G. and Sandmo, A., (1972), "Income Tax Evasion: A Theoretical
      Analysis", Journal of Public Economics, Volume 1 (3/4) November,
      pp. 323-338.

Arrow, K.J., (1970), Essays in the Theory of Risk-Bearing, North Holland.

Becker, G.S., (1968), "Crime and Punishment: An Economic Approach", Journal
      of Political Economy, Vol. 76(2), March/April, pp. 169-217.

Bentham, (1789), An Introduction to the Principles of Morals and Legislation,
      T. Payne, London.

Block, M.K. and Lind, R.C. (1975), "Crime and Punishment Reconsidered",
      Journal of Legal Studies, Volume IV(1) pp. 241-247.

Brown, W.W. and Reynolds, M.O.,(1973), "Crime and 'Punishment' :   Risk
      Implications", Journal of Economic Theory, Volume 6(5), October,
      pp. 508-514.

Buchanan, J.M. and Stubblebine, W.C., (1962), "Externality", Economica,
      N.5. Volume 29, No. 116, November, pp. 371-384.

Carr-Hill, R.A. and Stern, N.H. (1973), "An Econometric Model of the
      Supply and Control of Recorded Offences in England and Wales",
      Journal of Public Economics, Volume 2(4) November, pp. 289-318.

Carr-Hill, R.A. and Stern, N.H., (1976), "Theory and Estimation in Models
      of Crime and its Social Control and their Relations to Concepts
      of Social Output", pp. 116-147, in Feldstein and Inman (ed.)
      The Economics of the Public Services, published by MacMillan
      for the   International Economic Association.

Ehrlich, I., (1973), "Participation in Illegitimate Activites: A
      Theoretical and Empirical Investigation", Journal of Political
      Economy, Volume 81(3), May/June pp. 521-565.

Harris, J.R., (1970), "On the Economics of Law and Order", Journal of
      Political Economy, Volume 78(1) Jan/Feb. pp. 165-174.

Hart, H.L.A., (1968), Punishment and Responsibility, Clarendon Press,
      Oxford.

Heineke, J.M., (1975), "A Note on Modelling the Criminal Choice Problem",
      Journal of Economic Theory, Volume 10(1) February, pp. 113-116.

Kolm, S. Ch., (1973), "A Note on Optimum Tax Evasion", Journal of Public
      Economics, Volume 2(3), July, pp. 265-270.

Little, I.M.D. and Mirrlees, J.A., (1974), Project Appraisal and Planning
      for Developing Countries, Heinemann.

Sen, A. K., (1968), Choice of Techniques, Blackwell's , Oxford, 3rd Edition.

Srinivasan, T.N., (1973), "Tax Evasion: A Model", Journal of Public
      Economics, Volume 2(4), November, pp. 339-346.

Stigler, G.J. (1970), "The Optimum Enforcement of Laws", Journal of
      Political Economy, Volume 78/3), May/June, pp. 526-536.

Walker, N., (1972), <u>Sentencing in a Rational Society</u>, Penguin.

Economic Models of Criminal Behavior,
J.M. Heineke (ed.)
© *North-Holland Publishing Company, 1978*

CHAPTER FIVE

SUBSTITUTION AMONG CRIMES AND THE QUESTION OF DETERRENCE:
AN INDIRECT UTILITY FUNCTION APPROACH TO THE
SUPPLY OF LEGAL AND ILLEGAL ACTIVITY

J. M. Heineke*

Empirical investigations in recent years have amassed considerable

evidence that increasing expected costs or decreasing expected benefits

in a given illegal activity results in diminished participation in the

affected activity. But an important question remains unanswered before

policy recommendations can be drawn from such findings: to what extent

do individuals respond to changes in expected returns by moving from one

source of income to another? In this paper we estimate a system of supply

equations for the income-generating activities of burglary, larceny,

robbery and "legal work." Our interest lies in determining the degree of

substitutability or complementarity which exists between these alternative

sources of income and in assessing the "net" or system-wide response of

participation rates in the several income generating activities as

expected returns and costs vary.

*University of Santa Clara. The theoretical portion of this work was
supported under Grant #75-NI-99-0123 from the National Institute of Law
Enforcement and Criminal Justice, LEAA, U.S. Department of Justice to the
Hoover Institution at Stanford University. Points of view or opinions
stated in this document are those of the author and do not necessarily
represent the official position or policies of the U.S. Department of
Justice. I am especially indebted to Larry Lau for providing many useful
suggestions and criticisms and for several discussions concerning the
applicability of duality theory to decision problems with uncertain consequences. I would also like to thank Michael Block and Fred Nold who have
provided helpful comments and criticisms. Any remaining errors are the
responsibility of the author.

Introduction

One of the fundamental questions of interest to researchers studying

criminal behavior concerns the extent of any deterrent effects which may

be associated with different policy changes and sanctions. As one would

expect, and as Block and Heineke (1975) have recently shown, it is not

possible to establish the existence of deterrent effects from theoretical

considerations alone unless preferences are strongly restricted. The

situation is a familiar one: "uncertainty substitution effects" are

consistent with the deterrence hypothesis while "income uncertainty

effects" are qualitatively ambiguous.[1] Hence, as is usually the case in

models of household decision making, determination of both the magnitude

and the direction of supply and demand responses to parameter shifts is

an empirical proposition.

To this end a number of econometric investigations have been under-

taken in recent years, most of which have been supportive of the deterrence

hypothesis.[2] These studies have been of two general types: (1) studies

utilizing indices of overall criminal activity to measure the response of

offense levels to changes in policy parameters (see for example Orsagh

(1973), Sjoquist (1973), Carr-Hill and Stern (1973, 1976), and Phillips,

Votey and Maxwell (1972)); and (2) studies which have focused attention

---

[1]The terms "uncertainty substitution effect" and "income uncertainty
effect" were introduced by Block and Heineke (1973) to denote the stochastic
analogs to the terms in the traditional Slutsky decomposition.

[2]There has been some discussion concerning the validity of several of
the estimated "supply of offenses" equations. (See Nagin (1978), Fisher
and Nagin (1978) and Passell and Taylor (1977), for example.) Comments
have been essentially of two types: disagreement with identifying
restrictions, and comments revolving about the rather poor quality of
available data and the consequent difficulty of drawing valid inferences
from such data. See Nagin (1978) for a bibliography.

on particular crimes and used activity levels in those crimes to measure
the effects of changes in policy parameters. See, for example, Ehrlich
(1970, 1973, 1975), Vandaele (1975), and Avio and Clark (1976).

Models of the former type have rather obvious advantages and disad-
vantages. On the plus side one has the fact that since all criminal acts
are grouped into a single index, one automatically has a measure of the
system-wide response to any parameter shift in the model. So to some
extent the effects of a change in the sanction for, say, burglary, on
activity levels in other crimes have been accounted for. Of course, the
negative side of the "index approach" lies in the question of just how
much information is contained in movements of such an index. That is,
just how meaningful are changes in a broad index of criminal activity as
a measure of changes in the overall level of criminal activity, let alone
as a measure of changes in a society's well being? The problem is the
familiar one of weighting the components in an index, and in the case of
criminal acts this problem is manifestly exacerbated. Crimes against
persons and crimes against property must be assigned weights to obtain a
single number which serves to represent the total number of murders,
burglaries, rapes, robberies, etc.[3]

Of course models which rely on activity levels in single, relatively
well-defined crimes to measure the response of policy changes do not have
this problem and should be used as the basis for tests designed to assess
system-wide responses to policy changes. The point is that payoffs and

---

[3]The weighting problem is usually solved in reporting agencies by
assigning an equal weight to all crimes included in the index. For example,
the Uniform Crime Report's Index of Crime, prepared annually by the Federal
Bureau of Investigation, is calculated in this manner.

sanctions in one crime may affect the level of activity in other crimes,
and if so, changes in these payoffs and sanctions will have spillover
effects. This is especially true of property crimes where economic theory
leads one to suspect that the effort devoted to any one income-generating
activity depends upon the distribution of returns to that activity and in
general on the distribution of returns to all other competing sources of
income. Clearly, even if it can be established that increasing sanctions
and enforcement levels for a particular type of crime will decrease the
incidence of that crime, one must also be able to account for changes in
offense rates in other criminal activities which may be induced by the
original policy change, before general statements concerning system-wide
deterrence can be made. For example, will policy changes which decrease
mean returns to burglars result in fewer burglaries, but increases in
larceny, robbery and auto theft as individuals allocate more of their time
to these now relatively more favorable opportunities? Hence before
general conclusions concerning the overall deterrent effects of various
policies can be reached, researchers must come to grips with the question
of substitution among crimes as distributions of relative sanctions and
returns change. This problem is addressed most satisfactorily by estimating a system of joint supply equations and assessing the response of
the system as a whole to the policy changes of interest. None of the
studies mentioned above or any other published or unpublished study with
which we are familiar has attacked this problem.[4] The obstacle has certainly not been methodological, as the recent work on estimating demand

---

[4]We should point out that Ehrlich (1970) has made a limited effort to
estimate cross policy effects for several property crimes. He found all
cross effects to be insignificant. We report the Ehrlich estimates below.

systems is for the most part directly applicable to systems of activity supply equations. Instead the primary obstacle appears to be one of insufficient data and in particular insufficient data on returns to type of crime. Such information was available for the present study.

The discussion of the previous paragraphs indicates the desirability of building and estimating a model which does not rely on broad indices of criminal activity and at the same time treats the "supply" decision of criminal agents as a choice over competing sources of income and/or satisfaction. In what follows we model the joint activity supply decision of an individual confronted with a set of legal and illegal income-generating prospects and estimate the implied set of activity supply functions for the case of four income-generating prospects--a generic legal activity and three illegal activies: larceny, burglary and robbery. Attention is focused on measuring the degree of substitutability between the legal and various illegal activities. Obviously it is the extent of substitutability between activities which determines the information loss incurred when policy prescriptions are based upon a system representing fewer than the full range of income generating prospects confronting individuals.[5]

Outline of the Paper

We begin our investigation with a model of a single economic agent confronting the problem of allocating his time and income among n legal and illegal activities and m consumption possibilities, and derive the

---

[5]This point is hardly novel, but merely a restatement of the fact that "partial" analyses become less applicable as the degree of interdependence between commodities or activities increases.

implied system of activity supply and commodity demand equations. To

maintain the closest possible degree of contact between the underlying

economic model and the resulting econometric model, we exploit several

results from modern duality theory.[6] For our purposes the principal

advantage of adopting these duality results is that they permit straight-

forward derivation of a system of activity supply and commodity demand

equations which are consistent with utility maximizing behavior, simply

by differentiating the indirect utility function as opposed to explicitly

solving the utility maximization problem.[7] Among other advantages of

estimating an econometric model which is consistent with an underlying

utility maximization model is the substantial reduction in the number of

parameters which need to be estimated when utility maximization is the

maintained hypothesis and the restrictions implied by this hypothesis

are imposed.

We proceed by approximating the agent's indirect utility function

with a function which is quadratic in the logarithms of its arguments—

the transcendental logarithmic function.[8] This function provides a second

order approximation to an arbitrary direct or indirect utility function

and places no a priori restrictions on patterns or substitution between

activities.[9]

---

[6]The literature on duality theory is quite large and growing rapidly.
For a rigorous overview with an emphasis on applications see Diewert's
(1974) survey article and the followup paper by Lau (1974).

[7]We should note that for reasonably general functional specifications
for the direct utility function, obtaining explicit solutions to the
utility maximization problem is very complicated if it is possible at all.

[8]See Christensen, Jorgensen, and Lau (1971, 1973, 1975).

[9]See Lau (1974).

The agent's commodity demand functions and activity supply functions
for each legal and illegal income-generating activity are then derived and
integrated over the wealth distribution to obtain aggregate demand and
activity supply functions. We estimate a four-equation aggregate system
consisting of aggregate supply equations for legal activity, and the three
property crimes, burglary, larceny and robbery. To this end, we utilize
rather detailed published and unpublished information on values transferred
and the disposition of cases by type of crime furnished by the Uniform
Crime Reporting division of the Federal Bureau of Investigation and
estimates of the distribution of prison sentences across states by type
of crime which were computed from unpublished Uniform Parole Reports at
the Research Center for the National Council on Crime and Delinquency.

The Model

In this section we derive the system of activity supply and commodity
demand equations implied by the hypothesis that legal and illegal "labor
supply" decisions are made as if the individual's expected utility were
being maximized. In each period the agent decides which of the n income-
generating opportunities and m consumption possibilities confronting him
are to be undertaken and how intensively each is to be pursued. The
problem we address here differs from a traditional labor supply problem
in that returns to most criminal activities are fundamentally stochastic.
Seldom does an offender know the size of the gain to be realized from a
crime. Furthermore, there is always the possibility that the individual
will be arrested, convicted, and sentenced to jail or prison thereby
incurring the cost of a severely restricted opportunity set in addition
to any explicit costs incurred in his defense. From an empirical point

of view a major difficulty with building a model in which returns are
random lies in the apparent absence of a stochastic analog of Roy's
Identity (1974) in many decision making contexts. To a large extent the
existence of a stochastic analog to this identity depends upon how the
income-expenditure constraint is treated. More specifically, the fact
that returns and sanctions in each state of the world are uncertain means
that the decision maker's plans will often not be realized. In some
periods, surpluses will be generated, while in others deficits will be
incurred. It is therefore necessary to adopt some convention regarding
the relation between income and expenditures in the model. In what
follows we require expenditures to equal income only "on average."[10] Not
only does this appear to be a reasonable condition to impose upon the
income-expenditure relation as long as bankruptcy is disallowed, but in
addition it permits straightforward extension of Roy's Identity to a world
with stochastic "prices."[11]

We proceed as if consumption levels and time allocations to the
several legal and illegal activities were determined by an agent maximizing
utility subject to the requirements that expenditures equal income "on the
average" and that the total time allocated to all activities, including
leisure, be equal to total time available in the period. The following
definitions and notation will be used:

> W: The agent's wealth at the beginning of the period.
>
> t_i: The time allocated to activity i; $t \equiv (t_1, t_2, \ldots, t_n)$,
> where for convenience we denote t_n as legal activity.

---

[10]See Lau (1973) for a discussion of the duality between expected
direct and expected indirect utility functions under a similar budget
specification.

[11]The non-existence of bankruptcy has a long precedent. For example,
see virtually any of the portfolio models which have appeared in the
literature in recent years.

r_i: The unit return from activity i; $r \equiv (r_1, r_2, \ldots, r_n)$

$S_i(t_i, W)$: The monetary equivalent of the sentence if the agent is arrested for engaging in acticity i and convicted and sentenced to jail or prison. $S \equiv (S_1, S_2, \ldots, S_{n-1})$.[12] (Notice that S depends upon both the agent's wealth and his activity levels.) For convenience we assume S_i is proportional to t_i.

p_a^i: The agent's subjective probability of being arrested for engaging in acticity i; $p_a \equiv (p_a^1, p_a^2, \ldots, p_a^n)$. We have designated t_n as the time allocation to legal activity and assume $p_a^n = 0$. That is, we assume the probability of type one error is zero for individuals engaged exclusively in legal activity.

$p_{c/a}^i$: The agent's subjective probability of being convicted, given he is arrested for offense i; $p_{c/a} \equiv (p_{c/a}^1, p_{c/a}^2, \ldots, p_{c/a}^n)$.

x_j: The level of consumption of commodity j in the period; $x \equiv (x_1, x_2, \ldots, x_m)$.

P_j: The price of commodity j; $P \equiv (P_1, P_2, \ldots, P_m)$.

$U(t,x)$: The agent's utility indicator. We assume $U(\cdot)$ is monotonic, twice differentiable and strictly concave in t and x.

Given that the loss from a prison sentence is measured as its monetary equivalent, the individual's unit prospects from engaging in activity i are:

r_i: $1 - p_a^i p_{c/a}^i$

---

[12] See Block and Heineke (1975) and Block and Lind (1975a, 1975b) for a discussion of monetary equivalence and its applicability to the criminal choice problem.

$$r_i - s_i: \quad p_a^i p_{c/a}^i \qquad\qquad , \ i = 1,2,\ldots,n-1$$

$$r_n: \quad 1$$

Hence returns to illegal activity i in our model depend upon whether the agent is arrested or escapes; and if arrested, whether he is convicted and sentenced or is acquitted. In more detail, returns are r_i if the individual engages in illegal activity i and is either not arrested or is arrested but subsequently acquitted. This state occurs with probability $1 - p_a^i p_{c/a}^i$. If the individual is arrested and convicted for engaging in illegal activity i, returns are $r_i - s_i$ with probability $p_a^i p_{c/a}^i$.[13] The quantity $r_i - s_i \gtrless 0$. Finally, since $p_a^n = 0$, unit prospects from engaging in legal activity are r_n with probability one.

Given the contingencies and probabilities we have outlined, the agent's expected wealth is given by:

$$(1) \qquad W + \sum_1^n [(1 - p_a^i p_{c/a}^i) r_i + p_a^i p_{c/a}^i (r_i - s_i)] t_i$$

For notational simplicity, we define:

$$(2) \qquad \omega_i \equiv (1 - p_a^i p_{c/a}^i) r_i + p_a^i p_{c/a}^i (r_i - s_i)$$

$$\equiv r_i - p_a^i p_{c/a}^i s_i, \qquad\qquad i = 1,2,\ldots n$$

and

$$\omega \equiv (\omega_1, \omega_2, \ldots, \omega_n)$$

---

[13] There is no particular difficulty in expanding the model to include other contingencies. For example, the state "arrested, convicted and placed on probation" could be added or we could differentiate between the states "not arrested" and the state "arrested and acquitted." The only problem is an empirical one since data are not available on such outcomes.

Since $p_a^n = 0$, $\omega_n = r_n$, the return to legal endeavors. Equation (1), may now be written as:

(1') $W + \sum_1^n \omega_i t_i$.

Following Becker (1965), the formal problem is then:

(3) $\max_{t,x} U(t,x) - \lambda[\sum_1^m P_h x_h - W - \sum_1^n \omega_i t_i]$

subject to $\sum_1^n t_i \leq T$, where T is total time available in the period, $\sum_1^m P_h x_h$ are total concumption expenditures, and λ is a Lagrangean multiplier.

First order conditions for a maxima in t and x require:

(4) $\partial U/\partial t_i + \lambda \omega_i \leq 0$ $i = 1,2,\ldots,n$

$\partial U/\partial x_j - \lambda P_j \leq 0$ $j = 1,2,\ldots,m$

$\sum_1^m P_h x_h - W - \sum_1^n \omega_i t_i = 0$

$\sum_1^n t_i - T \leq 0$

We assume throughout that the last relation in (4) holds as a strict inequality. Since $U(\cdot)$ is strictly concave, a solution to (4) exists, is unique, and is given by:

(5) $t_k \equiv \phi_k(\omega,P,W)$ $k = 1,2,\ldots,n$

$x_i \equiv \psi_i(\omega,P,W)$ $i = 1,2,\ldots,m$

$L \equiv T - \sum_1^n \phi_k(\cdot)$

where L represents the individual's demand for leisure and $\phi_k(\cdot)$ and $\psi_i(\cdot)$

are differentiable functions of ω, P and W. Although we are assured of
the existence of supply and demand equations (5), it will generally not
be possible to solve for these functions explicitly unless $U(\cdot)$ is of a
particularly simple form. In other words, if one chooses a functional
form for $U(\cdot)$ that places relatively few restrictions on equations (5),
it will usually not be possible to actually solve first order conditions
for the implied demand and supply equations.

To surmount this problem one need only calculate the indirect utility
function and apply Roy's Identity (1947). The indirect utility function,
say $g(\cdot)$, gives the maximum utility the agent can attain when confronted
with expected returns ω, commodity prices P and wealth level W. By
definition:

(6) $U(\phi(\omega,P,W),\ \psi(\omega,P,W)) \equiv g(\omega,P,W)$

where ϕ and ψ are vectors of activity supply and commodity demand functions. Noting that $g(\cdot)$ is once differentiable in ω and P and assuming
that not all return and price derivatives of $g(\cdot)$ are zero, we have:

(7) $$t_k = \frac{-W\partial g/\partial \omega_k}{\sum_1^m P_h \partial g/\partial P_h + \sum_1^n \omega_j \partial g/\partial \omega_j} \qquad k = 1,2,\ldots,n$$

$$x_i = \frac{W\partial g/\partial P_i}{\sum_1^m P_h \partial g/\partial P_h + \sum_1^n \omega_j \partial g/\partial \omega_j} \qquad i = 1,2,\ldots,m$$

which are analogs to Roy's Identity for the utility maximizing problem (3)
and are the unique solution to that problem.

Aggregation

Equations (7) are of course activity supply and commodity demand
functions for one individual in the population under study. Since only
aggregated data are available for this study, it will be necessary to
adopt a set of assumptions which permit summation of individual offense
and demand equations into aggregate offense and demand equations corresponding to the same aggregates as those on which data are available.

A convenient starting point for this task is an assumption to the
effect that individuals are more or less homogeneous, except for their
wealth levels. More precisely, we assume that each individual confronts
the same commodity prices P, the same expected returns ω, and possesses
identical preferences, although we allow wealth levels to vary across
individuals, thus leading to differences in behavior over individuals.[14]

Now if wealth is distributed according to $f(W)$ and Q is the number
of individuals in the economy, then $Q\int_a^b f(W)dW$ is the number of individuals
with wealth levels between a and b. Under the above assumptions the aggregate or market supply of activity k, T_k, and the aggregate or market
demand for commodity s, χ_s, are given by:

$$(8) \qquad T_k(\omega,P;f) \equiv Q \int_o^\infty \phi_k(\omega,P,W)f(W)dW, \qquad\qquad k = 1,2,\ldots,n$$

and

$$(9) \qquad \chi_s(\omega,P;f) \equiv Q \int_o^\infty \psi_s(\omega,P,W)f(W)dW, \qquad\qquad s = 1,2,\ldots,m$$

---

[14]This approach may be considerably extended to include the case
where wealth and other characteristics of individuals are free to vary.

where ϕ_k and ψ_s are the individual activity supply and commodity demand

functions given in (5) and (7). Market wide supply elasticities are then:

(10) $\dfrac{\partial T_k}{\partial \omega_i} \dfrac{\omega_i}{T_k} \equiv \dfrac{Q}{T_k} \displaystyle\int_0^\infty \dfrac{\partial \phi_k}{\partial \ln \omega_i} f(W) dW,$ $i = 1, 2, \ldots, n$

(11) $\dfrac{\partial T_k}{\partial P_j} \dfrac{P_j}{T_k} \equiv \dfrac{Q}{T_k} \displaystyle\int_0^\infty \dfrac{\partial \phi_k}{\partial \ln P_j} f(W) dW,$ $j = 1, 2, \ldots, m$

with analogous expressions for market demand elasticities. Notice that

aggregate activity supply functions and aggregate demand functions depend

not only on the usual return and price variables but also on the moments

of the distribution of wealth. Hence if sample surveys of the population

are available so that sample moments of $f(W)$ can be computed, one can

estimate equation (8), thereby directly accounting for the effects of an

unequal distribution of wealth on the level of criminal activity.

The Translog Model

From an econometric point of view the aggregate supply functions and

commodity demand functions, (8) and (9), and the implied direct and cross

elasticities of supply and demand are only of limited interest until a

specific functional form has been assigned to the indirect utility

function $g(\cdot)$. The primary concern in choosing $g(\cdot)$ is that the chosen

class of functions be capable of approximating the unknown indirect

utility function to the desired degree of accuracy.[15] Because a central

concern of the present work is to study the extent of substitutability

---

[15] It is also desirable (less expensive) to choose functional forms
that yield supply equations which are linear in the parameters.

between alternative legal and illegal sources of income, it is important
to choose a functional form which does not a priori restrict substitution
possibilities. Any of the so-called "flexible" functional forms which
have appeared in the literature in recent years have this property.[16]

We now approximate the agent's indirect utility function with a
transcendental logarithmic function and hence, via equations (8), (9),
(10) and (11), approximate the implied aggregate activity supply functions,
commodity demand functions and corresponding elasticities. The translog
indirect utility function is defined as:[17]

$$(12) \qquad \ln g(\cdot) = \alpha_o + \sum_1^n \alpha_i \ln\omega_i + \sum_1^m \alpha_i' \ln P_i + \alpha_{m+1}' \ln W$$

$$+ \; 1/2 \sum_1^n \sum_1^n \beta_{ij}' \ln\omega_i \ln\omega_j \; + \; 1/2 \sum_1^m \sum_1^m \beta_{ij}' \ln P_i \ln P_j$$

$$+ \; \sum_1^n \sum_1^m \gamma_{ij} \ln\omega_i \ln P_j \; + \; \sum_1^n \Pi_i \ln\omega_i \ln W$$

$$+ \; \sum_1^m \Pi_j' \ln P_j \ln W + \mu (\ln W)^2$$

Application of identities (7) to equation (12) yields the following
system of individual demand and supply equations:

$$(13) \qquad t_k = \frac{-W(\alpha_k + \sum_1^n \beta_{ik} \ln\omega_i + \sum_1^m \gamma_{kj} \ln P_j + \Pi_k \ln W)\omega_k^{-1}}{\alpha + \sum_1^n \beta_i \ln\omega_i + \sum_1^m \beta_j' \ln P_j + \Pi \ln W} \;, \quad k = 1,2,\ldots,n$$

---

[16]In general, "flexible" functional forms are second order approximations to the primal or dual objective functions in optimization problems.
These functions include the generalized Cobb-Douglas function, Diewert
(1973), the generalized Leontief function, Diewert (1971), the transcendental logarithmic function, Christensen, Jorgensen and Lau (1971, 1973,
1975) and a number of hybrids.

[17]Given that income generation is viewed as "work," a necessary
condition for an internal solution to (4) is $\omega > 0$. Of course, the translog
indirect utility function is not defined for non positive expected returns.

$$x_s = \frac{W(\alpha_s' + \sum_1^m \beta_{sj}' \ln P_j + \sum_1^n \gamma_{is} \ln \omega_i + \Pi_s' \ln W) P_s^{-1}}{\alpha + \sum_1^n \beta_i \ln \omega_i + \sum_1^m \beta_j' \ln P_j + \Pi \ln W} , \quad s = 1,2,\ldots,m$$

where we have simplified notation by defining:

(14) $\alpha \equiv \sum_1^m \alpha_i' + \sum_1^n \alpha_j$

$\Pi \equiv \sum_1^m \Pi_i' + \sum_1^n \Pi_j$

$\beta_i \equiv \sum_1^n \beta_{ik} + \sum_1^m \gamma_{is}$ $i = 1,2,\ldots,n$

$\beta_j' \equiv \sum_1^m \beta_{sj}' + \sum_1^n \gamma_{kj}$ $j = 1,2,\ldots,m$

The parameter α_o cannot be identified as it has no effect on the agent's joint demand, time allocation decision.

Equations (13) are the empirical counterpart to equations (7) above. To arrive at the empirical counterpart to the aggregate activity supply and commodity equations given in (8) and (9) one need only substitute equations (13) into (8) and (9) and integrate. Integration of the result-ing equations is significantly simplified if the restriction

(15) $\Pi = 0$

is used.[18] Transforming aggregate activity supply functions into per capita value transferred functions by multiplying per capita illegal

----

[18]This restriction was suggested by Diewert (1974) in a slightly different context and has been used by Berndt, Darrough and Diewert (1976) to generate market demand functions.

activity supply functions by returns to the activity, we have:

$$(16) \quad \frac{\omega_k T_k}{Q} = \frac{-\int_0^\infty Wf(W)\,dW(\alpha_k + \sum_1^n \beta_{ik}\ln\omega_i + \sum_1^m \gamma_{kj}\ln P_j) - \Pi_k \int_0^\infty W\ln Wf(W)\,dW}{\alpha + \sum_1^n \beta_i \ln\omega_i + \sum_1^m \beta_j' \ln P_j}$$

$$k = 1,2,\ldots,n-1$$

Per capita legal earnings are given by:

$$(17) \quad \frac{\omega_n T_n}{Q} = \frac{-\int_0^\infty Wf(W)\,dW(\alpha_n + \sum_1^n \beta_{in}\ln\omega_i + \sum_1^m \gamma_{nj}\ln P_j) - \Pi_n \int_0^\infty W\ln Wf(W)\,dW}{\alpha + \sum_1^n \beta_i \ln\omega_i + \sum_1^m \beta_j' \ln P_j}$$

while per capita demand for commodity s is given by:

$$(18) \quad \frac{P_s X_s}{Q} = \frac{\int_0^\infty Wf(W)\,dW(\alpha_s' + \sum_1^m \beta_{sj}'\ln P_j + \sum_1^n \gamma_{is}\ln\omega_i) + \Pi_s' \int_0^\infty W\ln Wf(W)\,dW}{\alpha + \sum_1^n \beta_i \ln\omega_i + \sum_1^m \beta_j' \ln P_j}$$

$$s = 1,2,\ldots,m$$

If the wealth distribution $f(W)$ can be estimated, it will be possible to estimate the paramters of (16), (17), and (18) by more or less straight-forward regression techniques.

Using equations (16) and (17), we may calculate empirical counter-parts to the aggregate supply elasticities displayed as (10) and (11) above. These are:

$$(10') \quad \eta_{ki} \equiv \frac{\partial T_k}{\partial \omega_i} \frac{\omega_i}{T_k} = -\delta_{ik} + \frac{\lambda_1 \beta_{ik}}{\lambda_1 (\alpha_k + \Sigma \beta_{sk} \ln \omega_s + \Sigma \gamma_{kj} \ln P_j) + \pi_k \lambda_2}$$

$$- \frac{\beta_i}{\alpha + \Sigma \beta_s \ln \omega_s + \Sigma \beta_j' \ln P_j} \quad , \qquad i,k = 1,2,\ldots,n$$

and

$$(11') \quad \rho_{kj} \equiv \frac{\partial T_k}{\partial P_j} \frac{P_j}{T_k} = \frac{\lambda_1 \gamma_{kj}}{\lambda_1 (\alpha_k + \Sigma \beta_{ik} \ln \omega_i + \Sigma \gamma_{ks} \ln P_s) + \pi_k \lambda_2}$$

$$- \frac{\beta_j'}{\alpha + \Sigma \beta_i \ln \omega_i + \Sigma \beta_s' \ln P_s} \quad , \qquad \begin{array}{l} j = 1,2,\ldots,m \\ \\ k = 1,2,\ldots,n \end{array}$$

where λ_1 and λ_2 are given by:

$$(19) \quad \lambda_1 = \int_0^\infty Wf(W)dW$$

$$\lambda_2 = \int_0^\infty W \ln Wf(W)dW \quad ,$$

and

$$\delta_{ik} = \begin{cases} 0, & i \neq k \\ \\ 1, & i = k \end{cases}$$

Elasticities of supply with respect to mean wealth are given by

$$(20) \quad \eta_k \equiv \frac{\partial T_k}{\partial \lambda_1} \frac{\lambda_1}{T_k} = 1 + \frac{-\Pi_k \lambda_2}{\lambda_1 (\alpha_k + \Sigma \beta_{ik} \ln \omega_i + \Sigma \gamma_{kj} \ln P_j) + \Pi_k \lambda_2}$$

Finally, Allen elasticities of substitution (1938) associated with market supply functions may be calculated as

$$(21) \qquad \sigma_{ij} = \eta_{ij} \sum_i (\omega_i T_i / \omega_j T_j) - \eta_i \; , \qquad\qquad\qquad i,j = 1,2,\ldots,n$$

The restriction $\Pi = 0$ has been utilized throughout these calculations.[19]

Parameter Restrictions - In this section we set out the parameter restrictions implied by utility maximization in terms of the parameters of the
translog indirect utility function. Of course this more general functional
form may not be needed to adequately characterize the degree of substitution between crimes and it is of some interest to contrast the translog
model (a model of non-homothetic preferences) with several less general
systems. In particular, we estimate two additional models which are
increasingly special cases of the translog structure. These are the cases
of homothetic preferences and linear logarithmic (additive) preferences,
respectively. Hypotheses concerned with discriminating between these
models of nonhomethetic, homothetic and additive preferences are "nested"
and may be carried out according to straightforward, classical procedures.
In addition to the parameter restrictions implied by utility maximization,
in what follows we list sets of restrictions yielding models in which the
hypotheses of homothetic preferences and linear logarithmic preferences
are maintained.[20]

_____

[19] We remind the reader that η_{ij} is a measure of _gross_ substitution
between activities i and j while σ_{ij} is a measure of _net_ substitution.
It is for this reason that $\eta_{ij} \neq \eta_{ji}$, while $\sigma_{ij} = \sigma_{ji}$, for all i and j.

[20] It is interesting to note that linear logarithmic utility functions
yield double logarithmic supply and demand equations which in turn imply
zero cross elasticities, positive unitary income elasticities and negative
unitary direct elasticities. We make this point since the authors of each

If the theory of individual choice is valid, then the parameters α, β_i and β_j' appearing in the denominator of the per capita earnings and expenditure equations, equations (16)-(18), are equal in each equation. There are $n + m + 1$ such parameters in each of the $n + m - 1$ equations to be estimated, resulting in a total of $(n + m)(n + m - 1)$ restrictions of this type. Following the Jorgensen-Lau terminology, we term these equality restrictions.

In addition to the equality restrictions, if individuals make choices as if they were maximizing utility, then the second order coefficients β_{ij}, $\beta_{k\ell}'$ and γ_{st}, must be symmetric. That is,

$$\beta_{ij} = \beta_{ji} , \qquad i,j = 1,2,\ldots,n$$

(22) $$\beta_{k\ell}' = \beta_{\ell k}' , \qquad k,\ell = 1,2,\ldots,m$$

$$\gamma_{st} = \gamma_{ts}, \qquad s = 1,2,\ldots,n, \quad t = 1,2,\ldots,m$$

There are $(n + m)(n + m - 1)/2$ symmetry restrictions of this type.

Finally, utility maximization implies demand and supply functions are homogeneous of degree zero. This is accomplished with the following restrictions:

$$\sum_{i=1}^{n} \beta_{ik} + \sum_{j=1}^{m} \gamma_{kj} + \Pi_k = 0 , \qquad k = 1,2,\ldots,n$$

---

of the previous studies listed above have estimated double logarithmic supply equations while maintaining utility maximization. Although the linkage between the estimated aggregate supply equations and the model of individual choice is not explicit in these studies, if one assumes that aggregate supply equations were arrived at either by approximating the indirect utility function or by approximating the agent's supply equations themselves and aggregating the result over the population, then double logarithimc aggregate supply equations imply linear logarithmic preferences and severe restrictions on elasticities. See Jorgensen and Lau (1975a) for more detail.

$$(22') \quad \sum_{j=1}^{m} \beta'_{sj} + \sum_{i=1}^{n} \gamma_{is} + \Pi'_s = 0 \ , \quad\quad s = 1,2,\ldots,m$$

$$\sum_{i=1}^{n} \beta_i + \sum_{j=1}^{m} \beta'_j + \Pi = 0$$

If the per cȧpita earnings and expenditure equations, (16)-(18), were generated by individual utility maximizing behavior, the parameters of these equations must satisfy equality, homogeneity and symmetry restrictions.[21]

We next turn to the parameter restrictions implied by the several hypotheses concerning the functional structure of preferences. If the parameters β_i, $i = 1,2,\ldots,n$ and β'_j, $j = 1,2,\ldots,m$ are zero, the individual's indirect utility function is homothetic.[22] It is well known that homothetic preferences imply constant income elasticities of supply equal to one and hence the time allocated to each activity iṣ independent of the agent's income. In summary, the restrictions

$$(23) \quad \beta_i = \beta'_j = 0 \ , \quad\quad\quad i = 1,2,\ldots,n, \ j = 1,2,\ldots,m$$

imply homothetic direct and indirect utility functions.

Finally, if the agent's direct utility function is linear logarithmic then the indirect utility function is linear logarithmic and, in addition to restrictions (23), all second order parameters are restricted to be

---

[21]See Jorgensen and Lau (1975b) for a discussion of these restrictions and a detailed investigation of the functional structure of consumer preferences.

[22]In general a translog approximation to a homothetic function need not itself be homothetic. We have imposed what Jorgensen and Lau (1975a) term intrinsic homotheticity, in which case the translog approximation is itself homothetic.

zero. In summary, linear logarithmic preferences imply

(24) $\beta_{ik} = \beta'_{j\ell} = \gamma_{ij} = \Pi_i = \Pi'_j = 0$

$$i,k = 1,2,\ldots,n$$
$$j,\ell = 1,2,\ldots,m$$

Linear logarithmic utility implies that earnings shares for each activity
and expenditure shares for each commodity are constant.

The Econometric Model – In this section we specialize the n + m equation
model of per capita earnings and expenditures given above as equations
(16), (17) and (18) to the model which is to be estimated and provide the
stochastic specification needed for estimation.

   We had available for this study information on values stolen for the
four property crimes of robbery, burglary, larceny and motor vehicle
theft. We decided not to include a motor vehicle theft equation for two
reasons: First and foremost there is the question as to whether values
stolen adequately reflect the returns to many auto thieves due to the
large portion of all auto thefts which are for "joy-riding." More
precisely, available statistics indicate that approximately 85 percent
of all auto thefts fall into the "joy-riding" category and hence are what
Stigler has termed "consumption crimes" rather than "production crimes"
which are the subject of attention in this paper. Second, our "value
stolen" series are gross returns which have not been adjusted for
recoveries. This presents a problem for each of the property crimes
studied, but is especially acute for motor vehicle thefts where dollar
values per offense tend to be very large but where a large portion of all

stolen vehicles are recovered, causing the value stolen series to seriously
overestimate the return to the thief. To the extent that robberies,
burglaries and larcenies result in cash transfers, gross and net returns
will tend to be similar, since little cash is ever recovered. But since
burglaries in particular result in transfers of durables along with cash,
the returns to burglary will be over-estimated by the value of recovered
property. This wouldn't seem to be a serious problem since only about
fifteen percent of all burglaries are solved and of those solved, only a
small percent of the stolen property is recovered.[23]

For the reasons outlined in the last paragraph we include only the
crimes of burglary, robbery and larceny as possible sources of illegal
income along with a generic legal activity to represent legitimate
earnings. This gives a model with four activity supply equations and m
commodity demand equations in (if unrestricted) $2m^2 + 19m + 44$ parameters.
In an effort to keep the size of the model within the realm of estimation
possibilities, we aggregate all commodity demand equations into one, say
x, and normalize the returns to each activity and wealth with respect to
the price of this aggregate commodity, say P. Our model then becomes

$$(25) \quad \frac{\omega_k' T_k}{Q} = \frac{-\lambda_1'(\alpha_k + \sum_1^4 \beta_{ik} \ln\omega_i') - \Pi_k \lambda_2'}{\alpha + \sum_1^4 \beta_i \ln\omega_i'} \, , \qquad k = 1,2,3,4$$

$$(26) \quad \frac{X}{Q} = \frac{\lambda_1'(\alpha_1' + \sum_1^4 \gamma_{iP} \ln\omega_i') + \Pi_1' \lambda_2'}{\alpha + \sum_1^4 \beta_i \ln\omega_i'}$$

---

[23]Another problem here is the fact that estimated market values of
stolen merchandise overstate "fence" values.

where $\omega_i' \equiv \omega_i/P$, $\lambda_1' \equiv E(W/P)$ and $\lambda_2' \equiv E[(W/P)\ln(W/P)]$. Since equations
(25) and (26) are homogeneous of degree zero in the parameters a normal-
ization of parameters will be necessary to permit estimation. It is
convenient to set

(27) $\alpha = -1$

for this purpose.

The next step in implementing the econometric version of the model
is to provide a stochastic framework for the earning and expenditure
equations, (25) and (26). We do this by appending an additive disturbance to each of the five equations. These disturbances arise either as
a result of random errors in the maximizing behavior of individual agents
or as a result of the fact that the translog indirect utility function
only approximates underlying preferences; and due to the income-expenditure constraint, must sum to zero. We assume that noncontemporaneous
disturbances are uncorrelated both within and across equations and that
right hand side variables in equations (25) and (26) are uncorrelated
with the disturbances in each equation. The latter assumption assures
identification of the earnings and expenditure functions. It can be shown
that under a rather general model of the "market for illegal activities,"
activity supply functions will be identified merely by regressing the
observed number of offenses on expected returns as long as there is
sufficient variation in the cost of inputs and/or the production technologies of law enforcement agencies.[24] In this context, our assumption of

_____

[24]There appears to be sufficient variation in both input costs and
production technologies to provide the needed identifying restriction.
See Darrough and Heineke, Chapter 7, in the present volume.

zero correlation between right-hand variables and disturbances might be
interpreted as adopting such a model of the market for illegal activities
as a maintained hypothesis and finding the needed input price or production technology variation.[25]

Notice that it will be necessary to estimate only four of the five
equations since the budget constraint implies that the parameters of the
remaining equation can be determined from defintions (14) above. We have
chosen to estimate the four per capita earnings equations, in which case
the parameters of the expenditure function are given by

$$\alpha_1' = -1 - \alpha_1 - \alpha_2 - \alpha_3 - \alpha_4$$

$$\beta_{11}' = \beta_1' - \gamma_{1P} - \gamma_{2P} - \gamma_{3P} - \gamma_{4P}$$

(28)

$$\Pi_1' = -\Pi_1 - \Pi_2 - \Pi_3 - \Pi_4$$

$$\gamma_{iP} = \beta_i - \beta_{i1} - \beta_{i2} - \beta_{i3} - \beta_{i4} \, , \qquad\qquad i = 1,2,3,4$$

Earnings equations (25) comprises a complete econometric model of the
time and income allocation problem confronting the individual.

---

[25]The question of whether or not expected returns are exogenous hinges
primarily upon whether probabilities of arrest which enter these calculations are exogenous. The usual argument to the contrary has been in terms
of the "capacity" of police departments. Briefly, the argument goes that
as the number of offenses increases police resources are stretched increasingly thin and arrests per total offenses fall thereby yielding the
ubiquitous negative partial correlation between offense rates and probabilities of capture--but for the wrong reason. This argument requires
that offense levels explicitly enter police agency production functions
to account for agency capacity constraints. This hypothesis is tested and
rejected in Darrough and Heineke, ibid, utilizing results reported by
Phillips and Votey (1975) and results reported by Ehrlich (1973). Additional evidence supporting the exogeneity of expected returns is provided
by Wilson and Boland (1977), who find that police "capacity" is not related
to arrest rates for burglary, larceny, robbery and motor vehicle theft.

Our maintained hypothesis of utility maximizing behavior imposes twenty
equality restrictions (β_1, β_2, β_3, β_4 and β_1' must be equal in each
equation), ten symmetry restrictions

(29)

$$\beta_{12} = \beta_{21} \qquad \beta_{13} = \beta_{31} \qquad \beta_{14} = \beta_{41} \qquad \gamma_{P1} = \gamma_{1P} \qquad \gamma_{P3} = \gamma_{3P}$$

$$\beta_{23} = \beta_{32} \qquad \beta_{24} = \beta_{42} \qquad \beta_{34} = \beta_{43} \qquad \gamma_{P2} = \gamma_{2P} \qquad \gamma_{P4} = \gamma_{4P}$$

and five homogeneity restrictions

(29')

$$\sum_{i=1}^{4} \beta_{ik} + \gamma_{kP} + \Pi_k = 0 , \qquad\qquad k = 1,2,3,4$$

$$\sum_{i=1}^{4} \beta_i + \beta_1' = 0$$

which in conjunction with (28) reduces the number of parameters in the
system to be directly estimated from sixty to twenty-two.[26] From an
econometric point of view this dramatic reduction in the number of parameters to be estimated provides a powerful incentive for building econometric models which are consistent with utility maximization.

In the context of our five equation model the hypothesis of homothetic preferences yields the restrictions[27]

(30) $\beta_1' = \beta_1 = \beta_2 = \beta_3 = \beta_4 = 0$

and further reduces the total number of parameters to be directly estimated

---

[26] In completely unrestricted form the model consists of five equations each containing twelve parameters.

[27] See footnote 22 above.

to eighteen. Finally, the hypothesis of linear logarithmic utility
requires, in addition to homotheticity restrictions (30), that

$$(31) \qquad \beta'_{11} = \beta_{ik} = \Pi_k = \gamma_{iP} = \Pi'_1 = 0 \ , \qquad\qquad i,k = 1,2,3,4$$

reducing the number of parameters to be estimated to five.

The Data and Data Sources

Estimation of equations (25) and (26) requries information on expected
returns to burglary, robbery and larceny, the return and hours worked in
legal activity, the number of hours spent in the various illegal endeavors
and enough information on the wealth distribution to permit calculation of
E(W) and E(WlnW). Information allowing computation of estimates of average
returns, r_i, the probabilities of arrest and of conviction given arrest,
p^i_a, $p^i_{c/a}$, and the number of offenses by type was made available by the
Uniform Crime Reporting division at the Federal Bureau of Investigation
for the years 1967--1972. Theoretically, these data are reported to the
FBI either monthly or annually by every law enforcement agency in the
United States. At the micro level, this amounts to from nine to eleven
thousand reporting agencies. But for a number of reasons we chose to
aggregate reporting agencies into SMSA's. Primary among these reasons was
the need to match these data with sources for legal earnings and wealth
distribution information. In addition, aggregation lessens the problem of
spatial substitutability. More precisely, since returns to any one
criminal activity will in general differ from jurisdiction to jurisdiction,
one would expect substitution between small, contiguous jurisdictions.
Choosing SMSA's as the jurisdictional unit circumvents this problem to
some extent due to the fact that SMSA's are defined as self contained

labor markets and, with but few exceptions, are geographically separated.[28]

As indicated above, around ten thousand law enforcement agencies in
the United States are asked to record detailed information on offenses,
arrests, convictions, values stolen and much more by type of crime and to
report this information to the FBI. But there are no sanctions for non-
compliance and the information actually received by the FBI is quite
spotty. So as not to rely on SMSA's where only a small percent of the
total population was covered by reporting agencies, we have eliminated
from our sample all SMSA's in which less than fifty percent of the total
population was covered by reporting agencies. In addition, the need to
match our sample with other data sources forced us to eliminate all SMSA's
with under one quarter million in population. These aggregations and
deletions left us with 137 sample points over the seven year period.

Because the FBI data are on numbers of offenses by type and not on
the amount of time allocated to particular offenses, we assume that the
number of offenses committed of a particular type is proportional to the
time allocated to that activity. Expected returns to illegal activity i
were computed according to equation (2) above and is repeated here for
easy reference

(2) $\omega_i = r_i - p_a^i p_c^i / a S_i$ $i = 1,2,3$

From here on we designate burglary as illegal activity one, robbery
as illegal activity two, larceny as illegal activity three and activity
four will represent legal work. The variable r_i is measured using the

---

[28]Of course the problem of spatial substitution can never be
completely eliminated in a mobile population.

average value stolen in crime i, p_a^i is the ratio of the number of offenses
of type i that were cleared by arrest to the total number of known offenses
and $p_{c/a}^i$ is the ratio of the number guilty as charged to the number of
arrests for crime i.

The most difficult portion of the expected return calculation remains--
the monetary equivalent of a prison sentence of a given length. Prison
sentences for the criminal activities being studied here are set by the
state. Unfortunately, very little sentence length information is available
for the years covered in our sample. For this reason sentence lengths were
measured by the time served until parole for that portion of inmates who
were paroled, and were calculated from unpublished records at the Research
Center for the National Council on Crime and Delinquency. Parole information was available for thirty seven states plus the District of Columbia
and hence SMSA's in remaining states were eliminated from the sample.[29]
The monetary equivalent of a sentence of length S_i was computed as the
present discounted value of the income foregone per year--the discount
period given by the mean sentence for crime i. We used as the discount
rate, finance company unsecured loan rates as published in the Federal
Reserve Bulletin. Given the social and financial backgrounds of most
property crime offenders the unsecured finance company interest rate
probably fairly represents the cost of consuming future income in the
present. To the extent such individuals borrow to finance present consumption, this is the appropriate discount rate.

This leaves income foregone per year of imprisonment yet to be

---

[29] The states of Alaska, Colorado, Hawaii, Louisiana, Maryland,
Minnesota, Montana, New Hampshire, New Jersey, Oklahoma, Texas and
Washington are missing from the sample for this reason.

determined. We have used the mean (legal) income of households as the basis of our calculations. Even a cursary examination of the age-employment profile of property crime offenders indicates that many, if not most, offenders are either in their teens or not employed or both, and hence mean legal income will likely considerably overstate the loss suffered by these offenders. To deal with this problem we have defined "expected legal income" as the product of mean legal income and the percentage of individuals of high school age or older who are employed.[30] Mean income was calculated from the Internal Revenue Service's Statistics of Income: Individual Income Tax Returns. In odd numbered years this publication contains the number of returns and gross incomes broken down into twenty-four categories for each SMSA in our sample. It is reasonable to assume the income distribution remains invariant over two year periods and hence the IRS information is sufficient to characterize the income distribution. Since mean income calculated in this manner is mean household income these figures have been converted into personal incomes by dividing by the average family size. "Expected legal income" defined in this manner has been used to estimate the opportunity loss of a year's imprisonment in the empirical analysis which follows. Due to the very limited amount of information available on the distribution of wealth, we have also used the IRS measurements as a surrogate for the wealth distribution and have calculated estimates of $E(W)$ and $E(WlnW)$ from these data.

The remaining variables in equations (25) and (26) are legal earnings, the expected return to legal activity and the price of the aggregate

---

[30]We have approximated the number of persons employed in an SMSA with the BLS series "Employees on Nonagricultural Payrolls."

commodity which was used as a deflator for monetary valued variables.
Legal earnings were computed as the product of production worker wages
and the number of employees, while expected legal returns were computed
as production worker wages times the quotient of the number of employees
and the number in the labor force, the quotient being an estimate of the
probability of employment in the SMSA in question.[31] These series were
obtained from BLS Employment and Earnings statistics for most of the
points remaining in the sample. Finally, we used the BLS Urban Intermediate
Budget for a Family of Four, normalized at 1966, as P. Less than complete
information on sentence lengths, legal earnings and the deflator P reduced
the 137 remaining sample points to 61, upon which the parameter estimates
which follow are based.

Estimation

Our empirical results are based upon a cross section of approximately
ten large SMSA's each year for the years 1967-72. The included SMSA's
vary from year to year depending primarily upon the record keeping and
reporting behavior of the law enforcement agencies involved. We have
fitted the four per capita earnings equations under the stochastic specification discussed above.

The results of estimation are presented in Table I. The second
column of the table contains the estimated parameters of the unrestricted
translog model under the maintained hypothesis of utility maximization.
There are twenty two free parameters to be estimated directly. The

---

[31]In more detail these series are the "Average Hourly Wages of
Production or Nonsupervisary Workers on Private Nonagricultural Payrolls,"
"Employees on Nonagricultural Payrolls" and "Labor Force" series published
by BLS.

remaining parameters may be estimated indirectly via equations (28).
Column three contains estimates of the model's parameters under the joint
hypothesis of utility maximization and homothetic preferences. Homotheticity further reduces the number of directly estimated parameters to
eighteen. Finally, column four contains our estimate of the model under
the maintained hypotheses of utility maximization and linear logarithmic
preferences. Only five parameters are free in this case, four are
estimated directly, and one indirectly.

Statistical tests of the restrictions on the functional structure
of preferences are conditional upon the maintained hypothesis of utility
maximization and based upon the test statistic

$$(32) \qquad \Omega = \max L^R / \max L^{\overline{R}}$$

where $\max L^R$ is the maximum value of the likelihood function for the
model subject to the restrictions R and $\max L^{\overline{R}}$ is the maximum value of
the likelihood function for the model without restriction. Minus twice
the logarithm of Ω is asymptotically distributed as chi-squared with
number of degrees of freedom equal to the number of restrictions imposed.

Analysis of Results

Test Results - In Table II are presented the values of the test
statistic Ω for the two alternative models we have estimated along with
the number of degrees of freedom and the χ^2 critical value associated with
each test. We proceed by testing the homothetic model against the
unrestricted (nonhomothetic) model. If the hypothesis of homothetic
preferences is accepted, we test the hypothesis of linear logarithmic
utility conditional on the homotheticity hypothesis. If homotheticity

TABLE I. PARAMETER ESTIMATES FOR THE FIVE EQUATION
          EARNINGS-EXPENDITURE MODEL[32]

Parameters	Unrestricted Model	Homothetic Preferences	Linear Logarithmic Preferences
α_1	-29.528 (4.965)	-19.457 (3.961)	3.794 (.264)
α_2	-6.361 (1.683)	-4.161 (.938)	.459 (.086)
α_3	-9.710 (2.235)	-5.139 (1.316)	1.972 (.127)
α_4	1.968 (1.291)	2.704 (.765)	2.808 (.058)
β_{11}	4.300 (.487)	3.996	
β_{21}	.271 (.198)	.196 (.154)	
β_{31}	.405 (.204)	.270 (.203)	
β_{41}	.019 (.169)	-.017 (.167)	
β_{22}	.617 (.106)	.590	
β_{32}	.247 (.080)	.214 (.079)	
β_{42}	-.126 (.078)	-.136 (.078)	
β_{33}	1.294 (.122)	1.189	
β_{43}	-.027 (.085)	-.022 (.085)	
β_{44}	.906 (.225)	1.015	

TABLE I.   PARAMETER ESTIMATES FOR THE FIVE EQUATION
           EARNINGS-EXPENDITURE MODEL (Continued)

Parameters	Unrestricted Model	Homothetic Preferences	Linear Logarithmic Preferences
γ_{1P}	-5.779 (.748)	-4.445 (.581)	
γ_{2P}	-1.168 (.260)	-.864 (.197)	
γ_{3P}	-2.232 (.342)	-1.651 (.270)	
γ_{4P}	-.836 (.272)	-.840 (.258)	
β_1	-.782 (.319)		
β_2	-.159 (.111)		
β_3	-.362 (.149)		
β_4	-.063 (.083)		
Π_1	.782 (.319)		
Π_2	.159 (.111)		
Π_3	.362 (.149)		
Π_4	.0063 (.083)		

[32]Standard errors are in parentheses. (All coefficients are multiplied by 10^4.)

TABLE II.   TEST STATISTICS, DEGREES OF FREEDOM, AND χ^2
CRITICAL VALUES FOR THE ESTIMATED MODELS

Restrictions on Preferences	Degrees of Freedom	χ^2 Critical Value	Test Statistic, $-2\ln\Omega$
Homothetic Preferences	4	9.49	10.85
Linear Logarithmic Preferences	10	18.31	161.26

is rejected, testing terminates. The .05 level of significance is adopted
for these and all tests which follow.

The first row of Table II contains the relevant information for
testing the hypothesis of homothetic preferences conditional upon utility
maximizing behavior. The data support our earlier reservations with this
structure and the hypothesis of homothetic preferences is rejected.
Since the homotheticity hypothesis has been rejected our testing is
finished. We conclude that the unrestricted (nonhomothetic) model
provides the most satisfactory explanation of the data points in our
sample. All furhter discussion will be in terms of this model.

Elasticity Estimates - Using equations (10') and (20) we have calculated direct and cross elasticities of supply, η_{ij}, and wealth
elasticities of supply, η_i, at sample means. These calculations are
reported in Table III along with the associated standard errors.[33]   In

---

[33]Using η to denote the vector of direct, cross and wealth elastici-
ties, letting $\gamma \equiv (\alpha, \beta, \pi)$ represent the vector of all parameters entering
the model and denoting the variance-covariance matrix of $\hat{\gamma}$ with Z, stan-
dard error for the elements of η are calculated using $(\partial \eta / \partial \hat{\gamma}) Z (\partial \eta / \partial \hat{\gamma})^T$.

TABLE III. DIRECT, CROSS AND WEALTH ELASTICITIES OF SUPPLY*
            (at sample means)

Para-meter	Esti-mate	Para-meter	Esti-mate	Para-meter	Esti-mate	Para-meter	Esti-mate
η_{11}	2.051 (.723)	η_{12}	.066 (.038)	η_{13}	.099 (.059)	η_{14}	-.079 (.039)
η_{21}	.416 (.244)	η_{22}	1.947 (.460)	η_{23}	.378 (.125)	η_{24}	-.194 (.100)
η_{31}	.184 (.099)	η_{32}	.112 (.035)	η_{33}	1.565 (.566)	η_{34}	-.012 (.003)
η_{41}	-.068 (.030)	η_{42}	-.045 (.020)	η_{43}	-.010 (.003)	η_{44}	1.325 (.080)
η_{1}	-.841 (.348)	η_{2}	-1.347 (.582)	η_{3}	-.584 (.250)	η_{4}	.772 (.288)

*Standard errors are in parentheses.

Table IV we present the same matrix of elasticities after evaluating each
estimate at the .05 level of significance. The most striking result is
the apparent lack of interdependence between many of the sources of
income. "Own" expected returns seem to play a far larger role in determination of both legal and illegal activity levels than do the returns
in any competing or complementary activities. The suppliers of burglary
and robbery are especially sensitive to changes in own expected returns,
each with elasticities of about two. In addition, direct return elasticities for larceny and legal work are both considerably larger than unity.

    Next we note that wealth elasticities, with the exception of that
for legal work, are negative and quite large (in absolute value). These

SUBSTITUTION AMONG CRIME AND THE QUESTION OF DETERRENCE   189

TABLE IV.   RETURN AND WEALTH ELASTICITIES OF SUPPLY EVALUATED
AT THE .05 LEVEL OF SIGNIFICANCE

$$
\eta = \begin{bmatrix}
2.051 & 0 & 0 & -.079 \\
0 & 1.947 & .378 & -.194 \\
0 & .112 & 1.565 & -.012 \\
-.068 & -.045 & -.010 & 1.325 \\
\hline
-.841 & -1.347 & -.584 & .772
\end{bmatrix}
$$

estimates range from -1.347 for robbery to -.841 for burglary, indicating
that increases in wealth will tend to have deterrent effects on the
suppliers of burglary, robbery and larceny. The only somewhat unexpected
result here is the positive, although inelastic, response of legal
activity to wealth changes. Of course there is no reason to believe
that η_4 is a monotonic function and hence legal effort may increase in
wealth over some range and decrease over another. Overall we conclude
that own returns and wealth appear to be the major determinats of activity
levels in both legal and illegal pursuits.

As far as cross elasticities are concerned, we see (Table IV, row 4)
that although burglary, robbery and larceny are viewed as substitutes for
legal activity, changes in the expected returns to these crimes have
rather small effects on the supply of legal efforts. But this is much as
one might expect over any region of limited variation in returns and
follows from the fact that the majority of legal wage earners undoubtedly
are "specialists" in the provision of legal services[34] and for these

---

[34]Except for chiseling on income taxes perhaps.

individuals the expected losses accompanying a move from the legal
"corner" into a mixed effort allocation will be quite large. This will
be especially true of individuals with "clean" records where expected
losses are disproportionately high prior to the first arrest. Given
the low expected returns to property crimes (see Table V), one expects
that it would take large changes in these returns to induce the individuals in question to switch or mix occupations.

Turning next to the effects of variation in the legal wage rate,
we notice that burglary is somewhat more responsive to changes in legal
returns than legal activity is to changes in burglary returns. Comparing η_{42} and η_{24} indicates the same phenomenon, but to a much greater
extent, is operative between legal activity and robbery. The supply of
robbery is four times more responsive to variation in legal earnings
than is the level of legal activity to changes in the return to robbery.
In summary we estimate that legal activity is a substitute, albiet a
rather weak one, for each property crime studied and that the relationship is symmetric.

Continuing our examination of Table IV we see that no cross elasticity between burglary and other illegal sources of income is significantly different from zero. Hence the supply of burglars appears to
depend primarily upon own returns, wealth levels and to some extent
upon the returns to legal work. One possible explanation for this
result is definitional in origin. To see this consider the group of
burglars or potential burglars, who according to the estimates we have
presented, will respond quite strongly to increases in the expected
return to burglary. Now burglary is defined as a theft in which an
illegal entry is made, but the victim is not confronted, i.e., no force

is involved. But what if for some reason confrontation and force turn out to be unavoidable, e.g., some one is home (the planned burglary very likely becomes a robbery, i.e., force or implied force is involved) or the potential burglar finds it just as easy to steal from a parked automobile, the factory where he works or to shoplift at local business establishments (the planned burglary becomes a larceny). In such cases increases in the expected return to burglary lead to an increase in planned burglaries but a somewhat smaller increase in actual burglaries with the difference being unplanned increases in robbery and larceny. The point is that due to narrow definitional differences between crimes, increases in returns to one crime may well increase activity levels in other crimes. This is not to say that changes in returns do not lead to substitution, but rather that strong own elasticities and small definitional differences between crimes most likely smudge attempts to measure these effects.

This point is important enough, not only to our own efforts to measure the degree of interdependence between illegal activities but also to any future efforts, to merit amplification. The basic idea is that even if alternative illegal sources of income are substitutes, measurements of the extent of these efforts will in general tend to be understated, due to a complementarity bias imparted by the definitions of the activities involved. In other words, there will usually be simultaneous substitution and "complementarity" effects when expected returns change. If the two effects are of approximately the same magnitude, then measured effects will tend to support the independence hypothesis; if definitional blurring is relatively important, measurements will tend to support complementarity of the activities involved, etc.

Note that our estimates of η_{23} and η_{32} support the hypothesis that robbery and larceny are complements, although the relative magnitudes of the two estimates suggest that this conclusion may well be the result of definitional blurring as discussed above. More precisely, of all property crimes robbery and larceny are a priori the most likely pair to be independent. Now since one would expect that planned robberies could quite easily become actual larcenies, but that planned larcenies would only seldom become actual robberies, estimates of η_{23} should be considerably greater than those for η_{32}. This conclusion is supported by our estimates which are .378 and .112 respectively.

Finally, it may be appropriate to point out that although our estimates indicate only moderate substitution between crimes, we would be the first to admit that our measures of expected returns are very rough indeed. Even prior to our manipulations to transform average values stolen into "expected returns," we were informed by those responsible for UCR statistics at the FBI that the average value stolen series were ". . . at best a rough approximation to actual losses." It follows that this admonition holds a fortiori for our expected return series. More accurate return information, if the "definitional complementarity" we have noted could be netted out, would undoubtedly show a greater degree of substitutability among crimes than we have found.

Policy Implications - One of the purposes of this study was to measure the extent of any "system-wide" deterrent effects which may be associated with changes in sanctions and/or enforcement levels for a single crime. Such a measure must account for changes in offense rates in related illegal activities which are induced by a policy change in the activity in question. In what follows we measure the "system-wide" effects of policy changes by the response of the total value transferred in property crimes within the system, to the policy change in interest. By definition the total value transferred in the activities of burglary, robbery and larceny is given by

$$(33) \qquad V = \sum_{1}^{3} r_j T_j$$

If θ_i represents any parameter associated with the expected return to illegal activity i then the elasticity of V with respect to policy parameter θ_i is given by

$$(34) \qquad \frac{\partial V}{\partial \theta_i} \frac{\theta_i}{V} = (\frac{\partial \omega_i}{\partial \theta_i} \frac{\theta_i}{\omega_i} \sum_{j=1}^{3} r_j T_j \eta_{ji} + r_i T_i \frac{\partial r_i}{\partial \theta_i} \frac{\theta_i}{r_i})/V \ , \quad i = 1,2,3$$

Here we use θ_i to represent the "gross" return, r_i, the probability of arrest and conviction, p_{ac}^i, and the mean sentence, μ_i, associated with crime i.[35] Using Y to denote net income foregone per year of imprisonment and $\delta \equiv (1 + d)^{-1}$, where d is the annual discount rate, the elasticities of expected unit returns, $(\partial \omega_i/\partial \theta_i)$ (θ_i/ω_i), with respect to each of these parameters are

$$\frac{\partial \omega_i}{\partial P_{ac}^i} \frac{p_{ac}^i}{\omega_i} = - \frac{p_a^i p_{c/a}^i Y \int_0^{\mu_i} \delta^x dx}{\omega_i} = 1 - \frac{r_i}{i} \qquad 36$$

_____

[35]Since in our model elasticities of expected returns with respect to p_a, $p_{c/a}$ and p_{ac} are equal, we use p_{ac} as the probability measure in remainder of the paper.

[36]In terms of earlier definitions $Y \int_0^{\mu_i} \delta^x dx \equiv S_i$, the monetary equivalent of the mean sentence, if imprisoned for μ_i years.

$$(35) \quad \frac{\partial \omega_i}{\partial \mu_i} \frac{\mu_i}{\omega_i} = \frac{\partial \omega_i}{\partial p_{ac}^i} \frac{p_{ac}^i}{\omega_i} (\mu_i \delta^{\mu_i} \ln\delta / (\delta^{\mu_i} - 1))$$

$$\frac{\partial \omega_i}{\partial r_i} \frac{r_i}{\omega_i} = \frac{r_i}{\omega_i} \, , \qquad\qquad i = 1,2,3$$

Due to the fact that the income-expenditure constraint in our model is in terms of expected values, expected returns must always be positive and elasticities of expected returns with respect to probabilities of arrest and conviction will always be less than the same measurements with respect to gross returns, r_i. The magnitude of this difference is, however, an empirical proposition of some interest.

Because $(\partial T_k / \partial \theta_i)(\theta_i / T_k) = \eta_{ki}(\partial \omega_i / \partial \theta_i)(\theta_i / \omega_i)$, it is a simple matter to calculate market supply elasticities with respect to probabilities, mean sentence lengths and gross returns. Direct elasticities with respect to probabilities and sentence lengths may be of particular interest, in that these parameters have been estimated in other studies. Therefore, before presenting our estimates of the system wide effects of changes in the several parameters, we digress briefly and present estimates of these elasticities.

Using equations (35) we have

$$\frac{\partial T_k}{\partial p_{ac}^i} \frac{p_{ac}^i}{T_k} = \eta_{ki}(1 - \frac{r_i}{\omega_i}) \, , \qquad i = 1,2,3 \, , \ k = 1,2,3,4$$

$$(36) \quad \frac{\partial T_k}{\partial \mu_i} \frac{\mu_i}{T_k} = \eta_{ki}(1 - \frac{r_i}{\omega_i})(\mu_i \delta^{\mu_i} \ln\delta / (\delta^{\mu_i} - 1)) \, , \quad i = 1,2,3 \, , \ k = 1,2,3,4$$

$$\frac{\partial T_k}{\partial r_i} \frac{r_i}{T_k} = \eta_{ki} \frac{r_i}{\omega_i}^{37} \, , \qquad\qquad i = 1,2,3 \, , \ k = 1,2,3,4$$

---

[37]Since $r_4 = \omega_4$, for legal endeavors $(\partial T_k / \partial r_4)(r_4 / T_k) = \eta_{k4}$, $k = 1,2,3,4$.

Equations (36) indicate that the smaller is the expected loss from participating in a criminal activity, the smaller will be the supply response from increased probabilities of capture and conviction and from increases in the mean prison sentence. Therefore policies designed to affect the supply of illegal acts by altering a component of the expected return, will have the smallest impact when expected losses are small. It follows that jurisdictions with relatively low enforcement and sanction levels not only experience higher crime rates ceteris paribus than do similar jurisdictions with relatively high enforcement and sanction levels, but these jurisdictions also find that policy changes which are undertaken to lower crime rates have a smaller impact than the same policy change would have if inacted elsewhere.

In Table V, we report estimated market supply elasticities (evaluated at sample means) with respect to each of the policy parameters we have been discussing, along with our estimates of η_{ij}, reported earlier, for comparison. Column six of the table includes sample means for each of the variables used in these calculations. As the reader can see, mean probabilities of apprehension and conviction given apprehension, are quite low as are mean sentence lengths. Hence expected losses from participating in these activities are relatively small with the consequence that market supply elasticities with regrad to any of the parameters entering the expected loss will be considerably smaller than the corresponding elasticity with respect to the expected return. (See equations (36).) Table V bears out these statements. Estimates vary from the supply of larceny where changes in own probabilities and own sentence lengths are estimated to bring about -1.137 and -.914 responses, respectively, to the supply of robbery where the

TABLE V. MARKET SUPPLY ELASTICITIES WITH RESPECT TO ARREST AND CONVICTION PROBABILITIES, MEAN SENTENCE LENGTHS AND GROSS RETURNS (at sample means)

Parameter (θ_i)	Burglary Responses $(\partial T_1/\partial\theta_i)(\theta_i/T_1)$	Robbery Responses $(\partial T_2/\partial\theta_i)(\theta_i/T_2)$	Larceny Responses $(\partial T_3/\partial\theta_i)(\theta_i/T_3)$	Legal Work Responses $(\partial T_4/\partial\theta_i)(\theta_i/T_4)$	Sample Means*	Ehrlich's Estimates (2SLS, SUR) (Direct Effects Only) $(\partial T_i/\partial\theta_i)(\theta_i/T_i)$**
p_{ac}^1	-.343	0	0	0	.253 / .085	-.624, -.724
p_{ac}^2	0	-.834	-.051	0	.369 / .158	-1.112, -1.303
p_{ac}^3	0	-.274	-1.137	0	.184 / .317	-.358, -.371
μ_1	-.272	0	0	0	2.32	-.996, -1.127
μ_2	0	-.569	-.041	0	3.97	-.372, -.286
μ_3	0	-.187	-.914	0	1.92	-.602, -.654
ω_1	2.051	0	0	-.068	213.48	
ω_2	0	1.947	.112	-.045	163.53	
ω_3	0	.378	1.565	-.010	56.20	
r_1	2.394	0	0	-.079	249.33	
r_2	0	2.841	.163	-.066	238.67	
r_3	0	.653	2.703	-.017	97.03	
r_4	-.079	-.194	-.012	1.325	3.39	

*We have reported both probability means for each crime, p_a^i followed by $p_{c/a}^i$.

**See Ehrlich (1973).

same responses are -.834 and -.569 to the supply of burglary where own probability and own sentence length changes bring about supply responses of only -.343 and -.272 respectively.

In an earlier study Ehrlich (1973) has estimated own probability and own sentence length elasticities using OLS, 2SLS and SUR for each of the crimes we have studied. In the final column of Table V we report his 2SLS and SUR estimates of these parameters. As far as probability responses are concerned, we find that our estimates of the burglary and robbery elasticities are somewhat smaller than Ehrlich's (in absolute value), while our larceny elasticity estimate is somewhat larger than Ehrlich's. For sentence length elasticities, our estimates and Ehrlich's are fairly close for robbery and larceny, although our estimates for burglary are considerably smaller (in absolute value) than Ehrlich's. For several reasons one must be cautious in drawing conclusions from these comparisons. First, the Ehrlich estimates are based upon a cross section of states in 1960, while our sample is a mixed time series, cross section of SMSA's over the period 1967-1972. Second, Ehrlich's supply equations contain only own returns and hence parameter estimates will in general be biased--the direction of bias being determined by the relative strengths of the substitutability or complementarity relations between the activity in question and the omitted activities. Third, Ehrlich did not have information on convictions for his study and was forced to use the number imprisoned as a proxy for the number convicted in his measure of the probability of arrest and conviction.[38]

---

[38]In a still earlier study Ehrlich (1970) provides a few quite imprecise (i.e., statistically insignificant) estimates of cross policy effects on the supply of several property crimes. He has estimated

The last four rows of Table V give the response of each income
generating activity to changes in the gross returns to burglary, robbery,
larceny and legal work. As equations (36) make clear, these elasticities
will be larger than those we have been discussing. In the context of the
present study it appears that efforts by police departments directed to
lowering the "take," e.g., via public education programs or cracking
down on "fences" will have larger deterrent effects than the corresponding increases in probabilities of apprehension and conviction or
increases in sentence lengths. The responses of property crime to
changes in gross returns relative to similar changes in expected losses
(p_{ac}^i or μ_i) range from over three times as great for larceny to approximately nine times as large for burglary. We conclude that although
increases in probabilities of capture and conviction and increases in
the length of prison sentences will cause decreased participation in the
activities affected, even larger decreases may be obtained via actions
on the part of individuals to protect their property or actions on the
part of police directed to lowering the market value of stolen goods.

System-Wide Deterrent Effects - We now report our measurements of
the extent of "system-wide" deterrent effects associated with the several
policy instruments in our model. "System-wide" effects are measured by
the response of the total value illegally transferred, V, to the policy

market supply elasticities for burglary and robbery with respect to
probabilities of arrest and conviction and mean sentence lengths for
robbery, burglary and "theft" (auto theft plus larceny), respectively.
He finds robbery and burglary to be complements and "theft" to be a
substitute for burglary. Like Ehrlich, our estimates of these elasticities are also statistically insignificant, although our estimates
are both positive.

change of interest. Policy changes which affect expected returns alone
may be evaluated by means of the formulae set forth in equations (34)
above. In Table VI we report relative and absolute changes in total
value transferred due to changes in the probability of arrest and
conviction, to changes in gross returns and to changes in mean prison
sentence lengths. Due to the size of direct return effects and the
relative insignificance of cross effects it is obvious that increases
in probabilities of arrest and conviction, increases in mean sentence
lengths and decreases in gross returns will all have net or system-wide
deterrent effects. The magnitude of these effects is given in the
table. For example, a one percent increase in the probability of
apprehension and conviction for larceny will result in a .441 percent
reduction in the total value transferred, while a one percent increase
in prison sentence lengths will result in .354 percent reduction in
total value transferred.   But if instead the gross return to larceny
is reduced one percent, the reduction in value transferred is more than
five times as large. The differential response of crime rates to changes
in gross returns and changes in expected losses is most striking for the
crime of burglary, where changes in gross returns bring about a response
in burglaries ten to thirteen times larger than the corresponding changes
in the probability of apprehension and conviction and in sentence lengths.
For robbery, changes in gross returns have four to six times the impact
on value stolen as do probability and sentence length changes.

The last three columns in Table VI contain estimates of the absolute
change in the total value illegally transferred due to one percent
changes in the same policy instruments. To interpret these numbers recall

TABLE VI.   RELATIVE AND ABSOLUTE CHANGES IN TOTAL VALUES STOLEN DUE
TO ONE PERCENT CHANGES IN POLICY PARAMETERS
(at sample means*)

Activity	$\dfrac{\partial V}{\partial p^i_{ac}}(p^i_{ac}/V)$	$\dfrac{\partial V}{\partial \mu_i}(\mu_i/V)$	$\dfrac{\partial V}{\partial r_i}(r_i/V)$	$\dfrac{\partial V}{\partial p^i_{ac}}p^i_{ac}$	$\dfrac{\partial V}{\partial \mu_i}\mu_i$	$\dfrac{\partial V}{\partial r_i}r_i$
1	$-.177$	$-.140$	1.842	$-\$680,653$	$\$538,370$	$\$7,083,411$
2	$-.157$	$-.107$	$.649$	$-\$603,743$	$-\$411,468$	$\$2,495,729$
3	$-.441$	$-.354$	1.705	$-\$1,695,865$	$-\$1,361,307$	$\$6,556,579$
4	--	--	$.044$	--	--	$-\$167,616$

that our sample consists of approximately ten mid-sized SMSA's per year
for the seven years 1967 to 1972. Some SMSA's appear several times in
the sample, others appear but once, depending primarily upon reporting
behavior. The value V, the total value transferred, is the sum of total
amounts stolen in burglary, larceny and robbery over all SMSA's, over
all six years and is $384.55 million in 1966 dollars or approximately
sixty-four million dollars per year. We estimate that a one percent
change in the probability of arrest and conviction in 1967 would have
brought about, ceteris paribus, a reduction in value transferred of
between .603 and 1.695 million dollars, depending upon which probability
was changed. A similar reduction in the gross return to property crimes
would have resulted in a reduction in the total value transferred of
between two and one half million and seven million dollars.

The two entries in the last row of the table give the relative and
absolute response of the total value stolen to a one percent, say,
increase in the legal wage. We estimate that this would result in a

reduction in the total amount stolen of approximately four hundreths of one percent as some individuals engaged in property crime turn to legal work to generate income. In our sample this amounts to approximately one hundred seventy thousand dollars for each percentage change in the wage rate. This response is quite small due primarily to the fact that the supply of robbery is far the most sensitive to changes in the wage rate, but the proceeds to robbery constitute only about one tenth of the total value stolen. Since we have used the product of production worker wages and the number employed divided by the size of the labor force as our measure of the expected legal wage, it follows that a one percent increase in employment will also decrease total transfer by .044 percent.[39]

A slightly different way of assessing the overall deterrent effects of selected policy changes would be to calculate the change in the total amount stolen in all property crimes due to one more arrest or one more conviction for crime i. (These computations would of course be especially useful if one had estimates of the marginal costs of arrests and convictions by type of crime.[40]) Our results use the fact that $\partial V/\partial a_i = (\partial V/\partial p_a^i)(\partial p_a^i/\partial a_i) = (\partial V/\partial p_a^i)(1/T_i)$[41] and $\partial V/\partial c_i = (\partial V/\partial p_{c/a}^i) \cdot (\partial p_{c/a}^i/\partial c_i) = (\partial V/\partial p_{c/a}^i)(1/a_i)$, where a_i and c_i are the number of arrests and convictions for property crime i, respectively. In which case

---

[39] A one percent change in the number employed results in a one percent change in expected legal returns.

[40] See Darrough and Heineke, Chapter 7, in the present volume for estimates of marginal cost of "solution" functions, by type of crime.

[41] This calculation assumes that the probability of conviction given arrest is not affected by an additional arrest.

$$\frac{\partial V}{\partial a_i} = \frac{\partial \omega_i}{\partial p_a^i} \frac{1}{\omega_i} (\sum_j r_j T_j n_{ji})/T_i$$

(37)   , i = 1,2,3

$$\frac{\partial V}{\partial c_i} = \frac{\partial \omega_i}{\partial p_{c/a}^i} \frac{1}{\omega_i} (\sum_j r_j T_j n_{ji})/a_i$$

are responses of V to an additional arrest and to an additional conviction.
These formulae are evaluated at sample means and presented in Table VII
along with the response of V to a one year change in the length of the
prison sentence for crime i. Again, keep in mind that the "base" for
these calculations is the $384.55 million in total property transferred
over our sample.

From the table we see that one more arrest, ceteris paribus, leads
to an overall reduction in property stolen of between $256 and $756
depending upon the type of crime. Convictions have a considerably greater
impact with an additional robbery conviction resulting in a reduction in
property stolen of over forty seven hundred dollars, at the mean. The
analagous calculations for burglary and larceny convictions are $3,014 and
$1,466 respectively. In addition, we estimate that increasing the mean
length of prison sentences by one year will reduce the total amount stolen
from approximately $10.29 million for robbery sentences to approximately
$70.78 million for larceny sentences, in 1966 dollars.

Another question of interest concerns the response of total value
stolen to changes in the distribution of wealth. We address two hypothetical situations: First, we calculate the response of value transferred
to a change in the mean of the wealth distribution, λ_1, income and gross
returns, r_i, held constant. Second, we calculate the response of total

TABLE VII. THE RESPONSE OF TOTAL VALUES TRANSFERRED (AT SAMPLE MEANS)
            TO CHANGES IN THE NUMBER OF ARRESTS, CONVICTIONS AND THE
            LENGTH OF SENTENCE, BY TYPE OF CRIME

Property Crime i	$\partial V/\partial a_i$	$\partial V/\partial c_i$	$\partial V/\partial u_i$* (millions)
1	-$256.20	-$3,014.49	-$23.15
2	-$756.17	-$4,790.98	-$10.29
3	-$464.74	-$1,466.06	-$70.78

*A one year change in the mean sentence amounts to 43%, 25% and 52%
increases in time served, respectively.

value stolen to an equal percentage change in income, gross returns and
wealth. The result might be interpreted as the response of property crime
earnings to a secular increase in returns, income and wealth—given a
"passive" enforcement and sanctions policy which leaves enforcement levels
and sanctions unchanged.

The response of total value stolen to equi-proportional changes in
mean wealth, returns and income may be written as

$$(38) \qquad \frac{\partial v}{\partial \xi} \frac{\xi}{v} = (\sum_{j=1}^{3} r_j T_j (\sum_{i=1}^{4} \eta_{ji} + \eta_j + 1) d\xi/\xi)/V$$

where $d\xi/\xi$ represents an equal percentage change in mean income, wealth
and returns. In the first case where mean wealth alone changes equation
(38) simplifies to

$$(38') \qquad \frac{\partial v}{\partial \lambda_1} \frac{\lambda_1}{v} = (\sum_{k=1}^{3} r_k T_k \eta_k)/v$$

We find that a one percent increase in mean wealth, ceteris paribus, leads to a $\cdot 795$ percent decrease in total value transferred or approximately a three million dollar reduction over our sample. These computations are reported in Table VIII.

Turning to the second calculation, notice that a, say, one percent change in mean income and gross returns results in a one percent change in the expected return to all property crimes. If this is combined with an equal percentage change in mean wealth the result is equation (38). We find that, although increases in mean wealth alone have strong deterrent effects, if mean income and returns are also increasing, and enforcement and sanctions are left unaltered, then a one percent change in each of these factors leads to approximately a two percent _increase_ in total value transferred. (See Table VIII.) Obviously the increase in expected returns is sufficient to offset the negative effects on the supply of property crime caused by increased wealth. Over the sample such a secular increase in mean wealth, mean income and gross returns would result, _ceteris paribus_, in an increase in value stolen of more than eight million dollars.

TABLE VIII.   RELATIVE AND ABSOLUTE CHANGES IN TOTAL VALUE TRANSFERRED
              DUE TO ONE PERCENT CHANGES IN λ_1 and ξ
              (at sample means)

Elasticities of Total Value Stolen with Respect to Changes in		Changes in Total Value Stolen with Respect to a One Percent Change in (in millions)	
Mean Wealth $(\partial V/\partial \lambda_1)(\lambda_1/V)$	Mean "Returns," Income and Wealth $(\partial V/\partial \xi)(\xi/V)$	Mean Wealth $(\partial V/\partial \lambda_1)\lambda_1$	Mean "Returns," Income and Wealth $(\partial V/\partial \xi)\xi$
$-.795$	2.150	$-\$3.057$	$\$8,269$

Summary and Conclusions

In this paper we have used data gathered on a collection of medium
sized SMSA's for the years 1967-72 to estimate a simultaneous supply
system consisting of supply equations for burglary, robbery, larceny and
a generic legal activity. Three separate models were estimated corresponding to nonhomothetic, homothetic and additive preferences. We found
that if one maintains the utility maximization hypothesis, the data are
inconsistent with homothetic preferences and linear logarithmic preferences. We then computed direct and cross elasticities of supply and
wealth elasticities of supply, and found our estimates to be pretty much
consistent with expectations. Direct elasticities for each income
generating activity were positive and relatively large, while cross
elasticities indicated, among other things, that legal work is viewed as
an alternative income generating activity by those engaged in property
crime, although a rather poor alternative. As far as cross effects
between illegal income generating prospects are concerned, we have argued,
and found some supporting evidence, that narrow definitional differences
between crimes lead to a complementarity bias in cross elasticities--a
problem which must be confronted in future studies attempting to measure
the extent of substitutability between criminal activities.

Wealth elasticities for each illegal activity turned out to negative
and quite large in absolute value, indicating that increases in mean
wealth, ceteris paribus, will be accompanied by substantial reductions in
property crime rates. Comparing magnitudes of direct, cross and wealth
elasticity estimates led us to conclude that own returns and wealth are
the most important determinants of labor supply behavior--and especially
the supply of effort to illegal activity.

We used the response of the total value illegally transferred to a
policy change to measure system-wide effects of the policy change. We
found that each of the parameters entering the model possessed "net"
deterrent effects, but that altering gross returns to property crimes
through, say, policies directed to reducing the "fence" value of stolen
property or policies encouraging "self protection" paid far greater
deterrence dividends than the analogous policy changes affecting expected
losses. As always, much work remains to be done.

University of Santa Clara

BIBLIOGRAPHY

Allen, R. G. D., Mathematical Analysis for Economists. London: Macmillan, 1938.

Avio, K. L., and C. S. Clark, Property Crimes in Canada. Toronto: University of Toronto Press, 1976.

Becker, G., "The Allocation of Time," Journal of Political Economy, vol. 75, 1965, pp. 493-517.

Becker, G., "Crime and Punishment: An Economic Approach," Journal of Political Economy, March/April, 1968, pp. 169-217.

Berndt, E. R., M. N. Darrough and W. E. Diewert, "Flexible Functional Forms and Expenditure Distributions: An Application to Canadian Consumer Demand Functions," International Economic Review, vol. 18, no. 3, October, 1977, pp. 651-75.

Block, M. K., and J. M. Heineke, "The Allocation of Effort Under Uncertainty: The Case of Risk Averse Behavior," Journal of Political Economy, 81, March/April, 1973, pp. 376-85.

Block, M. K., and J. M. Heineke, "A Labor Theoretic Analysis of the Criminal Choice," American Economic Review, 65, June, 1975, pp. 314-25.

Block, M. K., and R. Lind, "Crime and Punishment: Reconsidered," Journal of Legal Studies, January, 1975, pp. 241-47.

Block, M. K., and R. Lind, "An Economic Analysis of Crimes Punishable by Imprisonment," Journal of Legal Studies, June, 1975, pp. 479-92.

Carr-Hill, R. A., and N. H. Stern, "An Econometric Model of the Supply and Control of Recorded Offenses in England and Wales," Journal of Public Economics, 1973, pp. 289-318.

Carr-Hill, R. A., and N. H. Stern," An Econometric Model of the Supply of Recorded Offenses in England and Wales," mimeo, 1976.

Christensen, L. R., D. W. Jorgensen and L. J. Lau, "Conjugate Duality and the Transcendental Logarithmic Production Function," Econometrica, 39, 1971, pp. 255-56.

Christensen, L. R., D. W. Jorgensen and L. J. Lau, "Transcendental Logarithmic Production Frontiers," Review of Economics and Statistics, 55, 1973, pp. 28-45.

Christensen, L. R., D. W. Jorgensen and L. J. Lau, "Transcendental Logarithmic Utility Functions," American Economic Review, 65, June, 1975, pp. 367-83.

Diewert, W. E., "An Application of the Shepard Duality Theorem: A
    Generalized Leontief Production Function," *Journal of Political
    Economy*, 79, 1971, pp. 481-507.

Diewert, W. E., "Separability and a Generalization of the Cobb-Douglas
    Cost, Production and Indirect Utility Functions," Technical Report
    86, IMSSS Stanford University, 1973.

Diewert, W. E., "Applications of Duality Theory," in M. D. Intriligator
    and D. A. Kendrick, eds., *Frontiers in Quantitative Economics*, Vol.
    II, North Holland, 1974.

Ehrlich, I., "Participation in Illegitimate Activities: A Theoretical
    and Empirical Investigation," Journal of Political Economy, 81, May/
    June, 1973, pp. 521-67.

Ehrlich, I., Participation in Illegitimate Activities: An Economic
    Analysis, unpublished Ph.D. dissertation, University of Chicago,
    1970.

Ehrlich, I., "The Deterrent Effect of Capital Punishment: A Question of
    Life and Death," *American Economic Review*, 65, June 1975, pp. 397-417.

Fisher, F., and D. Nagin, "On the Feasibility of Identifying the Crime
    Function in a Simultaneous Model of Crime Rates and Sanction Levels,"
    in Blumstein, et. al. (eds.), *Deterrence and Incapacitation: The
    Effects of Criminal Sanctions on Crime Rates*, National Academy of
    Sciences, 1978.

Jorgensen, D. W., and L. J. Lau, "The Integrability of Consumer Demand
    Functions," Discussion paper, Harvard Institute of Economic Research,
    May, 1975.

Jorgensen, D. W., and L. J. Lau, "The Structure of Consumer Preferences,"
    Annuals of Economic and Social Measurement, 4/1, 1975.

Lau, L. J., "Applications of Duality Theory: A Comment," in M. D.
    Intriligator and D. A. Kendrick, eds., *Frontiers in Quantitative
    Economics*, Vol. II, North-Holland, 1974.

Lau, L. J., "Econometrics of Uncertainty," Working Paper, Department of
    Economics, Stanford University, 1973.

Mathieson, D., and P. Passell, "Homocide and Robbery in New York City:
    An Economic Model," *Journal of Legal Studies*, 1976, pp. 83 - 98.

Nagin, D., "General Deterrence: A Review of the Empirical Evidence," in
    Blumstein, et. al. (eds.), *Deterrence and Incapacitation: The
    Effects of Criminal Sanctions on Crime Rates*, National Academy of
    Sciences, 1978.

Orsagh, Thomas, "Crime Sanctions and Scientific Explanation," *The
    Journal of Criminal Law and Criminology*, Vol. 4, no. 3, 1973.

Passell, P., and J. Taylor, "The Deterrent Effect of Capital Punishment," forthcoming, American Economic Review, 1977.

Phillips, L., H. L. Votey, Jr., and D. Maxwell, "Crime, Youth and the Labor Market," Journal of Political Economy, 1972.

Phillips, L., and H. L. Votey, "Crime Control in California," Journal of Legal Studies, June, 1975, Vol. IV, no. 2, pp. 327-49.

Roy, R., De l'Utilité: Contribution à la Theorie des Choix, Hermann et Cie, Paris, 1943.

Samuelson, P. A., "Using Full Duality to Show that Simultaneously Additive Direct and Indirect Utilities Implies Unitary Price Elasticities of Demand," Econometrica, October, 1965, 33, pp. 781-96.

Sjoquist, D. L., "Property Crime and Economic Behavior: Some Empirical Results," American Economic Review, 63, June, 1973, pp. 439-46.

U.S. Department of Justice, Law Enforcement Assistance Administration, Criminal Victimization in the U.S.: 1973 Advance Report, U.S. Government Printing Office, 1973.

U.S. Department of Labor, Bureau of Labor Statistics Bulletins No. 1370-11, 1375, 1570-5, 1570-7, U.S. Government Printing Office, assorted years from 1966-73.

U.S. Internal Revenue Service, Statistics of Income: Individual Income Tax Returns, U.S. Government Printing Office, 1969.

Vandaele, Walter, The Economics of Crime: An Econometric Investigation of Auto Theft in the United States, unpublished Ph.D. dissertation, University of Chicago, 1975.

Wilson, James W., and Barbara Boland, "The Effect of Police on Crime Rates," Urban Institute Working Paper, April, 1977.

Economic Models of Criminal Behavior,
J.M. Heineke (ed.)
© *North-Holland Publishing Company, 1978*

CHAPTER SIX

FACTOR DEMANDS IN THE PROVISION OF PUBLIC SAFETY

Llad Phillips

Introduction

The past twenty years has been a period of public concern with what
has been perceived as a deterioration in public safety, especially in big
cities. How have police departments in large cities responded to this
problem? To tackle this question we have to consider what it is that
police departments produce and how they go about producing it. This
question is examined in some detail in the next section, but suffice it
to say that an index of output is presumed to exist but is not measured.
The properties of an implicitly additive indirect production function
(developed by G. Hanoch, [11]) are investigated by estimating the factor
demand equations after algebraic substitution to eliminate the output
variable. This particular function was chosen because its properties
are general enough to allow for different elasticities of substitution
between factors and for nonhomotheticity, and yet it requires the estimation of fewer parameters than the more general translog or generalized Leontief functions.

The study utilizes quantity and price information for three factor
inputs: uniformed police officers, civilians, and police cars. The
latter variable represents the non-labor inputs. Time series and cross
section data for five big city police departments provide the information
base for the nonlinear least square estimations.

The matrices of elasticities of substitution and compensated price elasticities of demand are reported for the three factor inputs. A major finding of the study is the nonhomothetic nature of the production function. The meaning of nonhomotheticity is explored by estimating the production function with an appropriate alternative functional form, in particular, the nonhomothetic approximation to the Arrow-Chenery-Minhas-Solow constant elasticity of substitution production function. Using this device, non-homotheticity is captured by the translation of the origin, in contrast to the Hanoch function, where nonhomotheticity is captured by the output elasticities for each factor. A third alternative is suggested, namely that the nonhomotheticity may be capturing inefficiency due to feather-bedding. The dollar costs of inefficiency are calculated under the assumption that this is in fact the case.

Specifying Production Functions for Police Departments

As is the case with other service industries such as education and health care, the specification of the output of police departments is not easy. One possibility is to presume that public safety is indicated by the absence of crime, and define output or public safety as a function of the level of various crimes. Since the level of various crimes committed is not known for the past twenty years, the only available measure is the number of crimes reported to the police. Because the practice of reporting crimes may have varied in unknown ways during this period, and could have differed as well between cities, this creates some problems with using crime as a measure of output. This is simply because the ratio of known reported offenses to unknown true offenses could have differed between cities and over time, making reported offenses an unreliable measure of crime.

Another difficulty is that the police provide a number of services, some of which may be less related to public safety than others. Not only do the police patrol for the purpose of preventing crime and maintaining public order, they also patrol to monitor traffic. The police conduct criminal investigations but must also handle traffic accident investigations. Ostrom et al. have identified the provision of services such as these to citizens as what it is that police agencies produce.[1]

Another alternative measure of output used by a number of investigators of the economics of crime such as Ehrlich, and Votey and Phillips, is the fraction of crimes resulting in conviction or cleared by arrest.[2] While these measures are important since, as proxies for the likelihoods of apprehension and punishment, they in part determine deterrence, there may be some question whether police departments are concerned with deterrence or with "solutions" to crimes. With the latter argument in mind, Darrough and Heineke used the number of clearances by arrest as measures of output.[3]

The approach adopted in this paper is to presume that an index of output such as public safety exists. Using an implicitly additive indirect production function developed by Hanoch, which implies constant differences in the Allen partial elasticities of substitution between factors, it is possible to determine a great deal about the structure of the production function without specifying output.[4] Hence the results are independent of a questionable choice between the various alternative measures of output. These results include whether the production function is homothetic or not, the magnitudes of the elasticities of substitution and of the compensated price elasticities of demand. With an additional assumption that the finding of nonhomotheticity of the production function can be interpreted as due to featherbedding, it is possible to construct indices of unit costs and output (up to the returns to

scale) and to estimate the additional cost of law enforcement attributable
to inefficiency.

The provision of public safety, like many other service industries,
is labor intensive with the salary budget usually accounting for over 75%
of the total budget for most cities. The principal labor input is police
officers. They are assigned to a number of tasks including surveillance
and traffic patrol, criminal and accident investigations, and administration. In the past 15 or 20 years, big city police departments have increasingly made use of civilian employees, and the ratio of the number of
police officers to civilians has declined. Evidently civilians have been
substituted for police officers, at least in administration. It is interesting to note that this decrease in the relative use of police officers
has occurred while there has been a slight increase in the entry wage of
officers relative to civilians for some departments and little change in
this price ratio for others.

An important input to traffic patrol and (with the decline in the
use of sidewalk beats by police departments) to surveillance patrol is
the police car. This was used as an index of all non-labor inputs, such
as motorcycles, etc. In general, police departments experienced an increase in the entry wage of police officers relative to the price of
police cars during the last 20 years. Some police departments show a
declining ratio of police officers to patrol cars, others do not. Evidently there is a possible output as well as a substitution effect in the
demand for these factors. During this period, the price of vehicles
relative to the wage of civilians fell in general for police departments,
yet the ratio of vehicles to civilians rose at most moderately, and
often fell, for various departments.

Data for the quantities of these three inputs to police department
activities are available for from 9 to 11 years between 1960 and 1975 for
the four California cities of Long Beach, Oakland, San Diego and San
Francisco.[5] In addition, a complete time series from 1956 to 1975 was
available for Los Angeles.[6] The entry wage for police officers, as well
as total expenditures by police departments, was available in the annual
volumes of the Municipal Year Book. It is noteworthy that total expenditures increased considerably over this period. Inquiries to police
departments suggested that a reasonable classification for civilians
which reflected the nature of the job, and the entry wage, was typist
Class A, non-manufacturing. Data on weekly earnings for this occupation
were available by SMSA in Area Wage Surveys, published by the U.S. Bureau
of Labor Statistics. The price of vehicles (as standardized on a 4-door
Oldsmobile 98) was obtained from Automotive News, published annually.

Using these figures and given the trends in input ratios, input
prices and budgets as discussed above, the question remains whether the
structure of production and costs can be unravelled.

The Model

The economic view of police department behavior pursued in this paper
is to presume that departments act to minimize costs subject to the specification of an acceptable level of output (or vector of outputs) or, equivalently, act to maximize output(s) subject to a budget as determined by the
elected officials in the community. Thus it is presumed that the factor
prices, W_i, and the budget, C, are parametric or given.

This approach is implemented using the indirect production function
with the functional structure of implicit indirect additivity as developed
by Hanoch,

(1) $\quad G(y, q) \equiv \Sigma B_i q^{e_i b_i} y_i \equiv 1,$

with $\ln(q^{e_i} y_i)$ replacing $q^{e_i b_i} y_i^{b_i}$ if $b_i = 0$, and where q is output and

y is a vector of normalized input prices W, i.e.

(2) $\quad y \equiv \dfrac{W}{C}$

C is cost and B_i, b_i and e_i are parameters. The B_i are in the nature of

distribution parameters, the e_i output elasticities and the b_i determine

the elasticities of substitution. The B_i and e_i are restricted to be

greater than zero and b_i to be less than one with either all b_i less than

zero or all b_i between zero and one. Thus we have presumed that the cost

function dual to this indirect production function is linear homogeneous

in W (see [11] - p. 408). This hypothesis, which is consistent with

assuming police departments act to minimize costs subject to a specified

level of output, is maintained in this paper but was tested by Darrough

and Heineke (who specified a translog cost function) and found the hypo-

thesis that the cost function was linear homogeneous in W to be acceptable.[8]

In this formulation, output q can be considered a scalar such as

"public safety". An alternative would be to view output as an index of a

vector of outputs z, such as reported offenses, traffic accident investi-

gations, and other possible measures,

(3) $\quad q = q(z)$

where the latter assumption implies that the direct production function

dual to this indirect production function G can be expressed as

(4) $\quad q(z) = f(x)$

where x is the vector of inputs. This in turn presumes that the transformation function

(5) $t(z, x) = 0$

is separable, i.e.

(6) $t(z, x) = -q(z) + f(x) = 0$

This assumption of separability has several implications.[9] The first
is that the outputs are produced jointly. The work of Darrough and
Heineke is also relevant here. They specifically identified six outputs as clearances to burglaries, robberies, motor vehicle thefts,
larcenies, crimes against the person, and city size (as a proxy for
all other police services), respectively. Given this particular
specification of outputs, they tested for non-jointness of production
and found that production was joint.[10] The second implication of the
separability assumption is that "output price ratios or marginal rates
of transformation are independent of factor intensities or factor prices."
There is no evidence on this implication. Another condition for the
separability of the transformation function is that the cost function
be multiplicatively separable, i.e., a product of a function of output
times a function of factor prices. This will be the case only if the
production function is homothetic. Hence the property of homotheticity
bears on the assumption of whether output can be viewed as index of a
vector of outputs.

In summary, the choice of functional structure implied by G is
general enough to be consistent with the small amount of evidence
accumulated to date on the nature of police department production functions.

The ordinary Marshallian factor demand equations can be derived using Roy's Theorem of Identity,[11]

$$
(7) \quad X_i = \frac{\dfrac{\partial G}{\partial y_i}}{\sum_i y_i \dfrac{\partial G}{\partial y_i}} = \frac{G_i}{\sum_i y_i G_i} \qquad i = 1, 3, \text{ and } G_i \equiv \frac{\partial G}{\partial y_i},
$$

or

$$
(8) \quad X_i = \frac{B_i b_i q^{e_i b_i} y_i^{b_i - 1}}{\sum_i B_i b_i q^{e_i b_i} y_i^{b_i}} \qquad i = 1, 3
$$

where the subscripts of p, v and c will be used to indicate the inputs of police officers, police cars (indexing all vehicles, etc.) and civilian employees, respectively. Taking ratios of factor inputs to eliminate the denominator in Equation 8, we have,

$$
(9) \quad \frac{X_i}{X_k} = \frac{B_i b_i q^{e_i b_i} y_i^{b_i - 1}}{B_k b_k q^{e_k b_k} y_k^{b_k - 1}} \quad , \qquad i = 1, 2
$$

or in log linear form

$$
(10) \quad \ln \frac{X_p}{X_c} = \ln \frac{B_p b_p}{B_c b_c} + (e_p b_p - e_c b_c) \ln q + (b_p - 1) \ln y_p - (b_c - 1) \ln y_c
$$

and

$$
(11) \quad \ln \frac{X_v}{X_c} = \ln \frac{B_v b_v}{B_c b_c} + (e_v b_v - e_c b_c) \ln q + (b_v - 1) \ln y_v - (b_c - 1) \ln y_c
$$

If output q was readily definable for police departments, we could estimate equations (10) and (11). Instead, these two equations are used to eliminate output yielding

$$(12) \quad \ln \frac{X_p}{X_c} - \left(\frac{e_p b_p - e_c b_c}{e_v b_v - e_c b_c} \right) \ln \frac{X_v}{X_c} = \ln \frac{B_p b_p}{B_c b_c} - \frac{e_p b_p - e_c b_c}{e_v b_v - e_c b_c} \ln \frac{B_v b_v}{B_c b_c}$$

$$+ (b_p - 1) \ln y_p - \left(\frac{e_p b_p - e_c b_c}{e_v b_v - e_c b_c} \right) (b_v - 1) \ln y_v$$

$$- (b_c - 1) \left\{ 1 - \left(\frac{e_p b_p - e_c b_c}{e_v b_v - e_c b_c} \right) \right\} \ln y_c$$

or

$$(13) \quad \ln \frac{X_p}{X_c} - \varepsilon \ln \frac{X_v}{X_c} = K - a_p \ln y_p + \varepsilon a_v \ln y_v + a_c (1 - \varepsilon) \ln y_c$$

where

$$(14) \quad \varepsilon = \frac{e_p b_p - e_c b_c}{e_v b_v - e_c b_c} ,$$

$$(15) \quad K = \ln \frac{B_p b_p}{B_c b_c} - \varepsilon \ln \frac{B_v b_v}{B_c b_c}$$

and

$$(16) \quad a_i = (1 - b_i) \qquad\qquad i = 1, 3.$$

The economic implications of the b_i parameters can be developed using Allen's definition of the partial elasticity of substitution, σ_{ij},[12]

$$(17) \quad \sigma_{ij} = \frac{1}{S_j} \frac{W_j}{x_i} \frac{\partial x_i}{\partial W_j} + \frac{C}{x_i} \frac{\partial x_i}{\partial C}$$

where S_j is the share of input x_j in total cost,

$$(18) \quad S_j = \frac{W_j x_j}{C} = y_j x_j$$

If Roy's Identity (Eq. 7) is used to obtain the partial derivatives in Eq. 17 one obtains,[13]

$$(19) \quad \sigma_{ij} = \frac{\left[\sum_k y_k G_k\right] G_{ij}}{G_i G_j} - \frac{\sum_k y_k G_{ik}}{G_i} - \frac{\sum_k y_k G_{jk}}{G_j} + \frac{\sum_m \sum_k y_m G_{km} y_m}{\sum_k y_k G_K},$$

and using Eq. 8 to obtain σ_{ij} yields (see [11] - p. 412)

$$(20) \quad \sigma_{ij} = (1 - b_i) + (1 - b_j) - \sum_k (1 - b_k) S_k.$$

Note that if the number of factors is three or more it is possible for σ_{ij} to be negative, i.e., complements as well as substitutes are possible. From Eq. 20, the difference between two elasticities, σ_{ik} and σ_{jk} $(i \neq j \neq k)$ is constant,

$$(21) \quad \sigma_{ik} - \sigma_{jk} = (1 - b_i) = (1 - b_j),$$

providing the basis for the name of constant difference elasticity (CDE) production functions.

If the b_i are constant for all i, then (noting that the sum of the factor shares equal one, i.e., $\sum_k S_k = 1$) the elasticity of substitution is constant,

$$(22) \quad \sigma_{ij} = (1 - b), \quad b_i = b \quad \text{all } i$$

And the form of the production function is a non-homothetic CES unless the parameters e_i are equal ($e_i = e$ all i) in which case the production function is homogeneous. If b equals zero, i.e. a = 1 (recalling from Eq. 16 that a = 1 - b) then the production function is Cobb-Douglas. Thus one can estimate Eq. 13 subject to the constraint that

$$(23) \quad a_p = a_v = a_c = a$$

and use the likelihood ratio to test whether the elasticity of substitution is constant. If it is, one can use the t-statistic for the hypothesis that a equals one to test the hypothesis that the elasticity is equal to one.

In the case where the elasticity of substitution is constant ($b_i = b$, all i), it is instructive to use duality theory to obtain the cost function from the indirect production function G, where

$$(24) \quad G = \sum_i B_i q^{e_i b} y_i^b = \sum_i B_i q^{e_i b} \frac{W_i^b}{C^b} \equiv 1, \quad b_i = b, \text{ all } i$$

and

$$(25) \quad C = \left(\sum_i B_i q^{e_i b} W_i^b \right)^{1/b}$$

If the parameters e_i are equal for all i, then

$$(26) \quad C = q^e \left(\sum_i B_i W_i^b \right)^{1/b}$$

where $\left(\sum_i B_i W_i^b \right)^{1/b}$ is the unit cost function for the C.E.S. production function developed by Arrow et al. Thus the B_i are the distribution parameters and the parameter e determines the returns to scale. Note

from Eq. 25 that if the e_i are not equal then the cost function may not

be factored into a function of output q times a function of prices W, as

in Eq. 26, and hence from the duality theory of Shephard is not homothetic.[14]

In the case where all b_i are equal ($b_i = b \neq 0$) if the e_i differ, then the

parameter ε (as defined in Eq. 14) will differ from zero and ε can be used

to test for homothericity.

    Examining the case where the elasticity is constant and equal to one

($b_i = 0$, all i) the indirect production function G is

$$(27) \quad G = \Sigma B_i \ln (q^{e_i} y) \equiv 1$$

recalling from Eq. 1 that $\ln q^{e_i} y_i$ replaces $q^{e_i b_i} y_i^{b_i}$ if $b_i = 0$, or we may

write

$$(28) \quad q = \exp \left[\frac{1}{\Sigma e_i B_i} \right] \prod_i y_i^{-B_i / \Sigma e_i B_i}$$

which is the form of the indirect production function for the Cobb-Douglas.

(see [11] - p. 415).

From Eq. 28 we can derive the cost function,

$$(28') \quad C = \exp \left[\frac{-1}{\Sigma B_i} \right] q^{\Sigma e_i B_i / \Sigma B_i} \prod_i W_i^{B_i / \Sigma B_i}$$

where $\prod_i W_i^{B_i / \Sigma B_i}$ is the unit cost function for the Cobb-Douglas and the

degree of homogeneity is $\Sigma B_i / \Sigma e_i B_i$.

Estimation of the CDE Production Function

    Equation 13 was estimated for Long Beach, San Diego, Oakland and San

Francisco for selected years between 1960 and 1975 in a pooled time series

cross section estimation. Lack of data for the number of police cars was
the problem which limited the number of observations. The years 1960, '61,
'62, '64, '68, '69, '70, '71, and '73 were available for all four cities and
in addition the year 1974 was available for San Diego and years 1974 and 1975
for Oakland, making a total of 39 observations.

Equation 13 is non-linear in the parameters and was estimated using
the nonlinear least squares technique in the Time Series Processor (TSP)
program, version 2.7, on the IBM 370 at the Stanford Center for Information
Processing. As suggested by Hanoch, it was presumed that Equations 10 and
11 had error terms μ_p and μ_v, respectively, which were independent of the
y_i.[15] Hence Eq. 13 had an error term of the form $\mu_p - \varepsilon\mu_v$.

The estimates for the parameters in Eq. 13, using the 39 observations
for the four cities, are listed in Table 1.

Table 1:   CDE Estimates, 4 Cities

Coefficient	Estimate	Standard Error	t-Statistic
K	2.72	0.33	8.14
ε	0.585	0.135	4.34
a_p	2.91	0.657	4.43
a_v	2.52	1.12	2.25
a_c	1.68	1.62	1.03

with $R^2 = 0.769$ and the sum of the squared residuals SSR = 1.657. Eq. 13
was also estimated subject to four different constraints: (1) $a_p = a_v$,
(2) $a_p = a_c$, (3) $a_v = a_c$, and (4) $a_p = a_v = a_c$. The third constraint was
found not to reduce the likelihood function significantly ($R^2 = 0.768$, SSR
= 1.657).   The significance of the constraint was tested using a likelihood

ratio test and the Chi Square distribution. The statistic is the ratio of
the likelihood function of the residuals, constrained, to the likelihood
function unconstrained. The natural logarithm of this statistic multiplied
by minus two is distributed approximately Chi Square. Since the program was
inaccurate in calculating the likelihood function if the imposition of the
constraint reduced the likelihood function very little, the R^2 and sum of
squared residuals are reported in this case. An analysis of covariance
was conducted on the estimates of Eq. 13 subject to $a_v = a_c$ to determine if
there were a significant (1% level) reduction in the unexplained variance
if the parameters (K, ε, a_p, $a_v = a_c$) were allowed to be city-specific for
one or more cities. Estimating separate parameters for San Francisco proved
to be highly significant, reducing the total SSR to 0.321 with R^2 for Long
Beach, San Diego and Oakland of .8652 and for San Francisco of 0.9832. The
parameter estimates are indicated in Table 2.

Table 2:   CDE Estimates, Constrained, S.F. Separate
(Long Beach, San Diego, Oakland)

Coefficient	Estimate	Standard Error	t-Statistic
K	2.64	.160	16.5
ε	0.285	.050	5.72
a_p	2.00	.329	6.09
$a_v = a_c$	2.03	.279	7.30

(San Francisco)

K	2.83	.529	5.34
ε	0.877	.156	5.61
a_p	1.03	1.42	0.72
$a_v = a_c$	1.08	.723	1.33

Examining these estimates for San Francisco and the other three cities,

the parameters a_i appear to equal a constant a for both cases. Hence Eq. 13

was estimated subject to the fourth constraint (a_i = a, all i) with separate

parameters for San Francisco. This additional constraint did not lower the

likelihood function significantly either for San Francisco or the other

three cities (total SSR = 0.322). These results indicated the same nonhomo-

thetic CES production function for the three cities of Long Beach, San Diego,

and Oakland and a Cobb-Douglas production function for San Francisco. The

parameter estimates are listed in Table 3.

Table 3:   CDE Estimates, Constant Elasticity of Substitution
           (Long Beach, San Diego, Oakland)

Parameter	Estimate	Standard Error	t-Statistic
K	2.67	.147	18.2
ε	0.289	.045	6.24
$a_p = a_v = a_c$	2.08	.250	8.32

R^2 = 0.865

(San Francisco)

K	2.80	.394	7.12
ε	0.881	.135	6.51
$a_p = a_v = a_c$	1.12	.577	1.95

R^2 = 0.983

If, alternatively, the analysis of covariance is conducted using Eq. 13

before the imposition of constraints, a significant reduction in the unex-

plained variance is achieved by estimating separate parameters for San Francisco

(total SSR = 0.273). Equation 13 was then estimated subject to constraints
(with separate parameters for San Francisco). The fourth constraint
(a_i = a, all i) did not significantly reduce the likelihood function, and
the end results are the estimates reported above, which indicates the nonhomothetic CES for three cities and the Cobb-Douglas for San Francisco.

For the case of Long Beach, San Diego and Oakland, the matrix of
elasticities of substitution are given by:

$$
(29) \quad
\begin{bmatrix}
\sigma_{pp} & \sigma_{pv} & \sigma_{pc} \\
 & \sigma_{vv} & \sigma_{vc} \\
 & & \sigma_{cc}
\end{bmatrix}
=
\begin{bmatrix}
-.553 & 2.08 & 2.08 \\
(.066) & (.250) & (.250) \\
 & -18.30 & 2.08 \\
 & (2.20) & (.250) \\
 & & -17.20 \\
 & & (2.07)
\end{bmatrix}
$$

where the diagonal terms are determined from the condition of homogeneity
of degree zero for demand in terms of prices plus costs (Cournot aggregation):

$$
(30) \quad \Sigma S_i \sigma_{ij} = 0
$$

The standard errors are listed beneath the σ_{ij} estimates in parenthesis.
The factor shares S_i used in the calculation were the observed values
averaged over the three cities for all thirty observations where S_p = .790,
S_v = .102, and S_c = .108.

The corresponding matrix of compensated price elasticities is

$$
(31) \quad
\begin{bmatrix}
\dfrac{\partial x_i}{\partial W_i} & \dfrac{W_j}{x_i}
\end{bmatrix}_{i,\,j\,=p,v,c}
=
\begin{bmatrix}
-.437 & .212 & .225 \\
(.052) & (.026) & (.027) \\
 & -1.87 & .225 \\
 & (.22) & (.027) \\
 & & -1.86 \\
 & & (.22)
\end{bmatrix}
$$

where $\dfrac{\partial x_i}{\partial W_j}\dfrac{W_j}{x_i} = S_j\sigma_{ij}$. Note the low own price elasticity for police relative to vehicles and civilians.

The matrix of elasticities of substitution for San Francisco is

$$(32) \quad \left[\sigma_{ij}\right]_{i,\ j\ =\ p,v,c} = \begin{pmatrix} -.173 & 1.12 & 1.12 \\ (.089) & (.577) & (.577) \\ & -18.7 & 1.12 \\ & (9.63) & (.577) \\ & & -13.4 \\ & & (6.91) \end{pmatrix}$$

where the diagonal terms are calculated using the factor shares averaged over the observations with S_p = .8664, S_v = .0565, and S_c = .0771. Note that σ_{pp} is considerably smaller in absolute magnitude for San Francisco than for the other three cities while σ_{vv} is similar in magnitude and σ_{cc} is three-fourths as large. The compensated price elasticities for San Francisco are:

$$(33) \quad \left[\dfrac{x_i}{W_j}\dfrac{\partial W_i}{\partial x_j}\right]_{i,j\ =\ p,\ v,\ d} = \begin{pmatrix} -.150 & .063 & .086 \\ (.079) & (.0326) & (.044) \\ & -1.06 & .086 \\ & .544 & (.044) \\ & & -1.03 \\ & & (.532) \end{pmatrix}$$

The price elasticities are 1/2 to 1/3 as large (in absolute magnitude) for San Francisco as for the triad of Long Beach, San Diego and Oakland.

Twenty years of data, extending from 1956 through 1975, was available for the City of Los Angeles and was used to estimate Eq. 13. The estimates are reported in Table 4.

Table 4:   CDE Estimates
Los Angeles

Parameter	Estimate	Standard Error	t-Statistic
K	1.50	.315	4.75
ε	.366	.130	2.81
a_p	-.527	.254	-2.07
a_v	1.26	.683	1.84
a_c	-1.23	.426	-2.87

R^2 = .9610

Under global restrictions on the production function (Eq. 1), all of the a_i should be positive. The function could be locally valid with one of the a_i negative. Thus the estimates in Table 4 are not useful from an economic point of view. If Eq. 13 is estimated subject to the constraint a_i = a, all i, the likelihood function is reduced significantly (R^2 falls to 0.621). A constant elasticity form for the production function is not suitable for Los Angeles. If Eq. 13 is estimated subject to the constraint $a_v = a_c$, the likelihood function is not reduced significantly. The probability of getting a value higher than minus two times the logarithm of the likelihood function was 11% (X_1^2 = .11). The parameter estimates are reported in Table 5.

Table 5:   CDE Estimates, Constrained
Los Angeles

Parameter	Estimate	Standard Error	t-Statistic
K	2.21	.0075	295.3
ε	.625	.010	60.3
a_p	.0270	.0126	2.14
$a_v = a_c$	0.344	.00988	34.9

The elasticities of substitution can be calculated using Eq. 20,

$$
(34) \quad \left[\sigma_{ij}\right]_{i,\ j\ =\ p,\ v\ ,c} =
\begin{pmatrix}
-.091 & .263 & .263 \\
(.004) & (.011) & (.011) \\
 & & \\
 & -3.07 & .580 \\
 & (.126) & (.015) \\
 & & \\
 & & -1.56 \\
 & & (.053)
\end{pmatrix}
$$

and the corresponding compensated price elasticities calculated using Eq. 30,

$$
(35) \quad \left[\frac{\partial x_i}{\partial W_j}\frac{W_j}{x_i}\right]_{i,\ j\ =\ p,\ v,\ c} =
\begin{pmatrix}
-.068 & .025 & .042 \\
(.003) & (.001) & (.002) \\
 & & \\
 & -.294 & .093 \\
 & (.012) & (.002) \\
 & & \\
 & & -.251 \\
 & & (.009)
\end{pmatrix}
$$

where the factor shares used in the calculations were averaged over the observations (S_p = .7433, S_v = .0959, S_c = .1608). Note that the elasticities of substitution are smaller for Los Angeles than for San Francisco and the other three cities. Also, the own price elasticities of demand for civilians and vehicles for Los Angeles are one-third the size of those for San Francisco and one-sixth the size of those for the other three cities. The own price elasticity for police for Los Angeles is about one-half that for the other cities. Los Angeles is closer to a Leontief technology than the other cities with much less sensitivity to prices in determining factor demands.

Nonhomotheticity -- Another Approach

One of the major findings, both for the case of Los Angeles, and for
the case of Long Beach, San Diego and Oakland was the nonhomothetic nature
of the production function. This property was reflected in the output
elasticities or parameters e_i using Hanoch's CDE function. Another approach
is to approximate the nonhomotheticity using a homothetic function. A
device for doing this is to translate the origin. This approach has been
used in consumer expenditure studies where the amounts of the goods involved
in the translation were interpreted as "committed expenditures". (See [11],
p. 416 for a discussion and references.) For this interpretation to make
sense, the translated origin must lie below the observed quantities. This
approach is investigated for the insight it provides.

Since the production function for Long Beach, San Diego and Oakland
estimated using the CDE model was nonhomothetic with constant elasticity
of substitution, it is possible to estimate it using the CES function
developed by Arrow et al.[16] The nonhomotheticity can be approximated by
translation of the origin, i.e., measuring all factors as deviations from
fixed values.[17] Thus output q can be expressed as

$$(36) \quad q = \left[\sum_i d_i \, (x_i - x_i^o)^{-r} \right]^{-\nu/r}$$

where ν determines the degree of homogeneity (returns to scale), the
elasticity of substitution, σ_{ij} is

$$(37) \quad \sigma \equiv \sigma_{ij} = \frac{1}{1 + r} \, ,$$

the d_i are the distribution parameters, and the x_i^o are the fixed factor quantities which translate the origin. Using Wold's theorem (see [5]) the price demand functions are

$$(38) \quad \frac{\hat{W}_i}{C} = \frac{\frac{\partial q}{\partial x_i}}{\sum\limits_i x_i \frac{\partial q}{\partial x_i}} = \frac{d_i (x_i - x_i^o)^{-(r+1)}}{\sum\limits_i d_i (x_i - x_i^o)^{-r}}, \quad i = 1, 3$$

and taking ratios of prices to eliminate the denominator and solving for the factor ratio,

$$(39) \quad \frac{x_i - x_i^o}{x_j - x_j^o} = \left(\frac{d_i}{d_j}\right)^\sigma \left(\frac{W_i}{W_j}\right)^{-\sigma}$$

or

$$(40) \quad \frac{x_p - x_p^o}{x_v - x_v^o} = \left(\frac{d_p}{d_v}\right) \left(\frac{W_p}{W_v}\right)^{-\sigma}$$

i.e.,

$$(41) \quad \frac{x_p}{x_v} = \frac{x_p^o}{x_v} + \left[1 - \frac{x_v^o}{x_v}\right]\left(\frac{d_p}{d_v}\right)^\sigma \left(\frac{W_p}{W_v}\right)^{-\sigma}$$

and

$$(42) \quad \frac{x_v}{x_c} = \frac{x_v^o}{x_c} + \left[1 - \frac{x_c^o}{x_c}\right]\left(\frac{d_v}{d_c}\right)^\sigma \left(\frac{W_v}{W_c}\right)^{-\sigma}$$

Eq. 40 can be contrasted with Eq. 9, evaluating the latter when the b_i
are equal and the elasticity of substitution ($\sigma_{ij} = 1 - b \equiv \sigma$) is constant,

$$(43) \quad \frac{x_p}{x_v} = \frac{B_p}{B_v} \, q^{b(e_p - e_v)} \left(\frac{W_p}{W_v} \right)^{-\sigma}$$

the difference is that using the CDE model (Eq. 43), nonhomotheticity
is captured by the expansion elasticities e_i and the factor input ratio
depends upon output, while in the modified Arrow-CES model the nonhomotheticity is captured by the translation of the origin. The translation
device has been introduced into consumer demand studies as a means of
approximating nonhomotheticity. The translation parameters x_i^o are interpreted as committed expenditures in this context. Diewart has pointed out
that the nonhomothetic function is approximated by two homothetic segments,
i.e., a Leontief specification between the old and new origins, and, in the
case at hand, an Arrow-CES specification from the new origin (see [8], p. 508).

Since equations 41 and 42 are nonlinear in the parameters x_p^o, x_c^o, d_p/d_v,
d_v/d_c and σ, they were estimated using nonlinear least squares with the TSP
program for the 30 observations on the three cities of Long Beach, San Diego,
and Oakland. The results are reported in Table 6.

Table 6: CES Estimates

Equation 41

Parameter	Estimate	Standard Error	t-Statistic
x_p^o	816	202	4.05
x_v^o	236	130	1.83
d_p/d_v	2.49	1.14	2.18
σ	1.61	1.85	0.87

$R^2 = 0.833$, SSR $= 4.39$

Equation 42

Parameter	Estimate	Standard Error	t-Statistic
x^o_v	621	2132	.29
x^o_c	597	2006	.30
d_v/d_c	1.10	0.79	1.38
σ	0.43	2.03	.21

$R^2 = 0.357$, SSR = 1.37

Eq. 41 was reestimated constraining $\sigma = 2$, the elasticity of substituion
from the CDE estimates, see Table 3. This did not significantly affect the
likelihood function. The results are reported in Table 7. Based on the
results of reestimating Eq. 41, Eq. 42 was reestimated constraining $\sigma = 2$,
and $x^o_v = 220$. The latter being the value for X^o_v obtained for Eq. 41, see
Table 7. The likelihood function was not significantly reduced. The estimates
are in Table 7.

Table 7: CES Estimates, Constrained

Equation 41

Parameter	Estimate	Standard Error	t-Statistic
x^o_p	789	84	9.38
x^o_v	220	62	3.55
d_p/d_v	2.31	0.351	6.58

$R^2 = .832$, SSR = $4.42/\sigma = 2$

Equation 42

x^o_c	234	14	16.8
d_v/d_c	0.923	.067	13.7

$R^2 = 0.318$, SSR = $1.46/\sigma = 2$, $x^o_v = 220$

While the result for the elasticity of substitution σ is consistent
with the estimates from the CDE model, the estimates of the translated origin
$x_p^o = 789$, $x_v^o = 220$, and $x_c^o = 234$ tend to lie in the middle to upper part of
the distribution of the observations of the factor inputs for these three
cities. Since these parameters depend on scale, as would output if we could
estimate Eq. 10 in the CDE model, the parameters x_p^o, x_v^o, and x_c^o were allowed
to vary by city, keeping σ, d_p/d_v, and d_p/d_c common to all cities. The
results are reported in Table 8.

Table 8: CES Estimates, Separate Origins

Equation 41

Parameter	Estimate	Standard Error	t-Statistic
x_p^o - Long Beach	846	134	6.29
x_p^o - San Diego	1083	162	6.66
x_p^o - Oakland	805	78	10.31
x_v^o - Long Beach	250	109	2.29
x_v^o - San Diego	346	132	2.63
x_v^o - Oakland	285	64	4.48
d_p/d_v	2.35	0.385	6.11
σ	1.83	0.95	1.93

$R^2 = 0.965$, SSR = 0.927

Equation 42

x_v^o - Long Beach	105	6	17.2
x_v^o - San Diego	162	5	30.4
x_v^o - Oakland	210	9	23.3
x_c^o - Long Beach	148	19	7.81
x_c^o - San Diego	35	37	0.94
x_c^o - Oakland	293	20	15.0
d_v/d_c	0.720	.030	24.1
σ	4.71	.868	5.42

$R^2 = 0.916$, SSR = 0.180

Allowing the translation of the origin to differ by cities raises the
explained variance for both Equations 41 and 42, remarkably so in the latter
case. However, the new origin does not lie below the observations (input
values) for any of the three cities. Constraining the value of σ to 2 does
not lower the likelihood function significantly for either Eq. 41 or Eq. 42,
where the x_i^o are allowed to vary by city.

Equations 41 and 42 were estimated, not only allowing for separate origins
x_i^o for each city, but allowing these origins to vary with time, i.e.,

$$(44) \quad x_i^o = x_i^o \, (0) \, e^{\lambda_i t} \qquad i = 1, 3$$

The results for Eq. 41 are reported in Table 9, and the results for Eq. 42 in
Table 10. There was some difficulty in getting the estimates for Eq. 42 to
converge. Noting after 21 iterations that $x_c^o \, (0)$ and λ_i were not significantly
different from zero for Long Beach, these two parameters were constrained to
zero and convergence was achieved. Once again the time varying origins do
not lie below all of the observations for any of the three cities. Thus
it is difficult to interpret the nonhomotheticity in terms of "committed
resources". There is too much commitment   However, a good deal can be
learned from this exercise. First the elasticity of substitution is consistent with value of 2 estimated using the CDE function, even when the
translation of the origin is timevarying. Furthermore, note from Table 9
that the level of precommitment to police officers increases over time
for the cities of San Diego and Oakland. In contrast the precommitment
to vehicles is decreasing over time for Long Beach and San Diego and is not
different from zero for Oakland. These results suggest that much of the
"commitment" in resources is due to police officers rather than to civilians
and police cars. Perhaps the finding of nonhomotheticity for the estimated
production function is due to inefficiency caused by some phenomenon such as
featherbedding. This possibility is explored in the next section.

Table 9: Equation 41, Time-Varying Origins

Parameter	Estimate	Standard Error	t-Statistic
x_p^o – Long Beach	709	78	9.08
λx_p^o – Long Beach	-.00172	.0066	-.26
x_p^o – San Diego	624	76	8.16
λx_p^o – San Diego	.0311	.0072	4.29
x_p^o – Oakland	385	83	4.63
λx_p^o – Oakland	.0633	.0158	4.01
x_v^o – Long Beach	198	36	5.44
λx_v^o – Long Beach	-.0288	.0154	-1.87
x_v^o – San Diego	162	30	5.44
λx_v^o – San Diego	-.00149	-.0260	-.057
x_v^o – Oakland	39	37	1.07
λx_v^o – Oakland	.179	.059	3.04
d_p/d_v	2.05	.201	10.24
σ	2.57	0.591	4.34

R^2 = .985, SSR = .391

Note: The notation λx_p^o refers to the estimated exponential rate of growth

for the translation parameter (new origin) for x_p^o, i.e., x_p^o is

allowed to shift each period according to,

$$x_p^o (t) = x_p^o (o) \ e^{\lambda x_p^o t}$$

A similar interpretation is appropriate for λx_v^o and λx_c^o for each city.

Table 10:   Equation 42, Time-Varying Origins

Parameter	Estimate	Standard Error	t-Statistic
x_v^o - Long Beach	76	5	14.7
λx_v^o - Long Beach	-.0476	.0017	-2.83
x_v^o - San Diego	254	44	5.72
λx_v^o - San Diego	.0254	.0166	1.53
x_v^o - Oakland	194	11	17.3
λx_v^o - Oakland	.0167	.0092	1.82
x_c^o - Long Beach	constant = 0		
λx_c^o - Long Beach	constant = 0		
x_c^o - San Diego	607	201	3.03
λx_c^o - San Diego	-.0364	.0389	-0.93
x_c^o - Oakland	173	45	3.87
λx_c^o - Oakland	.0635	.0121	5.24
d_v/d_c	.564	.0580	9.72
σ	2.11	.61	3.40

$R^2 = 0.944$, SSR = .120

Note: The notation λx_p^o refers to the estimated exponential rate of growth
for the translation parameter (new origin) for x_p^o, i.e., x_p^o is
allowed to shift each period according to,

$$x_p^o (t) = x_p^o (o) \, e^{\lambda x_p^o t}$$

Could an Estimated Finding of Nonhomotheticity be Capturing Featherbedding?

In the context of production in public service industries, the estimation
of nonhomotheticity may be reflecting the presence of inefficiency. This
idea is developed by extending Norman Simler's and Paul Weinstein's analyses
of featherbedding and combining it with Diewart's discussion of the nonhomotheticity approximation.[18]

Why might law enforcement be inefficient? It is a public service
activity and insulated, at least partially, from the full force of market
competition. There is a tradition among police officers, not unlike that
of the military, of a son following the father's occupation. A history of
concern for employment possibilities for family and friends could have created
a higher ratio of police to other factors than warranted by efficiency.

Suppose the efficient technology in law enforcement is homothetic. At
a given factor price ratio, the expansion path is linear and passes through
the origin as illustrated by the ray OA in Figure 1, and the isoquant for
any output q may be obtained by radial expansion (or contraction) of the
isoquant for output q^o (illustrated in the figure).[19] Consider the point
B on the isoquant q^o which is off the expansion path OA. As Simler and
Weinstein point out, one could observe input usage at B because factor x_i
(say labor) insists that x_i^o workers be hired. Subject to this fixed demand,
as output expands we would expect the use of x_j to increase but not x_i until
the point C on the expansion path was reached, i.e., one would observe no
change in the use of factor x_i. Simler and Weinstein discuss another case
of featherbedding in which a fixed input ratio is imposed, as illustrated
by the ray OB in Figure 1. In this case, as output expands, input usage
will expand along this ray, i.e., one would observe a Leontief technology.
Intermediate to these two polar cases discussed by Simler and Weinstein,
are a number of possibilities. The impact of a given factor input usage
may decline over time with the consequence that the factor input ratio

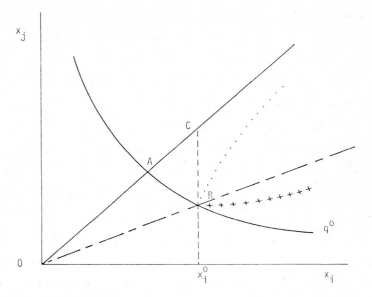

Figure 1. Nonhomotheticity as an approximation to a homothetic
technology with variable featherbedding.

moves away from ray OB toward the expansion path OC as illustrated by the
dotted line in Figure 1. Alternatively, the impact of factor x_i on efficiency
may worsen with the factor input ratio deviating even further from the expansion path, as indicated by the loci of plusses (+) in the figure.

Now recall Diewart's discussion of the approximation to nonhomotheticity. The segment OB can be viewed as the Leontief segment between the old
origin O and the new origin B, while the homothetic function being utilized
captures behavior beyond B. The latter may reflect sensitivity to prices
(if the factor price ratio is changing) plus the effects of output expanding
as modified by whether the impact of factor x_i on efficiency is lessening or
not. While a two segment approximation may be fair, additionally permitting
the translated origin to continue to shift over time may be even better.
Thus the finding of a nonhomothetic technology may reveal the existence of
inefficiency imposed by a factor(featherbedding) while the true technology
is homothetic. In summary, translation of the origin may be an approximation
to nonhomotheticity, but nonhomotheticity may also be an "approximation" to
the translation of the origin which may, in turn, approximate some phenomenon
such as featherbedding.

The estimates of section V are reinterpreted in this framework. The
translation of the origin is set to zero yielding a homothetic function
from which one can derive what the expansion path would be in the absence
of featherbedding. The implication of assuming that the nonhomotheticity,
as captured by the translation of the origin, reflects inefficiency due to
featherbedding are pursued in .the next section by comparing observed behavior with behavior in the absence of featherbedding (nonhomotheticity).

Aspects of Efficiency

1. Input Ratios, Featherbedding, and Relative Inefficiency

Given the assumption that the efficient technology in law enforcement

is homothetic, Eq. 39 and the estimates of σ, d_p, d_v and d_c obtained from

Equations 41 and 42 can be used to plot the efficiency loci of x_p/x_v, x_p/x_c,

and x_v/x_c. The actually observed loci can then be compared to these efficiency

loci to obtain a measure of the relative inefficiency of police departments

in allocating resources. Using the values of $d_p/d_v = 2.31$ and $d_v/d_c = 0.923$

from Table 7 when $\sigma = 2$, and implementing Eq. 39, one obtains

$$(45) \qquad \frac{x_p}{x_v} = (2.31)^2 \left(\frac{W_p}{W_v}\right)^{-2} \quad ,$$

$$(46) \qquad \frac{x_v}{x_c} = (.923)^2 \left(\frac{W_v}{W_c}\right)^{-2} ,$$

from which one can obtain,

$$(47) \qquad \frac{x_p}{x_c} = (2.13)^2 \left(\frac{W_p}{W_c}\right)^{-2}$$

The efficiency loci for the ratio of police to vehicles is plotted in

Figure 2 as the solid line with 95% confidence intervals indicated by the

dotted lines.[20]   There appear to be too many police relative to vehicles

for each of the three cities of Long Beach, San Diego and Oakland. Further-

more, the excess of police relative to vehicles increased for each of the

three cities between 1960 and 1973. This last result is also supported by

the estimates of the time-varying origins, as reported in Table 9, which

showed x_p^o increasing (or constant for Long Beach) and x_v^o decreasing (or not

different from zero for Oakland). Even though the price of police relative
to vehicles was increasing between 1960 and 1975, the ratio of police to
vehicles did not fall anywhere near as far as the efficient solution would
indicate as warranted.

In contrast to the result for police and vehicles, the data illustrated
in Figure 3 indicate that the observed ratio of vehicles to civilians straddle
the efficiency loci for all three cities. The estimates for Equations 41 and
42 are used to derive the efficiency loci for the ratio of police to civilians
illustrated in Figure 4. There is an excess of police to civilians for all
three cities. Even though the ratio of police to civilians fell between 1960
and 1975 in response to relative prices, it did not fall far enough to eliminate the excess of police to civilians. In summary, police officers appear
to be the principal source of featherbedding. Police departments had an excess of police officers relative to vehicles and civilians in 1960, and in
spite of some responsiveness to changes in relative prices, this excess has
been preserved into the middle '70's.

2. Output Indices

Maintaining the hypothesis that the efficient police department technology is homothetic, the Arrow-CES production function,

$$(48) \qquad q = \left[\sum_i d_i x_i^{-r} \right]^{-\nu/r}$$

can be exponentiated to determine an index of output, up to the returns to
scale ν,

$$(49) \qquad q^{1/\nu} = \left[\sum_i d_i x_i^{-r} \right]^{-1/r}$$

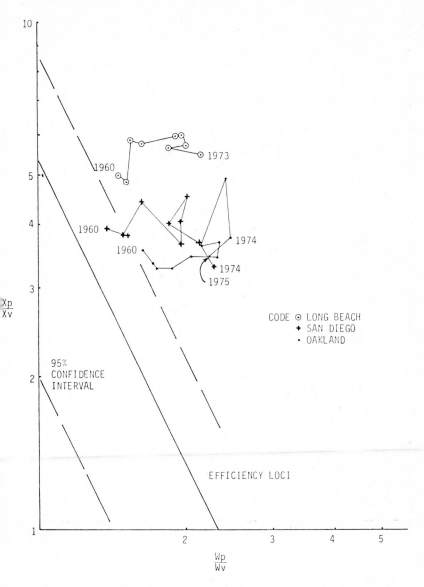

Figure 2. Efficiency loci, police to vehicles.

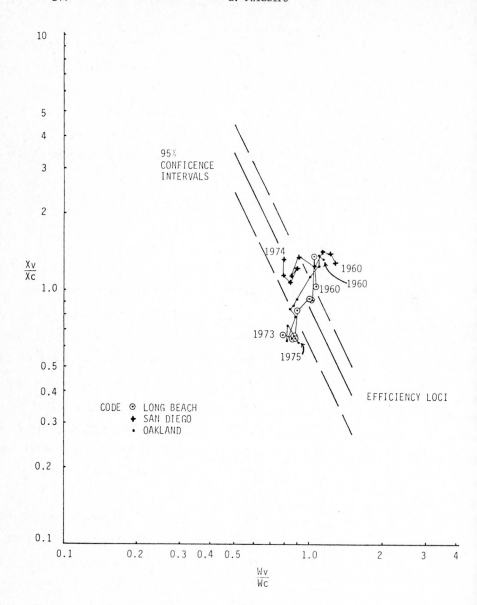

Figure 3. Efficiency loci, vehicles to civilians.

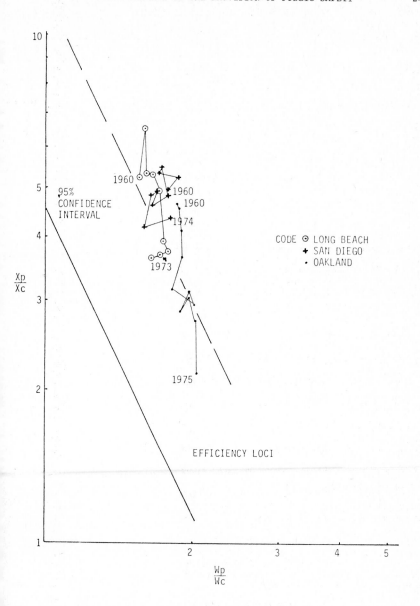

Figure 4. Efficiency loci, police to civilians.

The actual observed can be used to calculate $q^{1/\nu}$ since we presume that
police departments are technically efficient in using inputs to produce
output but simply use too many police relative to vehicles and civilians
to produce that output at minimum cost. The output indices calculated
using Eq. 49 are listed in Table 11 for Long Beach, San Diego and Oakland.
The value of r was -0.5 corresponding to $\sigma = 2$. The values of d_p, d_v and d_c
were obtained from the estimates in Table 7, noting that $\sum_i d_i = 1$.

Table 11:   Indices of Public Safety - $q^{1/\nu}$

Year	Long Beach	San Diego	Oakland
1960	257.1	366.4	378.5
1961	260.0	376.9	378.7
1962	266.5	378.7	365.7
1964	278.8	384.0	381.0
1968	347.0	493.2	403.5
1969	367.6	518.7	423.6
1970	383.9	517.8	438.0
1971	377.9	540.7	442.5
1973	363.3	609.5	418.7
1974		618.4	466.7
1975			460.5

In what sense are these indices of public safety, since they are
generally increasing between 1960 and 1975, the period when felony crime
was on the increase? Since inputs were growing during this period, it is
clear that an index of value added in public safety must be growing as well.
If such an index is to incorporate crime rates (average probabilities of

victimization), it would be necessary to incorporate potential crime rates
(priors) as well as actual crime rates (posteriors), perhaps using a measure
such as expected information. Value added would grow in this case if the
ratio of potential to actual crime increased. Alternatively, one might use
measures of police activity such as clearances, patrols, or investigations.
The exponential rates of growth per annum of the output indices in Table 11
are 1.5% for Oakland, 3.5% for Long Beach and 4.0% for San Diego. Since
some police services would grow more directly with population than others,
the output indices in Table 11 are divided by population and calculated on
a per thousand basis, as reported in Table 12. To make this output per
capita comparison meaningful we must assume constant returns to scale,
i.e., $\nu = 1$ (see footnote 21 concerning the reasonableness of this
assumption).

Table 12: Public Safety Per Thousand People

	Long Beach		San Diego		Oakland	
	1960	1970	1960	1970	1960	1970
$q^{1/\nu}$	257.1	383.9	366.4	517.8	378.5	460.5
tion	344,168	392,000	573,224	712,900	367,548	358,000
per thousand	.747	.979	.639	.726	1.03	1.29
offenses thousand	21.4	33.6	9.52	19.8	16.4	68.9

In per capita terms, Oakland has the highest level of public safety and
San Diego has the lowest. This may reflect the dependence of value added
upon potential as well as actual crime rates. The implied exponential rates
of growth between 1960 and 1970 for the per capita measure of public safety
are 1.3% for San Diego, 2.2% for Oakland and 2.7% for Long Beach. Thus most
of the growth in total public safety for San Diego was due to population increase.

3. Unit Costs and Absolute Efficiency

Duality theory may be utilized to develop what unit costs would be if
police departments used the cost minimizing quantities of inputs in response
to prices. The indirect production function dual to the Arrow-CES (Eq. 48) is

$$(50) \qquad q = \left\{ \sum_i \left(\frac{W_i}{C}\right)^{r/1+r} d_i^{1/1+r} \right\}^{-v(1+r)/r}$$

and the cost function dual to the production function is,

$$(51) \qquad C_e = q^{1/v} \left[\sum_i W_i^{r/1+r} d_i^{1/1+r} \right]^{1+r/r}$$

and, since the production function is homothetic, the cost function factors
into the term dependent upon output, $q^{1/v}$, and the unit cost function,

$$(52) \qquad \left[\sum_i W_i^{r/1+r} d_i^{1/1+r} \right]^{1+r/r}$$

Strictly speaking, this is only the unit cost function if there are constant
returns to scale.

Eq. 52 was implemented to calculate unit costs (in current dollars)
using the same parameter valus (based on Table 7) as were used to calculate
the output indices. The results are reported in Table 13. If one is willing
to maintain the hypothesis that the returns to scale in law enforcement are
constant, then the values in Table 13 provide the marginal costs of production
Since marginal costs do not differ greatly from city to city in a given year,
the amount of public safety enjoyed by the citizens in a particular city
would be determined by demand. This statement has to be qualified by the
proviso that all city police departments are equally efficient since the
unit costs presume a cost minimizing choice of inputs.   As we saw above this
is not the case, and we determine next that efficiency varies by city.

Table 13:   Unit Costs of Production*

Year	Long Beach	San Diego	Oakland
1960	$12,678	$11,795	$13,456
1961	13,036	12,666	13,954
1962	13,288	12,975	14,439
1964	13,917	14,027	15,329
1968	16,504	16,728	17,269
1969	17,252	17,408	19,024
1970	18,340	18,532	20,190
1971	18,971	18,997	20,782
1973	20,553	21,151	22,477
1974		23,232	24,010
1975			26,343

* Presuming constant returns to scale

The total cost of efficiently producing public safety C_e, given the factor prices P_i, can be determined by using Eq. 51, i.e., multiplying unit costs by the index of output. The actual cost C_o of producing this quantity of output given the inefficient mix of inputs actually used is given by the budget for each city. The ratio of these actual expenditures to the efficient total cost of production is listed in Table 14. Note that this ratio, C_o/C_e, does not depend upon assuming that the returns to scale are constant or known since $q^{1/\nu}$ is available from Eq. (49) to use in the formula for C_e given by Eq. (51).

Note that San Diego is the most efficient of the cities. Each of the cities has tended to become less efficient over time in an absolute sense. This is probably due to the fact that the cities historically had too many police relative to vehicles and civilians and as the price of police increased over time relative to vehicles and civilians, the cities become even more leveraged in their inefficiency. By 1973, public safety in Long Beach was costing the citizens twice as much as it should. In 1970, it was costing them 62% more than it had to, or $11.12 per capita of waste.

Table 14:   Cost Overrun Indices of Inefficiency, C_o/C_e

Year	Long Beach	San Diego	Oakland
1960	1.211	1.156	1.322
1961	1.270	1.138	1.346
1962	1.277	1.207	1.347
1964	1.315	1.255	1.086
1968	1.288	1.182	1.358
1969	1.280	1.262	1.203
1970	1.619	1.327	1.568
1971	1.770	1.387	1.555
1973	2.004	1.334	1.728
1974		1.344	1.816
1975			1.768

Note: The efficient costs C_e are calculated on the assumption
        that the efficient technology is homothetic.

Summary

Utilizing the actual quantities of inputs used and the prices at which they were purchased, a generalized constant difference of elasticity of substitution indirect production function was estimated for five cities. From these results it was possible to calculate elasticities of substitution

and compensated price elasticities. The most striking feature of the results
was the nonhomotheticity of the production function. For the case of three
cities which had a constant elasticity of substitution production function,
the nonhomothetic approximation of the Arrow-CES production function was
estimated. The finding of nonhomotheticity in the production function was
interpreted as resulting from inefficiency. Presuming that efficient behavior would be reflected by a homothetic production function for law enforcement, it was possible to calculate indices of output up to returns to
scale, as well as unit costs. Presuming that constant returns to scale
prevail in law enforcement, these can be interpreted as indices of public
safety and marginal costs, respectively. The product of the index of public
safety and unit costs determined the efficient cost of producing this particular level of output, and this efficient cost could be compared to the actual
cost to yield a dollar figure for inefficiency. In summary, using input
quantities and prices, it has been possible to determine all aspects of the
production function and cost function, excepting returns to scale. The
results suggest considerable inefficiency in large city police departments.
The amount of public safety that citizens enjoy in any particular city will
depend not only upon income and the price of substitutes, but upon the
inefficiency of their police department. This inefficiency will raise the
price and hence decrease the amount of public safety that otherwise would
be enjoyed.

Epilogue

   Two additional analyses may be of interest to the reader since in
previous sections the finding of nonhomotheticity was interpreted in terms
of inefficiency. The first analysis used the observed factor price information

for police officers, civilian employees and vehicles for the three cities of
Long Beach, San Diego, and Oakland. It was presumed the production function
was a homothetic Arrow-Chenery-Minhas-Solow CES function with the values for
the parameters d_i and σ. Using this assumed functional form and the observed
data for civilian employees, values were generated for police and vehicle
inputs, suitably randomized. This input data was generated under alternative
assumptions about cost inefficiency, i.e., that the factor input ratio deviated
by some multiple from the efficient expansion path. Then the Hanoch function
(Eq. 13) was estimated. The result was that the simulated inefficiency was
reflected in the expansion (or nonhomotheticity) parameter E of Eq. 13.
Thus the assumption in the text that the finding of nonhomotheticity could
be due to inefficiency is not unreasonable.

The second analysis was an attempt to directly estimate the presence
of cost inefficiency using an approach report by Lau and Yotopoulos.* In
this formulation the virtual price is presumed to be a constant proportion
of the actual price where this constant equals 1 in the case of efficiency.
The Hanoch function (Eq. 13), suitably modified was estimated using the
data for the cities of Long Beach, San Diego, and Oakland. The parameters
reflecting inefficiency were significant and indicated the use of too many
police relative to civilians. The production function still exhibited some
nonhomotheticity. Hence attributing all of the nonhomotheticity to inefficiency, as was done in section VII, probably overestimates the inefficiency.
Nonetheless, there evidently is relative cost inefficiency in big city police
departments in California. Further investigation is under way.

* L.J. Lau and P.A. Yotopoulos, "A Test for Relative Economic Efficiency
  and Application to Indian Agriculture," AER, V. 61 (1) pp. 94-109.

Notes

[1] See [14] , p. 3

[2] See [9] and [19]

[3] See [6]

[4] This of course may have proved possible using an alternative specification. For a discussion of the properties of the function used, see [11].

[5] Data on the number of 4-wheel police cars was obtained from [2] and [13] and by phone calls and written inquires to the police departments. The number of police officers and of civilian employees were obtained from [2] and [13] .

[6] Data for the quantity of inputs in the case of Los Angeles was obtained from [12].

[7] See [11] , p. 411

[8] See [6] , p. 29

[9] See [10] , p. 880

[10] See [6] , p. 31

[11] For a survey of duality theory applied to production see [5] or [7].

[12] See [1] , p. 512

[13] See [7] , p. 131

[14] See [15] , p. 412

[15] See [11] , p. 412

[16] See [3]

[17] See [11] , p. 416 and [8] , p. 509

[18] See [20] and [17] and [8] , p. 509

[19] See [16], pp. 30-36

[20]The variance of an input ratio such as that given for example by Eq. (39) or Eq. (45) can be calculated from the formula:

$\text{Var } y = \left(\frac{dg}{dx}\right)^2$ Var x where $y = g(x)$. See [11a], p.232. Applying this formula to Eq. (45), where y is $\frac{x_p}{x_v}$, x is $\frac{d_p}{d_v}$ whose estimated variance is given in Table 7, and σ is taken to be equal to 2 and given (see Table 7), we have:

$$\sqrt{\text{Var } \left(\frac{x_p}{x_v}\right)} = 2 \, \frac{\left(\frac{x_p}{x_v}\right)}{\left(\frac{d_p}{d_v}\right)} \, \sqrt{\text{Var } \frac{d_p}{d_v}} \; .$$

This formula can be evaluated at a particular price ratio W_p/W_v using Eq. (45) and the information in Table 7. The 95 percent confidence intervals are determined by plotting $X_p/X_v \pm 2.05 \sqrt{\text{Var } \left(\frac{x_p}{x_v}\right)}$.

[21]The evidence on returns to scale is limited, and in turn questionable, because of the specification of the cost functions used to estimate this property. For a discussion of the literature on this point see Darrough and Heineke[6]. Since one cost function study [14a] finds evidence of economies and another study [19a] finds evidence of slight diseconomies, the assumption of constant returns seems tenable.

References

[1]   Allen, R.G.D. Mathematical Analysis for Economists, St. Martin's Press
       Inc., New York, 1968.

[2]   Annual General Administrative Survey, prepared by the Kansas City Police
       Department for limited circulation, 1960, '62, '68, '69, '71, '73.

[3]   Arrow, K.J.; Chenery, H.B.; Minhas, B.S.; and Solow, R.M. "Capital-
       Labor Substitution and Economic Efficiency," Review of Economics
       and Statistics, Vol. 63, August 1961.

[4]   Automotive News, 1958-1975.

[5]   Blackorby, Charles, Primont, D. and Russell, R. Robert, "Application
       of Duality Theory to Consumer Preferences and Production Tech-
       nologies," Chapter 2 of manuscript.

[6]   Darrough, M.N. and Heineke, J.M.,"The Multi-Output Translog Production
       Cost Function: The Case of Law Enforcement Agencies," Chapter seven
       in present volume.

[7]   Diewert, W.E. "Applications of Duality Theory," in Frontiers of
       Quantitative Economics, Vol. II, edited by M.D. Intriligator
       and D.A. Kendrick, North-Holland Publishing Co., Amsterdam, 1974.

[8]   Diewert, W.E. "Intertemporal Consumer Theory and the Demand for Durables,"
       Econometrica, Vol. 42, No. 3 (May 1974).

[9]   Ehrlich, Issac, "Participation in Illegitimate Activites: A Theoretical
       and Empirical Investigation," Journal of Political Economy, Vol.
       81, 1973.

[10]   Hall, Robert E., "The Specification of Technology with Several Kinds of
       Output," Journal of Political Economy, Vol. 81, 1973.

[11] Hanoch, Giora, "Production and Demand Models with Direct or Indirect Implicit Additivity," Econometrica, Vol. 43, May 1975.

[11a] Kendall, M.G. and Stuart, A. The Advanced Theory of Statistics, Vol. I, 3rd edition Hafner Publishing Co., New York, 1969.

[12] Los Angeles Police Department, Statistical Digest for Los Angeles Police Department, 1956-1975.

[13] Municipal Year Book, 1956-1975.

[14] Ostrom, Elinor; Parks, Roger B.; and Whitaker, Gordon P. Policing Metropolitan America, Report prepared for the National Science Foundation Research Applied to National Needs, U.S. Government Printing Office, Washington, D.C.

[14a] Popp, D.O. and Sebold, F.D. "Quasi Returns to Scale in the Provision of Police Service", Public Finance, Vol. 27, No. 1, pp. 1-18, 1972.

[15] Shephard, Ronald W. "Comments by Ronald Shephard on 'Applications of Duality Theory,' by W.E. Diewart" in Frontiers of Quantitative Economics, Vol. II, edited by M. Intriligator and D. Kendrick, North-Holland Publishing Co., Amsterdam, 1974.

[16] Shephard, Ronald W. Theory of Cost and Production Functions, Princeton University Press, Princeton, N.J., 1970.

[17] Simler, Norman J. "The Economics of Featherbedding," Industrial and Labor Relations Review, Vol. 16, No. 1, October 1962.

[18] United States Department of Labor, Bureau of Labor Statistics, Area Wage Surveys.

[19] Votey, Harold L., Jr. and Phillips, Llad. "Police Effectiveness and the Production Function for Law Enforcement," The Journal of Legal Studies, Vol. I (2), June 1972.

[19a] Walzer, Norman "Economics of Scale and Municipal Police Service:
       The Illinois Experience", Review of Economics and Statistics,
       Vol. 54, No. 4, 1972, pp. 431-38.

[20] Weinstein, Paul A. "Featherbedding: A Theoretical Analysis,"
       Journal of Political Economy, Vol. 48, No. 4, August 1960.

Economic Models of Criminal Behavior,
J.M. Heineke (ed.)
© *North-Holland Publishing Company, 1978*

CHAPTER SEVEN

THE MULTI-OUTPUT TRANSLOG PRODUCTION COST FUNCTION:
THE CASE OF LAW ENFORCEMENT AGENCIES

M. N. Darrough and J. M. Heineke*

In this paper we study the relationship between costs, input prices

and activity levels in a sample of approximately thirty-five medium sized

city police departments for the years 1968, 69, 71 and 73. Our interest

lies in determining the functional structure of law enforcement production

technology.

Since efficient allocation of resources to activities requires knowl-

edge of relative incremental costs for the activities involved, we are

particularly interested in determining marginal cost functions for, and

rates of transformation between the various outputs. Since past studies

have adopted functional specifications which have implicitly maintained

strong hypotheses about the underlying technology, we adopt a quite general

functional specification which permits testing the appropriateness of these

hypotheses. In a more general context we model and estimate the structure

of production for a multiple output-multiple input firm in a manner which

*A portion of J. M. Heineke's participation in this study was supported
under Grant #75-NI-99-0123 from the National Institute of Law Enforcement
and Criminal Justice, LEAA, U.S. Department of Justice to the Hoover Institution at Stanford University. We are especially grateful to Erwin Diewert
and Lawrence Lau for their comments and suggestions on an earlier version of
the paper. We have also benefited from discussions with C. Blackorby, M. K.
Block and F. Nold. Points of view or opinions stated in this document are
those of the authors and do not necessarily represent the official position
or policies of the U.S. Department of Justice.

places few restrictions of first and second order parameters of the underlying structure.

Introduction

One question which arises immediately in any discussion of cost or
production functions associated with law enforcement agencies concerns the
appropriate measure of "output." Clearly police departments produce
multiple outputs (services) for a community, ranging from directing traffic,
quieting family squabbles, and providing emergency first aid, to preventing
crimes and solving existing crimes. In this study we view police output as
being of essentially two types: (1) general service activities as epito-
mized by the traffic control and emergency first aid care functions of
police departments; and (2) activities directed to solving existing crimes.
Strictly speaking, "solving existing crimes" is an intermediate output with
deterrence or prevention of criminal activity being the final product. But
due to the difficulty of measuring crime prevention we use the number of
"solutions" by type of crime as output measures.[1]

In the past few years a number of authors have, to one degree or
another, addressed the problem of determining the structure of production
in law enforcement agencies. Since under certain rather mild regularity
conditions there exists a duality between cost and production functions,
either the cost function or the production function may be used to
characterize the technological structure of a firm. The studies of
Chapman, Hirsch and Sonenblum (1975), Ehrlich (1970, 1973), Votey and
Phillips (1972) and Wilson and Boland (1977) all proceed by estimating

---

[1]See Chapman, Hirsch and Sonenblum (1975) for an attempt to measure
crime prevention as an output of police agencies.

production functions while Popp and Sebold (1972) and Walzer (1972) estimate cost functions. It is of some interest to briefly review the findings
of these authors.

Chapman, Hirsch and Sonenblum estimate a rather traditional production
function, at least from a theoretical point of view. All police outputs
are collapsed into one aggregate, which is then regressed on input use
levels utilizing data from the city of Los Angeles for the years 1956-70.
They find strongly increasing returns to scale--often a two to four percent
output response to a one percent change in input usage.

Ehrlich (1970, 1973) also uses an aggregate solution rate as the output
measure, but instead of employing traditional input measures he regresses
the aggregate solution rate on per capita expenditures on police, the
aggregate offense rate and a series of exogenous ("environmental")
variables. The expenditure variable is used as an index of overall input
use levels while Ehrlich includes the aggregate offense rate to measure
the effects of "crowding" or capacity constraints on output. The latter
is a substantial departure from a neoclassical approach in which the shape
of the production function itself will reflect diminishing returns as
capacity is pressed. But it is a specification that has been widely
adopted by those who have followed Ehrlich. (For example, see Vandaele
(1975) or Votey and Phillips (1972, 1975).) Using per capita expenditures
to measure the scale of output, Ehrlich finds that a one percent increase
in expenditures per capita leads to much less than a one percent increase
in the solution rate.

We should point out that two different arguments have been used for
including the offense level in police agency production functions. In
addition to the argument based upon police resource capacities, some

authors have justified inclusion of the offense level in the production
function using what is essentially the "fisheries argument," viz., that
the total number of fish in the ocean are a determinant of the number
caught. So if the number of offenses is high, then ceteris paribus, it
should be easier to obtain a solution than if there are but few offenses.
Obviously, the argument goes, if there are no offenses there can be no
solutions. But this is really not the question. The question is whether
in the neighborhood of observed solution levels, changes in the total
number of offenses would change solution levels.

Whichever rationale is used, the neoclassical production function is
then modified and written as $y = f(v_1, v_2, \ldots, v_m, 0)$, where y is the number
of solutions, v_i is the level of utilization of input i and 0 is the
number of offenses. One means of testing the appropriateness of this
specification is to assume that 0 does not belong in the production
function and then estimate the function $y/0 = f(v_1, v_2, \ldots, v_m)0^\gamma$, where y/0
is the solution rate. If γ is significantly different from minus unity,
the offense level probably influences solution levels. If not, one has
some evidence that the production function for solutions is independent of
the level of offenses.

Votey and Phillips (1975) report three estimates of the production
function $y/0 = \alpha v^\beta 0^\gamma$. Using their reported parameter estimates and
standard errors one cannot reject the hypothesis that $\gamma = -1$ in any one
of the estimated equations at the .05 level. In addition, Ehrlich's
(1973) estimate of γ is -.908 which again is not significantly different
from minus unity. We conclude, at least tentatively, that the production
of solutions does not depend upon offenses and do not consider the matter
further in this study.

Votey and Phillips (1972) estimate production functions which link solution rates for the property crimes of auto theft, burglary, larceny and robbery to input usage. As with Ehrlich and Vandaele, the authors include the level of offenses as an argument in the production function along with more traditional input measures.[2]

The Wilson and Boland study is similar to the work of Votey and Phillips (1972), in that they study the production of solutions to several property crimes. But instead of input levels as determinants of solutions, they utilize a "capacity" variable (the coefficient of which is uniformly insignificant) and variables meant to account for productivity differences between departments. Here as with Vandaele and Votey and Phillips (1972), the authors cannot address the question of scale economies due to the fact that only a subset of all outputs are included in these studies.

Finally, both Popp and Sebold, and Walzer estimate cost functions and attempt to measure scale economies. The former use population size in the police jurisdiction as their measure of "scale" along with a large number of demographic and environmental variables to estimate the per capita costs of police service. Given the appropriateness of these variables for explaining costs, the authors find diseconomies of scale throughout the entire range of population sizes. Of course the population variable provides a considerably different concept of scale than economists are accustomed to considering, and in fact, Walzer has argued that population size is a poor measure of scale for several reasons--the most important being a tendency on the part of police administrators to determine man-

---

[2]This is primarily an expository paper and only graphical analyses of the estimated functions are reported. Hence it is not possible to perform tests of the sort discussed in the previous paragraphs.

power needs as a proportion of population size. In such a case there is
obviously a strong bias toward constant returns to scale. In his study
Walzer recognizes that offenses cleared, accidents investigated, etc.,
all make up the output of a police department. But instead of estimating
a multiple output cost function, he creates an "index of police service"
by collapsing all outputs into one.[3] The estimated cost function contains
the offense rate as an argument in addition to measures of input prices,
input usage and several variables meant to pick up externally determined
differences in productivity. Using the service index to measure output
Walzer finds evidence of economies of scale, although they seem to be
rather slight. Interestingly enough he also finds that input costs are
not significantly related to overall production costs.

Outline of the Paper

     A number of strong hypotheses concerning the production structure of
law enforcement agencies have been implicitly maintained in the studies
we have sketched. First, the arguments entering cost and production
functions have for the most part differed considerably from what one would
expect from classical production theory. In addition, in the one case
where input costs do enter the cost function (Walzer), linear homogeneity
in input costs has not been imposed on the estimated cost function. One
possible explanation for these deviations from classical production and
cost specifications is that classical theory and cost minimizing
behavior in particular, is not capable of explaining observed choices in
public agencies. While this appears to be a plausible hypothesis, it is

---

[3]The weights used are average times spent on each type of activity.

also a testable hypothesis.[4] In what follows we test the propostion that

the law enforcement agencies make input and output decisions in a cost

minimizing manner.

Second, each of the estimated production functions upon which we have

reported is either linear or linear logarithmic. Such functions may be

viewed as first order approximations to an arbitrary production function.

It is well known that first order approximations severely restrict admis-

sable patterns of substitution among inputs and admissable rates of trans-

formation among outputs as well as having other undesirable empirical

implications.[5] An additional problem with linear logarithmic production

or cost functions arises if one is interested in determining the extent

of scale economies, since these functions do not permit scale economies

to vary with output. We noted above that each of the production studies

surveyed included the offense rate or level as an argument. A possible

explanation for this inclusion might be based upon the restrictiveness of

the chosen functional forms and a consequent attempt on the part of the

authors to provide output responses which do vary with the scale of opera-

tion, in functions which do not naturally possess this property. For

these reasons and others we adopt a second order approximation to the

underlying cost and production structure thereby leaving the various

elasticity measures of common interest free to be determined by the data.[6]

---

[4]This hypothesis is explicit in Wilson and Boland, p. 8, who state,
"In our view, police departments do not behave in accordance with the
economic model of the firm."

[5]For example, linear logarithmic production functions imply input
expenditure shares which are independent of the level of expenditure, while
linear production functions imply perfect input substitutability and consequently rule out internal solutions to the cost minimization problem.

[6]In the Popp and Sebold, and Walzer studies the production cost
function is specified to be quadratic in the scale argument although all
other second order parameters are restricted to be zero.

Third, the Chapman, Hirsch and Sonenblum, Walzer and Ehrlich studies all utilize a single output aggregate. If the results of such aggregate studies are to be used for decision purposes, it is desirable that the aggregate measure be a consistent index over all police outputs. In what follows we estimate a multiple output cost function and test whether the various subsets of outputs may be consistently aggregated into single categories.

Fourth, the Wilson and Boland, Votey and Phillips (1972) and Vandaele studies each implicitly maintain the hypothesis of nonjoint outputs by estimating separate production functions for different types of solutions. Again, instead of maintaining this hypothesis we estimate a general multiple output function and then test the nonjointness hypothesis.

To summarize, in this study we characterize the structure of production in a combined cross section and time series analysis of U.S. Police departments, test for the existence of consistent aggregate indices of police output, for nonjointness of output, and for consistency of our estimated equations with the optimizing behavior of classical theory. In addition, we calculate (1) the marginal and average costs for solutions to the property crimes of burglary, robbery, larceny and motor vehicle theft, and for solutions to crimes against the person; (2) marginal rates of transformation between these activities; and (3) an estimate of scale economies based upon the response of total cost to simultaneous variation in all police outputs. In the next two sections we provide definitions, theorems and the conceptual structure which underpin the parameter estimation and testing which follow.

Theoretical Background

The following definitions and theorems provide precise meaning to many of the concepts discussed above and the basis for testing the hypotheses of interest.

Let $F(y,v) = 0$ represent the production possibility frontier, where y is an n vector of outputs and v is an m vector of inputs. We assume that F is continuous at least twice differentiable, nonincreasing in y and nondecreasing in v. In addition, let $C(y,w)$ be the associated production cost function, where w is an m vector of input prices.

Theorem 1: $C(y,w) = \min_{v \in L(y)} w^T v$

where $L(y) = \{v \mid F(u,v) \geq 0$ is the input requirement set and T denotes transposition. The function $C(y,w)$ is unique and is a positive linear homogeneous, differentiable and nondecreasing function of input prices, w. (See Uzawa (1964) or Shephard (1953).)

We denote the sets of n outputs and m inputs as $N = \{1,2,3,\ldots,n\}$ and $M = \{1,2,\ldots,m\}$ and partition these sets into ρ and σ mutually exclusive and exhaustive subsets, respectively, $N = \{N_1, N_2, \ldots, N\}$ and $M = \{M_1, M_2, \ldots, M_\sigma\}$. The elements of N_i are denoted Y_i, the elements of M_j, V_j.

Definition 1: If marginal rates of transformation between any two outputs from the subset N_k are independent of all other outputs not in N_k, and all inputs, then the production function is separable (weakly) with respect to the partition $\{N_k, N_\ell, \forall \ell \neq k\}$. A similar definition holds for input partitions. Formally, the production function $F(u,v) = 0$ is output separable with respect to the partition $\{N_k, N_\ell, \forall \ell \neq k\}$ iff

(1) $\partial(\partial F/\partial y_i / \partial F/\partial y_j)/\partial y_p = 0$,

       $\partial(\partial F/\partial y_i / \partial F/\partial y_j)/\partial v_q = 0$, $i,j \in N_k$, $p \notin N_k$ and $\forall q$,

and is input separable with respect to the partition $\{M_r, M_s, \forall s \neq r\}$ iff

(2) $\partial(\partial F/\partial v_i / \partial F/\partial v_j)/\partial v_t = 0$,

       $\partial(\partial F/\partial v_i / \partial F/\partial v_j)/\partial y_u = 0$, $i,j \in M_r$, $t \notin M_r$ and $\forall u$.

Theorem 2: Separability with respect to the output partition $\{N_k, N_2, \ldots, N_\rho\}$ and the input partition $\{M_1, M_2, \ldots, M_\sigma\}$ is necessary and sufficient for the production function to be written as $F(y,v) = F^*(h_1(Y_1), \ldots, h_\rho(Y_\rho), g_1(V_1),$ $\ldots, g_\sigma(V_\sigma))$ where h_i and g_j are called __category__ functions and are functions of the elements of N_i and M_j only. (See Goldman and Uzawa (1964).)

Definition 2: A technology with production function $F(y,v)$ is __nonjoint__ if $F(\cdot)$ may be decomposed into functions $y_i = f_i(v^i)$, $i = 1,2,\ldots,n$ with the property that $f_i(v^i)$ is independent of y_j, $i \neq j$, and $\sum_1^n v^k = v$. So to show that a technology is nonjoint, the functions $f_i(\cdot)$ must exist and be free of any economies or diseconomies of jointness. As Hall (1973) has pointed out, this does not require physically separable processes producing the various outputs, nor does the fact that two or more outputs are produced in the same plant rule out nonjointness.

Theorem 3: A technology is __nonjoint__ iff the joint cost function can be written as $C(y,w) = C_1(y_1,w) + C_2(y_2,w) + \ldots + C_n(y_n,w)$. (See Hall (1973).)

Definition 3: Aggregation is said to be __consistent__ if the solutions to a problem at hand are identical regardless of whether one uses aggregate indices or the micro level variables.

Definition 4: If a function is separable and each of the category functions is homothetic, the function is said to be homothetically separable.

Theorem 4:∧ Homothetic separability is sufficient for consistent aggregation. (See Blackorby, Primont and Russell (1977a).)

Hicks' Aggregation Theorem: "If the prices of a group of goods change in the same proportion, that group of goods behaves just as if it were a single commodity." (See Hicks (1946, p. 312-3).)

Motivation of Agencies

We next present two alternative models of the decision process of law enforcement agencies. One model focuses on input decisions, the other on output decisions. It should be kept in mind that the model chosen to represent agency behavior will likely have a major influence on the values of estimated parameters. Hence one should consider the alternative specifications with one eye on statistical tractability and data limitations, and the other on the "realism" of the implied decision process.

Cost Minimization - The formal structure provided by the cost minimization behavioral hypothesis can be imposed on the estimation process in several ways. To begin, we generalize the traditional cost minimization paradigm to include the multiple output firm. In particular, we assume that law enforcement agencies are given a vector of outputs which is minimally acceptable to the community and are instructed to provide at least that level of service at minimum cost.[7] Formally the agency's problem is to

(3) $\min_{v} w^T v$ s.t.) $F(y^0,v) = 0$

where y^0 is the minimally acceptable output vector. Optimization problem

(3) provides the system

(4) $\dfrac{w_i}{w_j} - \dfrac{\partial F/\partial v_i}{\partial F/\partial v_j} = 0$,   ∀ $i,j = 1,2,\ldots,m$, $i \neq j$

       $F(y^0,v) = 0$

of m equations which may be used in estimating F. If equations (4) are

assumed to be associated with a well behaved minimum, we know that a solu-

tion for v as a function of w and y^0 exists. In addition, as long as

input prices are exogenously determined as far as an individual agency is

concerned, the solution yields the m endogenous factor demands as functions

of strictly exogenous variables. Because factor demands are simultaneously

determined, disturbances, given by the stochastic specification into which

the model must eventually be imbedded, will be correlated across equations.

As a consequence, it will usually be necessary to treat the solution to (4)

as system for purposes of parameter estimation, if efficiency is a

criterion.

   Two other points concerning the system implied by equations (4) are

of interest: First, if (4) can be solved for the v_i as functions of w and

y^0, these functions may well be nonlinear in the parameters. This need

not be a major obstacle, but for large systems nonlinear estimation is

----

   [7]In a democratic society, voters through their elected representa-
tives provide this information.

expensive and one is never sure of convergence to a global maximum.
Secondly, and more important, is the fact that although we know a solution
to (4) exists in principle, this is cold comfort to the econometrician
charged with estimating $F(\cdot)$. Since for even modestly general functional
specifications for $F(\cdot)$, it will generally be impossible to express the v_i
as explicit functions of w and y^0.

An alternative to the approach we have just described for estimating
the production structure is to focus on the cost function rather than the
production function. If one maintains the hypothesis of cost minimization,
the duality between cost and production functions implies that once one
function is given the other is uniquely determined.[8] So it matters not a
whit which function is estimated, and the choice of estimating the cost
function or the production function should be made on purely statistical
grounds.

One way of proceeding to estimate the production cost function would
be to use OLS to directly estimate $C(y,w)$. Since both w and y are exogenous in the present framework, OLS is an appropriate procedure. In
contrast to the system we have just discussed this is a welcome respite.
But a caveat must be added: If cost minimization is a maintained hypothesis and if $C(y,w)$ is estimated via OLS, then one ends up not exploiting
information available in the maintained hypothesis which might have been
used to add precision to parameter estimates. Furthermore, unless there
is significant variation in y and w across the sample, multicollinearity
could be a problem. An additional advantage of imposing the structure
implied by cost minimization is that the resulting restrictions across

---

[8] See Diewert (1974).

parameters will help circumvent multicollinearity problems which may be present.

The economical way to impose the structure implied by cost minimization is to call upon Shephards' Lemma (1953) which gives cost minimizing factor demands as a function of the partial derivatives of the cost function with respect to input prices:

(5) $v_i = \partial C / \partial w_i$ $i = 1, 2, \ldots, m$.

In general, estimation of (5) may not be sufficient to determine all of the parameters of the production cost function.[10] This can be remedied merely by including $C(\cdot)$ as an equation in the system to be estimated. In which case the system of interest is

(6) $v_i = \partial C / \partial w_i$, $i = 1, 2, \ldots, m$

       $C = C(y, w)$.[11]

Recall that a maintained hypothesis of this section has been that law enforcement agencies are assigned minimal output requirements and that input prices are exogenous as far as any single agency is concerned. In this case, right hand variables in system (6) will be uncorrelated with stochastic disturbances in the econometric version of (6). Hence estimation of equations (6) will most assuredly identify the parameters of the

---

[9] Of course this same information was also present in system (4) above.

[10] For example, if $C(y, w)$ is a polynomial in y and w, parameters associated with terms in elements of y alone will be missing from equation (5).

[11] Note that equations (6) are not independent. Linear homogeneity of $C(\cdot)$ in w implies $\sum_1^m w_j \partial C / \partial w_j = C$. Multiplying the ith equation in (6) by w_i and summing we have $\sum_1^m w_i v_i = \sum_1^m w_i \partial C / \partial w_i = C$, since $\sum_1^m w_i v_i = C$.

cost function. But since the v_i are simultaneously determined, disturbances will be correlated across equations as before, necessitating estimating (6) as a simultaneous system.

Value Maximization - In this section we provide an alternative framework within which the structure of law enforcement production technology could be estimated. The model is essentially a value maximization model and of course still implies that input decisions are reached in a cost minimizing manner. The value maximization model has the advantage of not requiring that police decision makers to take the community's final output vector as a datum. Indeed the focus of the model shifts from determination of optimal input usage given an output vector, to determination of the optimal mix of outputs.

To this end we assume in this section that police administrators, either implicitly or explicitly, assign "seriousness" weights to crimes by type and use these weights along with the costs of solving crimes by type to determine the solution mix. This might be termed a "bounty hunter" model of police decision making since resources are allocated to solutions by type as if police remuneration were proportional to the "value" of solved crimes and assumes that police decision makers are primarily interested in solutions and not deterrence.[12] We believe that on a day to day basis a strong argument can be made that police administrators are primarily concerned with solutions and not deterrence and that for property crimes average values stolen are likely to be reasonable approximations to

_____

[12]Michael Block has suggested this terminology which is particularly descriptive of the model.

the weights used in allocating resources to solving property crimes.

Using P_i to represent the "value" to police of a solution to a crime of type i, $P \equiv (P_1, P_2, \ldots, P_n)$, the police agency's decision problem is

(7) $\max_y P^T y - C(y,w).$[13]

Decision problem (7) provides the familiar system

(8) $P_i - \partial C / \partial y_i = 0 ,$ $i = 1,2,\ldots,n$

which may be used as a basis for estimting $C(y,w)$. As was the case with equations (5) above, if $C(y,w)$ is approximated with a polynomial in y and w, equations (8) alone may not be sufficient to determine the cost function. This can be remedied by including $C(y,w)$ itself in the system to be estimated. In which case

(9) $P_i - \partial C / \partial y_i = 0 ,$ $i = 1,2,\ldots,n$

        $C - C(y,w) = 0$

is the system of interest. In the circumstances we have outlined it is reasonable to assume that P is determined jointly by the activities of police and offenders in earlier periods--i.e., P is a vector of predetermined variables. Assuming that input costs are exogenous, equations (9) determine the n endogenous solution levels as functions of exogenous and predetermined variables.

One problem in implementing this system in an econometric context is

---

[13]There is a constraint on the decision problem which we have not taken into account: Viz., that $C(y,w) \leq A$, where A is the agency's budget for the period.

obvious: The weights to be given the various types of solution are at best difficult to obtain. But as we have indicated above, in the case of property crimes average values stolen probably provide reasonable approximations to the seriousness of these crimes in the eyes of the police. Although for the case of "crimes against the person," e.g., homocide, rape and assualt, no such convenient measure is available.

To circumvent this problem we assume that there exists functions C^* and f such that the cost function may be written as

$$(10) \qquad C = C^*(f(y_1, \ldots, y_p, w), \ y_{p+1}, \ldots, y_n, w)$$

where $y_1, \ldots, y_p$ represent solutions to crimes against property and y_{p+1}, $\ldots, y_n$ represent solutions to crimes against the person and the service activities performed by police. That is, we assume that solutions to crimes against property are functionally separable from all other police activities. As we indicated above (*Definition 1*), this is equivalent to requiring that marginal rates of transformation (MRT) between solutions to all pairs of property crimes be invariant to the level of nonproperty crime solutions and to the level of other police services provided, e.g., traffic control, emergency first aid, etc.[14] In this case, optimization (7) may be treated as two problems: The optimal level of property crime solutions relative to non property crime solutions and services is determined in a first step after which a second optimization is performed to determine the optimal mix of property crime solutions. (See Strotz

---

[14]Recall that $\dfrac{\partial C(y,w)/\partial y_i}{\partial C(y,w)/\partial y_j} = \dfrac{\partial F(y,v)/\partial y_i}{\partial F(y,v)/\partial y_j} \equiv \dfrac{-\partial y_j}{\partial y_i}$

(1957).) System (9) then becomes

(11) $P_i - \partial C^*/\partial y_i = 0$, $i = 1,2,\ldots,p$

$\quad\quad C - C^*(F(y_1,y_2,\ldots,y_p w), y_{p+1},\ldots,y_n,w) = 0$

and is estimated below for the case of four property crimes, burglary,
robbery, motor vehicle theft and larceny, an aggregate of crimes against
the person and an aggregate service indicator.

We have chosen to estimate the production cost function utilizing
equations (11) rather than (6) for several reasons: First, costs in law
enforcement agencies tend to be predominately labor costs (approximately
ninety percent). And as one would expect, salaries of police employees
by rank are highly correlated. Therefore, it will most likely not be
possible to estimate more than one or two input demand equations if
structure (6) is imposed. In addition, we approximate C* with a second
order expansion in the logarithms of y and w and factor demand equations
will impose no restrictions across the coefficients of $\ln y_i$ and $\ln y_i \ln y_j$.
If these terms are highly collinear, which is likely to be the case, then
system (11) is preferrable since it places restrictions across coefficients
of terms in y and hence reduces the collinearity between the elements of y.
Another reason for choosing (11) as the basis for estimation is that it
explicitly addresses the output mix problem rather than assuming that the
decision is exogeneous to police administrators as in (6).

The Translog Model

From an econometric point of view equation system (11) is only of
limited interest until a specific functional form has been assigned to the

cost function $C^*(y,w)$. The primary concern in choosing a functional form for C^* is that the chosen class of functions be capable of approximating the unknown cost function to the desired degree of accuracy. In widespread use in the literature in the past few years are the class of so called "flexible" functional forms which includes the generalized Leontief function, the generalized Cobb-Douglas function, the transcendental logarithmic function and many hybrids.[15] These functions are all second order approximations to arbitrary differentiable, primal or dual objective functions and in particular place no restrictions on elasticities of substitution between inputs or elasticiteis of transformation between outputs and allow returns to scale to vary with the level of output. We have chosen to approximate $C^*(y,w)$ with a translog function due primarily to the fact that most past studies of law enforcement agency production technology have adopted linear logarithmic production structures--a special case of the translog structure.[16]

The translog cost function may be written as

$$(12) \quad \ln C(y,w) = a_0 + \sum_1^n a_i \ln y_i + \sum_{n+1}^{n+m} b_i \ln w_i + \frac{1}{2} \sum_1^n \sum_1^n \alpha_{ij} \ln y_i \ln y_j$$

$$+ \frac{1}{2} \sum_{n+1}^{n+m} \sum_{n+1}^{n+m} \beta_{ij} \ln w_i \ln w_j + \frac{1}{2} \sum_{n+1}^{n+m} \sum_1^n \gamma_{ij} \ln y_i \ln w_j.$$

---

[15] See Diewert (1971, 1973, 1974) and Christensen, Jorgensen and Lau (1971, 1973, 1975).

[16] These studies have utilized linear logarithmic production functions which in turn imply linear logarithmic production cost functions. This property of linear logarithmic primal and dual functions is termed self duality. The linear logarithmic function is the only self dual translog function.

Our maintained hypothesis of functional separability (see equation (10))

between property crime solution and all other activities of the police

agency implies the following restrictions on equation (12):

(13) $\alpha_{ij} = 0$, $i = 1,2,\ldots,p$, $j = p+1,p+2,\ldots,n.$ [17]

We proceed by testing the estimated cost function for consistency

with cost minimization. Then we test for the existence of one or more

consistent indices of output, and test the hypotheses of nonjoint outputs,

constant returns to scale and a linear logarithmic production structure

each conditional upon the cost minimization hypothesis. We have chosen

to proceed in this manner due to the fact that we view the translog cost

function only as an approximation to the true underlying cost function and

hence tests will necessarily be only approximate. In addition, the power

of the tests we have utilized is not known for finite samples.

Consistency of our model with cost minimization implies that $C(y,w)$

be linear homogeneous in input prices and that the matrix of second order

---

[17]See Berndt and Christensen (1974) for more detail on these conditions. We have imposed what is called linear separability of property crime solutions from other activities, which implies $\ln C(y,w) = \ln C_1(y_1,y_2,\ldots,y_p,w) + \ln C_2(y_{p+1},y_{p+2},\ldots,y_n,w)$ where $\ln C_1$ and $\ln C_2$ are translog functions (see Blackorby, Primont and Russell (1977b)). Functional separability may also be achieved via a set of nonlinear restrictions (see Berndt and Christensen (1974)). However, Blackorby, Primont and Russell have shown that if one assumes that the translog function exactly represents the underlying cost or production function, then nonlinear separability implies $\ln C(y,w) = F(D_1(y_1,y_2,\ldots,y_p,w), D_2(y_{p+1}, y_{p+2},\ldots,y_n,w))$ where D_1 and D_2 are linear logarithmic functions. Such linear logarithmic "aggregator" functions are highly restrictive. In this paper we have assumed only that the translog function approximates the underlying structure, in which case nonlinear separability does not appear to be as restrictive. Nonetheless we consider only the case of linear separability throughout the paper.

coefficiencts be _symmetric_. Linear homogeneity of C in w places the following restrictions on the translog cost function.

$$(14) \quad \sum_i^m b_i = 1 \; , \quad \sum_j^m \beta_{ij} = \sum_i^m \beta_{ij} = \sum_j^m \gamma_{ij} = 0$$

Symmetry implies

$$(15) \quad \begin{array}{ll} \alpha_{ij} = \alpha_{ji} \; , \quad \beta_{ij} = \beta_{ji} \; , \quad \forall \; i,j \\[2mm] \gamma_{ij} = \gamma_{ji} \; , \qquad\qquad i = 1,2,\ldots,n \text{ and } j = n{+}1, n{+}2, \ldots, n{+}m \end{array}$$

It will also be of interest to test for _constant returns to scale in_ output. Constant returns to scale imply

$$(16) \quad \sum_i^n a_i = 1 \; , \quad \sum_j^n \alpha_{ij} = \sum_i^n \alpha_{ij} = \sum_i^n \gamma_{ij} = 0$$

A test of the nonjoint production hypothesis may be based upon the restrictions[18]

$$(17) \quad \alpha_{ij} = -a_i a_j \; , \qquad\qquad i,j = 1,2,\ldots,n, \; i \neq j.$$

Finally the underlying production function is linear logarithmic if

$$(18) \quad \alpha_{ij} = \beta_{ij} = \gamma_{ij} = 0 \; , \qquad \forall \; i,j \;[19]$$

---

[18]This is easily seen by writing C = exp(lnC) and requiring $\partial^2 C / \partial y_i \partial y_j = 0$. The restrictions given as (17) hold at $y_i = y_j = w_k = 1$, $\forall i,j,k$. Since nonjointness is a global property of production structures, it must hold at every point. Therefore rejecting nonjointness at a point is sufficient for rejecting nonjointness globally. For the same reason, acceptance of restrictions (17) is an inconclusive test of the nonjoint production hypothesis.

[19]This follows from the fact that linear logarithmic production functions imply linear logarithmic cost functions and vice versa. This property is termed _self duality_.

The Econometric Model

In this section we specialize the n output, m input production model
to the model which is estimated and provide the stochastic specification
model for estimation. We had available for this study information on
annual police budgets for the years 1968, 1969, 1971 and 1973 for a sample of
approximately thirty two medium size cities; the average wages of officers
by rank, the number of crimes of type i cleared by arrest ("clearances")
and the average value stolen for each of the property crimes in the FBI
index.[20] The police budget and wage information was gathered by the Kansas
City Police Department and circulated for use by participating cities under
the title of the Annual General Administrative Survey. The data on clearances and average values stolen are from unpublished sources at the FBI.
We have used clearances by arrest for the seven index crimes reported in
the Uniform Crime Reports as our measures of "solutions." In particular,
we have called burglary clearances (solutions), y_1, robbery clearances, y_2,
motor vehicle theft clearances, y_3, and larceny clearances, y_4. We have
used the aggregate number of homicide, rape and assault clearances to
represent solutions to crimes against the person and have labeled this
output, y_5. Finally, a very large component of the output of all law
enforcement agencies is the rather mundane but important service functions--
directing traffic, investigating accidents, breaking up fights, providing

---

[20] We also had information on fleet sizes and compositions and the type
of computer services available. We have assumed that unit rental costs
are approximately equal across cities and hence need not be explicitly
considered in the estimation. We also attempted to treat differences in
available computer services as differences in production technology using
dummy variables. Coefficients on these variables tended to be uniformly
insignificant lending credence to the often voiced proposition that modern
technology has yet to be effectively utilized in law enforcement. The
largest city in our sample is Houston, Texas, (1,230,000), the smallest is
Birmingham, Alabama (300,000). Mean population over the sample is 561,000.

emergency first aid, etc. We group all such service functions together as y_6. There is some question as to the appropriate measure of these activities. We have adopted the hypothesis that the quantity of services of the type we have been discussing is proportional to the size of the city in which the agency is located. This gives a cost function with six outputs and a still unspecified number of input prices.

We had available wage information on eight grades of police officers from patrolman to chief. As one might expect these wage series are highly collinear. To test for the existence of a Hicksian price index we computed correlation coefficients between the wages of the various ranks and found very high coefficients. For example the correlation between wages of patrolmen and a weighted average of the wages of all other ranks is .955. Unfortunately, there does not appear to be a way of testing whether a sample correlation is significantly different from one since the distribution of this statistic is degenerate at that point. But with correlation this high it appears safe to assume the conditions for Hicks' aggregation are fulfilled and hence we use a weighted average of all police wages as an aggregate measure of unit labor costs, denoted w.[21]

The translog cost function of (12) above may now be written as

$$(19) \quad \ln C^*(y,w) = a_0 + \sum_1^6 a_i \ln y_i + b \ln w + \frac{1}{2} \sum_1^6 \sum_1^6 \alpha_{ij} \ln y_i \ln y_j$$

$$+ \frac{1}{2} \beta \ln w^2 + \frac{1}{2} \sum_1^6 \gamma_i \ln w \ln y_i$$

---

[21] We have constructed a price index for each of the cities in the sample based upon BLS Intermediate Family Budget data and have used this index to tranform cost and wages series into "real" terms. This transformation has the added benefit of correcting for heteroscedasticity if increasing prices lead not only to increases in mean costs but also to increases in the variance of costs.

where $\alpha_{15} = \alpha_{16} = \alpha_{25} = \alpha_{26} = \alpha_{35} = \alpha_{36} = \alpha_{45} = \alpha_{46} = 0$ due to the imposed functional separability of property crime solutions and all other police activities.

Symmetry and linear homogeneity of C* in w would impose the further restrictions on (19)

(20)
$$b = 1 \, , \qquad \beta = 0 \, , \qquad \gamma_i = 0 \, , \qquad i = 1,2,\ldots,6$$

$$\alpha_{ij} = \alpha_{ji} \, , \qquad i,j = 1,2,\ldots,6$$

while constant returns to scale implies

(21) $\sum_1^6 a_i = 1 \, , \quad \sum_i^6 \alpha_{ij} = \sum_j^6 \alpha_{ij} = 0 \, , \quad \forall i,j \quad \text{and} \quad \sum_1^6 \gamma_i = 0.$

If property crime solutions are nonjoint then

(22) $\alpha_{ij} = -a_i a_j \, , \qquad i,j = 1,2,3,4,5,6 \, , \qquad i \neq j$[22]

The latter imposes only seven additional restrictions, since the α_{ij} are symmetric. Given cost minimization, a linear logarithmic production structure would imply

(23) $\alpha_{ij} = 0 \qquad\qquad i,j = 1,2,\ldots,6$

Finally, given the hypothesis of functional separability between property crime solutions and all other police activities there are a total of eleven possible groupings of property crime solutions which might be considered for indexing. Our question here is not whether an index exists in any of these cases because an index can always be found, but whether a

---

[22]See footnote 18 above.

consistent index exists.[23] The eleven candidates for aggregation and

indexing are displayed in Table I along with the implied linear separa-

bility restrictions. It is important to keep in mind that the existence

of an aggregate (a functionally separate group) does not necessarily

imply existence of a consistent index for the aggregate. (See *Theorem 4*).

For the case at hand, system (11) may be written as

$$
(24) \quad P_i y_i / C^* = a_i + \sum_1^6 \alpha_{ij} \ln y_j + \gamma_i \ln w , \qquad i = 1,2,3,4
$$

$$
\ln C^* = a_0 + \sum_1^6 a_i \ln y_i + b \ln w + \frac{1}{2} \sum_1^6 \sum_1^6 \alpha_{ij} \ln y_i \ln y_j + (\beta/2) \ln w^2
$$

$$
+ \sum_1^6 \gamma_i \ln w \ln y_i
$$

where $\alpha_{ij} = 0$, $\alpha_{ji} = 0$, $i = 1,2,3,4$, $j = 5,6$. (The first four equations

---

[23]An example of such a question is whether it is possible to aggregate
burglary, robbery and larceny solutions into a composite category such as
"non automobile theft" solutions. Given the numbers of burglary, robbery
and larceny solutions and their imputed values, how does one derive quantity
and value indices for "non automobile theft" solutions? Suppose burglary
solutions, robbery solutions and larceny solutions are separable from other
police outputs and input prices, then the cost function may be written as
$C(y,w) = C(h(y_1,y_2,y_4), y_3,y_5,y_6,w)$. In addition, if h is homothetic then
y_1, y_2 and y_4 may be aggregated into a category. The quantity index for
sample point $\bar{y}^* \equiv (y_1^*,y_2^*,y_4^*)$ is determined by the function $h(\cdot)$ and the
values of (y_1^*,y_2^*,y_4^*). Since the index should be linear homogenous in $\bar{y}$,
the problem is to find a function ϕ such that $\phi(h(\bar{y}))$ is linear homogeneous
in y. The quantity (solution) index is then $\phi(h(\bar{y}^*))$ at $\bar{y}^*$. The corresponding value (price) index is $\bar{P}^* = (P_1^* y_1^* + P_2^* y_2^* + P_4^* y_4^*)/\phi(h(\bar{y}^*))$.
Evaluating two "nonautomobile theft" solution vectors (y_1^*,y_2^*,y_4^*), and
(y_1^o,y_2^o,y_4^o), given $\bar{P}^*$ and $\bar{P}^o$, but without knowledge of the function $h(\cdot)$,
is the analog to the more traditional index problem.

TABLE 1. PARAMETER RESTRICTIONS FOR LINEAR FUNCTIONAL SEPARABILITY[24]

Aggregate	Parameter Restrictions	Aggregate	Parameter Restrictions
(y_1, y_2)	$\alpha_{13} = \alpha_{14} = \alpha_{23} = \alpha_{24} = \gamma_1 = \gamma_2 = 0$	(y_1, y_2, y_3)	$\alpha_{14} = \alpha_{24} = \alpha_{34} = \gamma_1 = \gamma_2 = \gamma_3 = 0$
(y_1, y_3)	$\alpha_{12} = \alpha_{14} = \alpha_{23} = \alpha_{34} = \gamma_1 = \gamma_3 = 0$	(y_1, y_2, y_4)	$\alpha_{13} = \alpha_{23} = \alpha_{34} = \gamma_1 = \gamma_2 = \gamma_4 = 0$
(y_1, y_4)	$\alpha_{12} = \alpha_{13} = \alpha_{24} = \alpha_{34} = \gamma_1 = \gamma_4 = 0$	(y_1, y_3, y_4)	$\alpha_{12} = \alpha_{23} = \alpha_{24} = \gamma_1 = \gamma_3 = \gamma_4 = 0$
(y_2, y_3)	$\alpha_{12} = \alpha_{24} = \alpha_{13} = \alpha_{34} = \gamma_2 = \gamma_3 = 0$	(y_2, y_3, u_4)	$\alpha_{12} = \alpha_{13} = \alpha_{14} = \gamma_2 = \gamma_3 = \gamma_4 = 0$
(y_2, y_4)	$\alpha_{12} = \alpha_{23} = \alpha_{14} = \alpha_{34} = \gamma_2 = \gamma_4 = 0$	(y_1, y_2, y_3, y_4)	$\gamma_1 = \gamma_2 = \gamma_3 = \gamma_4 = 0$
(y_3, y_4)	$\alpha_{13} = \alpha_{23} = \alpha_{14} = \alpha_{24} = \gamma_3 = \gamma_4 = 0$		

[24]These restrictions are conditional on the functional separability of property crime solutions and all other police activities. Under the cost minimization hypothesis, see equation (20), the aggregate (y_1, y_2, y_3, y_4) is automatically separable from other outputs and input prices. Moreover, the parameter restrictions for separability are identical for (y_1, y_2) and (y_3, y_4), for (y_1, y_3) and (y_2, y_4) and for (y_1, y_4) and (y_2, y_3). Hence only seven tests need be undertaken.

here give the value of y_i solutions to property crime i as a proportion of
total police expenditures.) The next step in implementing the econometric
version of the model is to provide a stochastic framework for equations (24).
We do this by appending classical additive disturbances to each of the five
equations in the model. These disturbances arise either as a result of
random error in the maximizing behavior of police administrators, or as a
result of the fact that the translog function provides only an approximation
of the "true" underlying production structure. We assume that noncontemporaneous disturbances are uncorrelated both within and across equations. We
make no other assumptions about the distribution of disturbances other than
they be uncorrelated with right hand variables in each equation.[25]

Empirical Results

   We have fitted the five equations of system (24) under the stochastic
specification outlined above. There were 125 observations available for
estimating each equation in the system. Since no assumption has been made
concerning the distribution of disturbances, our estimation procedure may
be thought of as multiequation, nonlinear least squares. In the computations we used the Gauss-Newton method to locate minima. The results of all
estimations that are conditional upon cost minimization are presented in
Table II. We have not reported the parameter estimates for the unrestricted
model, although the results are discussed below.

   The estimates reported in column two contain no restrictions other than
than symmetry and homogeneity of C* in input prices and entails estimating

_____

[25]The latter is in fact a rather strong assumption which may be
eliminated by using a set of instrumental variables to generate "predicted"
values of y_i, say $\hat{y}_i$, and then replacing y_i with $\hat{y}_i$ when estimating system
(24).

M.N. DARROUGH and J.M. HEINEKE

TABLE II. PARAMETER ESTIMATES FOR FOUR COST MODELS[26]
(CONDITIONAL UPON COST MINIMIZATION)

Parameter	Symmetry & Homogeneity	Symmetry & Homogeneity & Nonjoint Outputs	Symmetry & Homogeneity & Linear Logarithmic Costs	Symmetry & Homogeneity & Constant Returns to Scale
a_0	-114.974 (33.466)	5.150 (4.201)	-4.469 (1.092)	-.5043 (1.307)
a_1	-.0606 (.0166)	-.0794 (.0075)	.0292 (.0016)	.0171 (.0021)
a_2	-.0068 (.0039)	-.0053 (.0011)	.0065 (.0003)	.0088 (.0007)
a_3	-.0724 (.0216)	-.0771 (.0086)	.0459 (.0026)	.0653 (.0031)
a_4	-.0327 (.0100)	-.0376 (.0035)	.0198 (.0009)	.0102 (.0013)
a_5	-1.944 (1.210)	-.4885 (1.136)	.2448 (.0376)	.4338 (.3991)
a_6	19.080 (5.291)	.1020 (.0722)	.9113 (.0902)	.4646 (.3992)
b	1	1	1	1
α_{11}	.0246 (.0020)	.0235 (.0016)		.0214 (.0015)
α_{22}	.0033 (.0004)	.0031 (.0004)		.0032 (.0004)
α_{33}	.0293 (.0024)	.0298 (.0023)		.0199 (.0020)
α_{44}	.0126 (.0009)	.0127 (.0008)		.0117 (.0007)
α_{55}	.0191 (.0524)	-.0028 (.0535)		.0313 (.0607)
α_{66}	-1.461 (.4214)	.0308 (.0468)		.0313 (.0607)
α_{12}	-.0020 (.0006)	-.00042 (.00009)		-.0027 (.0005)
α_{13}	-.0064 (.0017)	-.00613 (.00075)		-.0123 (.0015)
α_{14}	-.0048 (.0010)	-.00299 (.00034)		-.0063 (.0008)
α_{23}	-.0003 (.0005)	-.00041 (.00009)		-.0013 (.0004)
α_{24}	.0013 (.0004)	-.00020 (.00004)		.0008 (.0003)
α_{34}	-.0028 (.0010)	-.00290 (.00037)		-.0062 (.0008)
α_{56}	.1501 (.0997)	.04984 (.09617)		-.0313 (.0607)

[26]Standard errors are in parentheses.

twenty parameters. Given the primarily cross section nature of the data, the model fits quite well with R^2 figures of .72 for the cost function and .35, .13, .30 and .27 for the value of solution equations $P_i y_i / C^*$, $i = 1,2,3,4$, respectively.

In columns three, four and five are reported parameter estimates for the cases of nonjoint outputs, linear logarithmic costs and constant returns to scale, each conditional on the cost minimization hypothesis. Column three contains our estimates of the translog production structure when nonjointness of outputs is imposed. These restrictions reduce the number of parameters which must be directly estimated to thirteen. (See equations (17).) The linear logarithmic cost function (column four) was estimated primarily to contrast the functional form of the cost function presented in this paper with that implied by the linear logarithmic production functions which have been estimated in the majority of earlier papers.[27] The total number of parameters to be estimated is now reduced to seven. The final column contains our estimate of the model with constant returns to scale imposed.

Our tests of the various hypotheses which have been discussed are based upon the test statistic

(25) $\lambda = \max L^R / \max L^{\bar{R}}$

where $\max L^R$ is the maximum value of the likelihood function for the model with restrictions R and $\max L^{\bar{R}}$ is the maximum value of the likelihood function without restriction. Minus twice the logarithm of λ is

---

[27]Recall that a linear logarithmic production function is self dual and hence implies a cost function of the same functional form.

asymptotically distributed as chisquared with number of degrees of freedom
equal to the number of restrictions imposed. Logarithms of the likelihood
function are given in Table III for each of the model specifications to be
evaluated. Throughout we choose a critical region based upon the .01
level of significance.

We now report the results of statistical tests performed on the estimated models. As we noted previously, the model was estimated in unrestricted form conditional only upon the maintained hypothesis of functional
separability of property crime solutions from other police activities. We
have contrasted this specification with the model implied by cost minimization (i.e., the model with symmetry and linear homogeneity of input prices
imposed). Our interest here of course lies in determining whether our
sample is consistent with cost minimization (or more generally with value
maximization). Without the minimization (or maximization) hypothesis the
"share" equations of system (24) above are interpreted as the average
(observed) value of property crime solutions as functions of solution
activity levels and as a proportion of total agency budgets.

Symmetry and linear homogeneity in input prices impose fifteen
restrictions in addition to those imposed by the functional separability
of property crime solutions from all other police activity. The $\chi^2_{.01}$
critical value is 30.58. As is evident from Table III, minus twice the
logarithm of the likelihood ratio falls far into the critical region of
the test. Our sample appears to be inconsistent with cost minimizing
(and consequently value maximizing) behavior on the part of police
decision makers. Nonetheless, as we have indicated earlier, we will
proceed with all other tests conditional upon the cost minimization
hypothesis. We have chosen this approach due first to the fact that the

TABLE III. ESTIMATED VALUES OF THE LOGARITHM OF THE LIKELIHOOD FUNCTION[28]

Model	Ln of Likelihood Function	Functional Separability Imposed[29]				
		Aggregate	Ln of Likelihood Function	Aggregate	Ln of Likelihood Function
Unrestricted	1,696.65	(y_1,y_2), (y_3,y_4)	1,610.48	(y_1,y_3,y_4)	1,625.19
Symmetry and Homogeneity in Input Prices	1,633.58	(y_1,y_3), (y_2,y_4)	1,612.21	(y_2,y_3,y_4)	1,611.41
Nonjointness	1,620.66	(y_1,y_4), (y_2,y_3)	1,618.59		
Linear Log-arithmic Costs	1,483.57	(y_1,y_2,y_3)	1,612.90		
Constant Returns to Scale	1,600.13	(y_1,y_2,y_4)	1,626.77		

[28]All entries under Logarithm of Likelihood Function in Table III conditional upon symmetry and homogeneity in input costs except the entry for "Unrestricted."

[29]See footnote 24 above.

translog cost function is but an approximation to the true cost structure

and hence in this sense our test result is only approximate; second, due

to the fact that our maintained hypothesis of functional separability of

property crime solutions from all other police activity is a strong

assumption and could possibly have distorted the result of our test;

third, due to the fact that average values transferred may not accurately

reflect departmental evaluation of outputs; and forth, due to the fact

that we are uncertain as to the power of the likelihood ratio test in

finite samples. Finally we note that past studies indicate that tests of

the symmetry restriction tend to be very difficult to pass. Any one of

these factors could cause us to reject the structure implied by cost

minimization when in fact it is true. Of course, still another and

perhaps more fundamental reason for proceeding conditional upon cost

minimziation is the lack of interpretation and the shallowness of expla-

nation one must be content with once the behavioral hypotheses underlying

equation systems are abandoned.

Conditional upon cost minimization we next test the validity of the

hypothesis of nonjoint outputs--a hypothesis which has been maintained in

a great many past studies. Munus twice the logarithm of the likelihood

ratio is 25.84. Since nonjointness entails seven additional restrictions,

the hypothesis is easily rejected. We conclude that one may not go about

estimating separate production functions or separate cost functions for

each of the outputs of police agencies. The interaction between outputs

must be accounted for if one is to adequately characterize the structure

of cost and production in this "industry."

It is instructive to contrast the linear logarithmic cost and

production structure implied by these data, with our more general model.

Columns two and four of Table II contain parameter estimates for the two cost models of interest in this test. The linear logarithmic specification is overwhelmingly rejected. The fact that twice the logarithm of the likelihood ratio for this test is 300.02 is an accurate indication of the magnitude of the loss in explanatory power resulting from adopting the Cobb-Douglass functional form for C*.

We next test the hypothesis that the underlying production function exhibits constant returns to scale. The logarithm of the likelihood function associated with this model is reported in Table III. According to equation (21) above, linear homogeneity in outputs imposes seven additional restrictions on the model.[30] The value of the test statistic is 66.90 and hence these data lend no support to the constant returns hypothesis.[31]

Parameter estimates for the models associated with each of the ten possible output aggregates are presented in Table IV with corresponding logarithms of likelihood functions tabulated in Table III. As above, we test these restrictions conditional on the validity of the cost minimization hypothesis. To begin our tests we choose the prospective aggregate (y_1, y_2, y_4) with the largest likelihood function. Minus twice the logarithm of the likelihood ratio is 13.62 in this case. Since there are only three additional restrictions the chisquare (.01) critical value is 11.34 and functional separability of burglary, robbery and larceny

---

[30] Symmetry of the α_{ij} reduces the restrictions in (21) from thirteen to seven. Recall that $\gamma_i = 0$ is already imposed.

[31] According to Table V, returns to scale at the sample mean are $1/\varepsilon = .923$ which turns out to be not significantly different from one. Obviously this does not imply constant returns to scale throughout the relevant output region.

TABLE IV. PARAMETER ESTIMATES: LINEAR HOMOGENEITY, SYMMETRY AND FUNCTIONAL SEPARABILITY IMPOSED[32]

Parameter	Potential Output Aggregates						
	(y_1,y_2) or (y_3,y_4)	(y_1,y_3) or (y_2,y_4)	(y_1,y_4) or (y_2,y_3)	(y_1,y_2,y_3)	(y_1,y_2,y_4)	(y_1,y_3,y_4)	(y_2,y_3,y_4)
a_0	-89.877 (7.299)	-98.632 (7.314)	-104.181 (7.357)	-94.451 (7.289)	-106.927 (7.385)	-107.259 (7.406)	-99.692 (32.993)
a_1	-.1225 (.0137)	-.1339 (.0129)	-.0730 (.0171)	-.1275 (.0122)	-.0698 (.0170)	.0669 (.0163)	-.1296 (.0140)
a_2	-.0076 (.0032)	-.0161 (.0036)	-.0088 (.0027)	-.0095 (.0032)	-.0101 (.0039)	-.0083 (.0023)	-.0161 (.0036)
a_3	-.1256 (.0167)	-.1290 (.0171)	-.1253 (.0160)	-.1230 (.0170)	-.1268 (.0156)	-.0804 (.0205)	-.1287 (.0176)
a_4	-.0655 (.0077)	-.0767 (.0082)	-.0402 (.0098)	-.0702 (.0073)	-.0407 (.0100)	-.0359 (.0095)	-.0731 (.0082)
a_5	-1.746 (1.026)	-1.882 (1.030)	-2.093 (1.038)	-1.734 (1.025)	-1.764 (1.039)	-2.187 (1.042)	-1.954 (1.195)
a_6	15.321 (.5877)	16.798 (.5891)	17.615 (.5939)	16.037 (.5870)	17.873 (.5945)	18.059 (.5964)	16.979 (5.219)
b	1.0	1.0	1.0	1.0	1.0	1.0	1.0
α_{11}	.0213 (.0018)	.0257 (.0019)	.0190 (.0017)	.0262 (.0020)	.0214 (.0017)	.0229 (.0019)	.0214 (.0018)
α_{22}	.0035 (.0004)	.0029 (.0003)	.0028 (.0004)	.0033 (.0004)	.0034 (.0004)	.0024 (.0003)	.0030 (.0004)
α_{33}	.0287 (.0022)	.0318 (.0023)	.0267 (.0023)	.0310 (.0023)	.0266 (.0023)	.0298 (.0024)	.0300 (.0022)
α_{44}	.0125 (.0009)	.0118 (.0093)	.0123 (.0008)	.0115 (.0009)	.0123 (.0008)	.0126 (.0009)	.0129 (.0009)

TABLE IV. PARAMETER ESTIMATES: LINEAR HOMOGENEITY, SYMMETRY AND FUNCTIONAL SEPARABILITY IMPOSED (CONTINUED)

Parameter	Potential Output Aggregates						
	(y_1,y_2) or (y_3,y_4)	(y_1,y_3) or (y_2,y_4)	(y_1,y_4) or (y_2,y_3)	(y_1,y_2,y_3)	(y_1,y_2,y_4)	(y_1,y_3,y_4)	(y_2,y_3,y_4)
α_{55}	.0176 (.0512)	.0211 (.0514)	.0123 (.0519)	.0235 (.0511)	.0159 (.0518)	.0162 (.0521)	.0152 (.0517)
α_{66}	-1.172 (.4224)	-1.293 (.4201)	-1.361 (*)	-1.226 (*)	-1.367 (.4182)	-1.395 (*)	-1.310 (.4158)
α_{12}	-.0010 (.0005)			-.0010 (.0006)	0.0020 (.0005)		
α_{13}		-.0043 (.0015)		-.0048 (.0015)		-.0066 (.0017)	
α_{14}			-.0049 (.0009)		-.0060 (.0009)	-.0038 (.0010)	
α_{23}			-.0003 (.0004)	.0004 (.0004)			-.0005 (.0004)
α_{24}		.0005 (.0004)			.0013 (.0004)		.0009 (.0004)
α_{34}	-.0019 (.0008)					-.0022 (.0010)	-.0022 (.0008)
α_{56}	.1339 (.0873)	.1423 (.0876)	.1634 (.0883)	.1301 (.0872)	.1368 (.0883)	.1695 (.0887)	.1509 (.0984)

*Collinearity problems prevented estimates of this standard error.

[32]Standard errors are in parentheses.

solutions from the remaining outputs and from input prices is narrowly

rejected. Perusal of Table III indicates that all other potential aggre-

gates are rejected. Our sample does not support the existence of a

category function for any aggregate.

Although the sufficient conditions for consistent aggregation of

outputs via homothetic separability are not met, another possibility for

consistent aggregation remains--the values for y_1, y_2 and y_4, (P_1, P_2, P_4),

(or for that matter, the values of any subgroup of (y_1, y_2, y_3, y_4)) are

perfectly correlated. (See *Theorem 4* and the *Hicks' aggregation Theorem*

above.) We have calculated the correlation matrix for P to check for the

possibily of a Hicksian aggregate. The correlations are r_{12} = .065,

r_{13} = .065, r_{14} = .901, r_{23} = .197, r_{24} = .014 and r_{34} = 0.026. (Of

course, such calculations permit testing only pairwise groupings of out-

puts in the first step.) The question here is whether .901 is significantly

different from 1.0. It is not possible to test this proposition as the

distribution of the sample correlation coefficient is degenerate at 1.0.

However, .901 seems distant enough from 1.0 to conclude that y_1 and y_4

may not be treated as a single output. We conclude that the data in our

semple does not support the existence of a consistent output aggregate.

Hence future efforts directed to estimating cost and production functions

for law enforcement should attempt to determine the appropriateness of

summing police outputs into aggregates prior to using such measures.[33]

---

[33]The hypotheses of nonjoint production, linear logarithmic costs,
constant returns to scale and functional separability of the several
aggregates were also tested against the unrestricted model. In each
case these hypotheses were rejected.

Marginal Costs, Rates of Transformation and Returns to Scale

The marginal cost function for activity i is given by $\partial C^*/\partial y_i =$ $(\partial \ln C^*/\partial \ln y_i)(C^*/y_i)$, $i = 1,2,3,4,5$, and may be calculated using the formula

$$(26) \quad \partial \hat{C}^*/\partial y_i = (a_i + \sum_1^6 \alpha_{ij}\ln y_j + \gamma_i \ln w)(e^{\ln C^*}/y_i) \, , \quad i = 1,2,\ldots,5.$$

As indicated, (26) will be valid for each of the crime solving outputs, $y_1, y_2, \ldots, y_5$ but not for y_6. Recall that the sixth output was an aggregate of the "non-crime solving" services provided by police. Since we have postulated only that the production of this output is proportional to population size, it will be possible to determine $\partial C^*/\partial y_6$ only up to this factor of proportionality.

The rate of transformation of output i for output j gives the number of solutions to crimes of type i which must be forgone for an additional solution to a crime of type j, given fixed levels of all other outputs. Formally, the rate of transformation between outputs i and j may be written as $-\partial y_i/\partial y_j = (\partial C^*/\partial y_j)/(\partial C^*/\partial y_i)$, $i,j = 1,2,\ldots,5$, $i \neq j$, and may be calculated using the formula

$$(27) \quad -\frac{\partial y_i}{\partial y_j} = \frac{(a_j + \sum_1^6 \alpha_{jk}\ln y_k + \gamma_j \ln w)y_i}{(a_i + \sum_1^6 \alpha_{ik}\ln y_k + \gamma_i \ln w)y_j} \, , \quad i,j = 1,2,\ldots,5,, \; i \neq j$$

As with marginal cost functions, it will not be possible to obtain transformation rates between output six and other outputs.

Traditional measures of scale economies (or diseconomies) are predicated on the single output firm and must be modified for use here. We measure scale economies as the inverse of the percentage response of costs to a small equal percentage change in all outputs. That is, if

(28) $\varepsilon \equiv dC*/C* = \sum_{1}^{6} (\partial \ln C*/\partial \ln y_i)(dq/q)$,

where dq/q is the percentage change in outputs, then $1/\varepsilon$ is the usual measure of economies of scale.[34] ε measures the percentage response of costs to an equal percentage change in all solutions and in the service output.[35]

Defining average cost functions for the various outputs presents something of a problem in the case of multiple output production structures. We have calculated the average cost of solutions of type i by evaluating

(29) $[C*(\bar{y}_1,\ldots,\bar{y}_i,\ldots,\bar{y}_6,\bar{w}) - C*(\bar{y}_1,\ldots,\min y_i,\ldots,\bar{y}_6,\bar{w})]/(\bar{y}_i - \min y_i)$

where an overbar indicates a sample mean and min y_i is the minimum sample value of y_i.[36] This approach holds input prices and all outputs, except y_i, constant and yields the average value of the increment in costs over the region between the minimum value of y_i and the mean of y_i.

In Table V we have evaluated the cost responsiveness function, ε, marginal cost functions, average cost functions and marginal rates of transformation between outputs at sample means.

We find that estimated marginal costs are lowest for solving larcenies

---

[34] E.g., if $dq/q = 1$, and $\varepsilon < 1$ at y*, then the production function exhibits increasing returns to scale at the output mix y*, etc.

[35] The proportionality between population size and y_6 causes no problem in calculating returns to scale since the percentage change in y_6 is equal to the percentage change in population size.

[36] $C*(y,w) \equiv e^{\ln C*(y,w)}$

TABLE V.   MARGINAL AND AVERAGE COSTS OF OUTPUTS, RATES OF TRANSFORMATION
AND COST RESPONSIVENESS FUNCTIONS AT SAMPLE MEANS[37]

MC_1 \$ 786.70	AC_1 \$ 662.80	MRT_{12} .743	MRT_{24} .605
MC_2 \$ 584.89	AC_2 \$ 720.34	MRT_{13} 3.82	MRT_{25} 12.94
MC_3 \$3,065.29	AC_3 \$ 3,367.77	MRT_{14} .449	MRT_{34} .115
MC_4 \$ 353.94	AC_4 \$ 332.87	MRT_{15} 9.62	MRT_{35} 2.47
MC_5 \$7,569.61	AC_5 \$13,097.40	MRT_{23} 5.24	MRT_{45} 21.39
			ε 1.083

at \$353, followed by those for robbery at \$584, burglary at \$786, motor
vehicle solutions at \$3,065 and solutions to crimes against the person at
\$7,569.[38]

Rates of transformation between outputs at sample means range from
.11 between motor vehicle theft solutions and larceny solutions to twenty-
one between larceny solutions and solutions to crimes against the person.
Hence, the estimated cost function predicts that on average it will be
necessary to forego between eight and nine larceny solutions to solve one
additional motor vehicle theft (at the mean) and approximately twenty-one
larceny solutions to solve an additional crime against the person.

----

[37]Standard errors were calculated for ε and for marginal cost functions at this point. Each was highly significant at the .01 level.

[38]Of course the model insures that "on average" marginal costs are
equal to values stolen. Notice that this does not imply that marginal
costs evaluated at the mean are equal "on average" to values transferred.
More importantly, our interest in this study is primarily in the structure
of law enforcement production technology and hence not local properties of
marginal and average cost functions.

Similar interpretations hold for the other transformation rates.

Unit costs of clearing larcenies are $332, followed by burglary at $662, robbery at $720, motor vehicle solutions at $3,367 and solutions to crimes against the person at $13,097. Comparing marginal cost estimates with associated average costs, indicates that marginal costs of solving robberies, auto thefts and crimes against the person are below average costs and hence unit costs are falling (at the sample mean) for these activities. Marginal costs are greater than average costs for solving burglaries and larcenies, indicating rising unit costs (at the sample mean) for these activities.

We have estimated the value of ε to be 1.083, which turns out to be not significantly different from unity. But as Figure 1 indicates, scale economies vary greatly over the sample with decreasing, then constant, then increasing returns to scale as output levels increase. Sample values of ε range from 1.62 to .53. To the extent that small cities have low solution levels, it appears that "large" cities have technological advantages in the provision of police services.

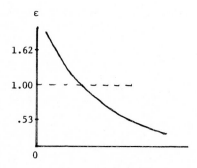

Figure 1

Cost Responses: All Police Activities

In interpreting this finding one should keep in mind that the cities in our sample range in size from approximately one third million to only a little over one million. Therefore one should not conclude that very large American cities experience increasing returns to scale in the provision of police services, since scale diseconomies may appear as city size continues to increase.[39]

Summary and Conclusions

In this paper we have adopted the economic model of an optimizing firm as a framework for characterizing the production structure of a sample of medium sized U.S. law enforcement agencies. Unlike previous studies we have begun with a second order approximation to an arbitrary multi-output-multi-input production possibilities function. This rather general functional specification has permitted us to test a number of hypotheses which have been implicitly maintained in earlier work. Of particular interest are the findings that, at least in our sample, the decisions of police administrators seem to be inconsistent with cost minimization. We also rejected the hypothesis of nonjoint production. If this result is upheld in future studies, and there seems to be reason

---

[39]In the past few years there has been considerable discussion concerning the share of the total police budget going to non-crime solving activities. All parties seem to agree that the share is high and has been increasing. For example, unpublished studies by the Vera Institute of Justice and the Cincinnati Institute of Justice indicate that police officers spend only about 15 to 20 percent of their time in crime solving activities. To provide additional information on this point, we have calculated $AC_6(\bar{y},\bar{w}) \cdot \bar{y}_6 / C(\bar{y},\bar{w})$ to measure the budget share of activity six--non-crime solving activities. (This calculation assumes that unit costs of these police services are approximately constant up to $\bar{y}_6$. See equation (29) above.) We find that the budget share of non-crime solving activities is slightly more than 80 percent at the sample mean--a result strikingly consistent with the stidies mentioned.

to suspect that it will be, estimation of separate production and/or cost
functions for the different outputs of police agencies is effectively
precluded. In addition, we strongly rejected the hypothesis of constant
returns to scale and found that scale economies varied considerably with
activity levels--which in turn pointed up the inappropriateness of maintaining a Cobb-Douglas production structure in studies of law enforcement
production technology. We also found that our sample did not support the
existence of a consistent index for any one of the possible sub-aggregates
of outputs. This finding makes explicit that the usual aggregation of all
police outputs into one measure is accompanied by a loss of information.
All tests of functional structure were performed conditional on cost
minimizing behavior, although the same results are forthcoming in tests
against the unrestricted model.

Finally, we calculated returns to scale, marginal costs, average
costs and marginal rates of transformation at the sample mean. As always
much work remains to be done. Among the more challenging and potentially
promising tasks is to disaggregate the "crimes against the person" output
and to incorporate these variables directly into the decision problem
underlying estimation. Initial work in this area seems to indicate that
unit costs for clearing homicides are an order of magnitude greater than
that of any other police activity.

University of Santa Clara

REFERENCES

Annual General Administrative Survey, prepared by Kansas City Police
Department for limited circulation, 1968, 1969, 1971, 1973.

Berndt, E. R., and L. R. Christensen, "The Translog Function and the
Substitution of Equipment, Structures and Labor in U.S. Manufacturing
1929-68," Journal of Econometrics, pp. 81-113, 1974.

Blackorby, C., D. Primont and R. Russell, "Dual Price and Quantity
Aggregation," Journal of Economic Theory, 14, pp. 130-48, 1977.

Blackorby, D., D. Primont and R. Russell, "On Testing Separability
Restrictions with Flexible Functional Forms," Journal of Econometrics,
1977, vol. 5, pp. 195-209.

Chapman, J. I., W. Z. Hirsch and S. Sonenblum, "Crime Prevention, the
Police Production Function and Budgeting," Public Finance, Vol. XXX,
no. 2, 1975, pp. 197-215.

Christensen, L. R., D. W. Jorgensen and L. J. Lau, "Conjugate Duality and
the Transcendental Logarithmic Production Function," Econometrica,
39, pp. 255-56, 1971.

Christensen, L. R., D. W. Jorgensen and L. J. Lau, "Transcendental
Logarithmic Production Frontiers," Review of Economics and Statistics,
55, pp. 28-45, 1973.

Christensen, L. R., D. W. Jorgensen and L. J. Lau, "Transcendental Logarithmic Utility Functions," American Economic Review, 65, pp. 367-83,
1975.

Diewert, W. E., "Aggregation Problems in the Measurement of Capital."
Paper presented to the Conference on Research in Income and Wealth,
National Bureau of Economic Research, Toronto, 1977.

Diewert, W. E., "Applications of Duality Theory," in Frontiers of Quantitative Economics, Volume II, eds. M. Intriligator and D. A. Kendrick,
North Holland Publishing Co., 1974.

Diewert, W. E., "An Application of the Shephard Duality Theorem: A
Generalized Leontief Production Function," Journal of Political
Economy, 79, pp. 481-507, 1971.

Diewert, W. E., "Separability and a Generalization of the Cobb Douglas
Cost, Production and Indirect Utility Functions," Technical Report
No. 86, IMSSS, Stanford University, 1973.

Ehrlich, I., Participation in Illegitimate Activities: An Economic
Analysis. Unpublished dissertation, Columbia University, 1970.

Ehrlich, I., "Participation in Illegitimate Activities: An Economic Analysis," in Essays in the Economics of Crime and Punishment, edited by G. Becker and W. Landes, NBER, 1975.

Ehrlich, I., "Participation in Illegitimate Activities: A Theoretical and Empirical Analysis," Journal of Political Economy, 81, pp. 521-67, 1973.

Goldman, S., and H. Uzawa, "A Note on Separability in Demand Analysis," Econometrica, 32, pp. 387-98, 1964.

Hall, R. E., "The Specification of Technology with Several Kinds of Output," Journal of Political Economy, 81, pp. 878-92, 1973.

Hicks, J. R., Value and Capital, Oxford: 2nd ed., Clarendon Press, 1946.

Jorgensen, D. W., and L. J. Lau, "The Structure of Consumer Preferences," Annals of Economic and Social Measurement, 4/1, 1975, pp. 49-101.

Lau, L. J., "Applications of Duality Theory: A Comment," in M. P. Intriligator and D. A. Kendricks, eds., Frontiers in Quantitative Economics, Vol. II, North-Holland, 1974.

Phillips, L., and H. L. Votey, "Crime Control in California," Journal of Legal Studies, June 1975, Vol. IV, no. 2, pp. 327-49.

Popp, D. O., and F. D. Sebold, "Quasi Returns to Scale in the Provision of Police Service," Public Finance, Vol. 27, no.11, pp. 1-18, 1972.

Shephard, R. W., Cost and Production Functions, Princeton University Press, 1953.

Strotz, R. H., "The Empirical Implication of a Utility Tree," Econometrica, April 1957, pp. 269-80.

U. S. Department of Justice, Federal Bureau of Investigation, Uniform Crime Reports for the U.S., Printed Annually from 1933, Washington, D.C., Government Printing Office.

U.S. Department of Labor, Bureau of Labor Statistics, Family Budgets, Annual, Washington, D.C. Government Printing Office.

Vandaele, Walter, "The Economics of Crime: An Econometric Investigation of Auto Theft in the United States," unpublished Ph.D. dissertation, University of Chicago, 1975.

Votey, H. L., and L. Phillips, "Police Effectiveness and the Production Function for Law Enforcement," Journal of Legal Studies, Vol. 1, 1972, pp. 423-36.

Walzer, Norman, "Economies of Scale and Municipal Police Services: The Illinois Experience," Review of Economics and Statistics, Vol. 54, no. 2, 1972, pp. 431-38.

Wilson, James Q., and Barbara Boland, "The Effect of Police on Crime Rates," Urban Institute Working Paper, April, 1977.

Economic Models of Criminal Behavior,
J.M. Heineke (ed.)
© *North-Holland Publishing Company, 1978*

CHAPTER EIGHT

AN ECONOMETRIC MODEL OF AUTO THEFT IN THE UNITED STATES

Walter Vandaele[1]

1. Introduction

In this paper we develop an industry supply and demand model of the
economics of crime. The model is not restricted to one particular crime
category; it is sufficiently general to be relevant to many types of
crime. The model is empirically tested with U.S. annual data on auto
theft, and used both for forecasting and for policy implementations.

In developing the model we built on previous work by Becker (1968)
and Ehrlich (1970, 1972, 1973, 1975b), but constructed the model as an
economic industry supply and demand model with a market for factors of
production, including illegal labor services, a production sector that
produces illegal goods and services, and a product market for these goods
and services. A crime prevention sector is also included in the model.

The pioneering article that forms the basis for this work and for
the work of several others is Becker (1968), "Crime and Punishment: An

[1]This paper is based on my Ph.D. dissertation (Vandaele 1975). I
would like to thank the members of my thesis committee: A. Zellner
(chairman), G. S. Becker, and P. Pashigian. Helpful comments were also
received from L. Benham, I. Ehrlich, J. M. Heineke, B. Landes, G. Lewis,
M. Nerlove, S. Peltzman, M. Reid, G. W. Schwert, R. Smith, and G. Stigler.
The preparation of this paper was partly facilitated by the Belgian American
Educational Foundation, the Ford Foundation, the Belgian National Science
Foundation (National Fonds voor Wetenschappelijk Onderzoek), the H.G.B.
Alexander Research Foundation, the National Science Foundation under grants
GS-2347, GS-40033 and SOC76-15546, the National Bureau of Economic Research,
and the Division of Research, Graduate School of Business Administration,
Harvard University.

Economic Approach," in which, using a cost-benefit approach, he answered
the question: "[H]ow many offenses *should* be permitted and how many
offenders *should* go unpunished?"[2] The desire to participate in illegitimate activities is treated within the same framework as the desire to
participate in legitimate activities, except that persons consider the
risk of punishment associated with illegitimate activities. Several
economists investigated empirically the relationship between criminal
and other income-yielding activities. The first major publications
analyzing the effects of economic variables, such as income and employment,
on juvenile delinquency were written by Fleisher (1963, 1966a, 1966b).
Smigel-Leibowitz (1965) and Ehrlich (1967, 1970, 1973) used cross-sectional
data to analyze the supply of illegitimate activities of seven index crimes.[3]
Church (1970), Press (1971), Swimmer (1972, 1974), Ozenne (1972, 1974),
Phillips, Votey, Jr., and Maxwell (1972), Bartel (1974, 1975), Heineke
(1978), and Landes (1978), also deal with an empirical analysis of crime.
For a review of some of this literature and some additional references,
see Palmer (1977) and Nagin (1978).

   Ehrlich's (1975b) capital punishment paper led to several other
publications evaluating capital punishment as well as other deterrents.
For a survey and an evaluation of this literature, see the National
Academy of Sciences report of the Panel on Research on Deterrent and
Incapacitative Effects (Blumstein, et al., eds., 1978). For more recent
work on capital punishment, see Ehrlich (1977).

   Most of the works noted above used U.S. data. Data for other countries

---

[2]Becker (1968), p. 170

[3]The FBI index crimes are murder, rape, assault, robbery, burglary,
larceny and auto theft.

have been used in Ahamad (1967), Robert and Bombet (1970), Zeegers (1971),
Carr-Hill and Stern (1971, 1973), Avio and Clark (1976), and Wolpin (1977),
among others.

Although different studies asked different questions, many of the
empirical studies mentioned above share a major defect: They develop only
partial analyses. Most of the studies do not take interdependence into
account. For example, in most of the studies the probability of arrest
is treated as an exogenous variable. However, probability of arrest
influences protection expenditures, which are in turn influenced by the
crime index. Neglecting this simultaneity will generally lead to biased
and inconsistent estimates of the parameters. More important, the neglect
of this and other interdependencies can result in misleading and incorrect
conclusions.

In this paper we will develop a simultaneous equation model for the
economics of crime. In section 2 we derive and analyze a theoretical
economic model of crime along the lines of a standard industry supply
and demand model. Estimates for the auto theft model are obtained and
discussed in section 3. In that section we also present model forecasts,
both within and outside the sample period. Section 4 contains some policy
uses of the model.

2. The Economic Model of Crime

Our economic model of crime is analogous to an economic industry
supply and demand model. It is formulated in real terms with product and
factor markets, but is augmented with a crime prevention sector. The
theoretical analysis is not restricted to one particular crime category
since the model is general enough to be relevant to many types of crime.

However, we pay particular attention to auto theft, the crime analyzed
empirically.

Figure 1 represents the simultaneous equation model of the crime
sector. At the upper right of the figure is the demand for the illegal
product. In the product market this demand will generate a supply of an
illegal product. Influences emanating from the crime prevention sector
will affect the interaction of supply and demand. Given a certain level
of illegal activity in the product market, a criminal could be arrested
and convicted -- there is a probability of unsuccessful illegal transaction --
and, if convicted, he could receive a fine ranging from incarceration to
a monetary fine.[4] Therefore the probability of unsuccessful illegal transaction and the fine, denoted by π_1 and f_1 respectively, will influence the
product market, but at the same time will be influenced by the level of
criminal activity.

In the production sector illegal labor time and capital service[5] will
be used to produce the final product. The crime per se constitutes a major
part of the production sector activities. Again, there is an interaction
with the prevention sector, as the criminal can be arrested while producing
the final product--for example, a thief can be arrested while stealing a
car. Furthermore, the activity level in the production sector will have a

---

[4]For a discussion of conditions under which prison sentences may be
expressed in monetary equivalents, see Block and Heineke (1975) and in
particular Block and Lind (1975a, 1975b). In particular, if the individual
contemplating the commission of a crime has a wealth only equal to the required subsistence level to sustain a free man over his lifetime, a monetary
equivalent does not exist. This does not imply that for such an individual
a fine is incapable of deterring the crime. In our analysis, we will assume
that monetary equivalents do exist.

[5]To keep Figure 1 simple, we have omitted capital services.

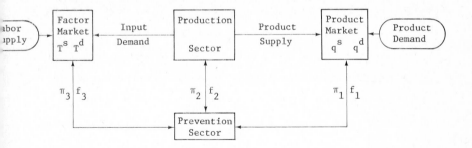

Symbols

T^s =   supply of illegal labor time,

T^d =   demand for illegal labor time,

q^s =   supply of illegal product,

q^d =   demand for illegal product,

π_1, π_2, π_3 =   probability of unsuccessful illegal transaction in the product market, of unsuccessful activity in the crime production sector, and of unsuccessful operations in the factor market, respectively,

f_1, f_2, f_3 =   as with the π's, but f is the fine in the different sectors of the crime economy. The fine can be a monetary fine as well as incarceration.

Fig. 1.--The Crime Industry

feedback effect on its probability of arrest and fine. Finally, the crime
industry model is completed with the factor market. In this market, the
demand for illegal labor interacts with the supply and generates an equilibrium wage rate. The prevention sector also influences this third sector
of the crime model.

The auto theft industry model can be described in broad outline as
follows. Buying and selling of stolen cars takes place in the product
market. Stolen cars are produced in the production sector: auto theft
is an activity of the production sector. In the illegal labor factor
market, those planning to work for the auto theft industry offer their
services to the production sector. The prevention sector interacts with
these three markets: the police can arrest individuals for buying and
selling stolen cars, can apprehend thieves for stealing cars, or can make
raids on places where illegal labor services are transacted.

This is the skeleton of the model. In the next section we explain
the demand equation for an illegal product. In section 2.1.2, the derivation
of the illegal product supply equation is given, along with the derived
demand for labor in the crime industry. Section 2.2 analyzes individuals'
supply of illegal labor to the factor market. Section 2.3 contains the
formulation of the crime prevention sector.

2.1. The Crime Product Market

2.1.1. The Demand for an Illegal Product

The demand curve for the illegal product, be it a stolen radio, a
stolen automobile, heroin, or even murder or rape, is fundamental to all
illegal activities. This demand curve shows the quantity of the illegal

product that will be purchased per unit of time at each price, *ceteris paribus*. In general, the crime per se - a burglary, for example - is not transacted in the product market, but the finished product - a stolen radio - is.

Furthermore, a person supplying an illegal product may be the same one who demands it. Similar phenomena can be found in the economic literature. An example is the new approach to consumer choice, where abandoning the traditional separation between production and consumption makes households producers as well as consumers.

For no reason has the demand for an illegal product to differ fundamentally from that of any legal good, and therefore we postulate that demand theory can be applied to illegal goods. Both legal and illegal goods can be combined with the consumer's own time and other inputs in a household production function to produce a set of basic commodities. We assume that the consumer maximizes the utility derived from different combinations of these commodities, subject to his budget constraint. Therefore, the demand for an illegal good depends on the real price of the illegal product, p, the real prices of commodities closely related to the illegal good, p^c, and real income, y. Specific factors associated with the demand for illegal goods, such as probability of arrest, and conviction and fines, are also entered into the demand equation. A consumer of an illegal good can be arrested and convicted for participating in an illegal transaction. The probability of unsuccessful transactions in the product market, π_1, and the fine when convicted, f_1, are therefore additional variables in the demand function.[6] The fine represents both the monetary fine and the discounted cost of imprisonment.

The demand equation of individual i for an illegal good is summarized
as

$$q_i^d = d_i \ (p, \ p^c, \ y_i, \ \pi_{1i}, \ f_{1i})$$

where q_i^d = quantity of an illegal good demanded per unit of time by the ith
individual; p = real price of the illegal good; p^c = a vector of real prices
of substitutes and complements; y_i = real income of the ith individual; and
π_{1i} = probability of unsuccessful transactions in the product market and
f_{1i} = fine, both π_{1i} and f_{1i} as perceived by the ith individual.

Expressing the demand in per capita terms, we obtain

$$(2.1) \qquad q^d = d \ (p, \ p^c, \ y, \ \pi_1, \ f_1)$$

where q^d = per capita quantity demanded of an illegal product; p = real
price of the illegal product; $p = P/P_o$, with P_o the general price level
and P the nominal price of the illegal product; $p^c = P^c/P_o$ is a vector
of real prices of commodities closely related to the illegal product
where P^c is the vector of nominal prices; $y = Y/P_o$ is the real per capita
income; π_1 = probability of unsuccessful illegal transaction in the
product market; and f_1 = real monetized fine.

---

[6]In this analysis we abstract from the possibility of bribery. For
a discussion of the effects of bribery, see Becker and Stigler (1974),
and Pahigian (1975).
  We refer to Parkin and Wu (1972) for an analysis of the consumer's
choice when faced with an unwanted contingency, that is, when the utility
depends upon the "state of the world" in which the consumer happens to be.
For a theoretical foundation of the conditional expected utility approach,
see Luce and Krantz (1971). This approach differs from an analysis given
in Ehrlich and Becker (1972) where the household "production function
fully incorporates the effects of the environment" (p. 624, fn. 5). The
utility function is therefore independent of the state that occurs.

Since only aggregate data are available for this study, it will be necessary to adopt a set of assumptions which permit an aggregate demand equation. A convenient assumption is that individuals are more or less homogeneous, except for their wealth effects. In general the aggregate demand equation depends on the distribution of income, and not simply on the mean of the distribution. However, under reasonable assumptions it can be shown that a consistent aggregation would lead to an aggregate function depending on the mean of the distribution.[7]

Next, we apply economic theory in discussing the possible algebraic signs of the partial derivatives of (2.1). However, as no empirical study deals with the demand curve for illegal products, we can only make comparisons with the properties of a demand equation for a legal product. *Ceteris paribus*, the price elasticity of demand should be negative. The algebraic signs of the cross price elasticities are determined by the commodities considered. The demand for stolen automobiles depends upon the price of gasoline (complement) and the price of legal cars (substitute). For complements the price elasticity is negative, whereas for substitutes the price elasticity is positive.

For the algrbraic sign of the coefficient of real income, y, it is presumed that the illegal product is a normal good, that is, the quantity consumed increases as income increases. However, it could be argued that the illegal product is an inferior good; as income increases, the quantity consumed decreases. As their incomes increased, people could shift from stolen cars toward legal cars and consume fewer stolen cars, leaving the prices unchanged.

---

[7]One of the assumptions is that if aggregate income changes, each individual will share in the change in proportion to its income. For a more detailed analysis, see Tobin (1950).

2.1.2. The Supply Function of an Illegal Product

One of the important innovations of our model is a production sector, with an illegal product as output. We distinguish between a crime and the result of a crime, the illegal product. The criminal act is looked upon as a product transformation curve that converts labor and capital inputs into the final good, the illegal product.

This production sector can be composed of individual proprietorships, partnerships, corporations, or combinations thereof. The jth firm produces a single illegal product, using as factor inputs illegal labor time, t_j, and capital services, c_j. Also, because the activity is illegal, the probability of an unsuccessful transaction in the crime production sector, π_2, as well as the fine when arrested and convicted for producing illegal goods, f_2, will affect production. With an increase in π_2 and f_2, the crime industry will have to take more precautionary measures in order for its members to be arrested and fined. And so the larger the values of π_2 and f_2, the smaller the output of the production process. Note that we distinguish between the probability of an unsuccessful transaction in the production market, π_1, and that in the crime production sector, π_2.

Let q_j be the quantity of illegal output by the jth firm. The production function is then written as

$$(2.2) \qquad q_j = f_j(c_j, t_j, \pi_2, f_2)$$

where the symbols are defined as in the previous paragraph.

The variables π_2 and f_2 are not under direct control[8] of the jth firm, but act as shift variables in the firm's production function. Also

---

[8] The probability of arrest, π_2, is exogenous with respect to the jth firm, but not with respect to the whole crime industry.

assume that the production function is continuously differentiable at
each point of the economic region of the inputs. Further, these derivatives have the following properties:

$$\frac{\partial f_j(.)}{\partial c_j} \equiv mp_c > 0, \qquad \frac{\partial f_j(.)}{\partial t_j} \equiv mp_t > 0,$$

$$\frac{\partial f_j(.)}{\partial \pi_2} < 0, \qquad \frac{\partial f_j(.)}{\partial f_2} < 0$$

where $f_j(.)$ is short notation for f_j (c_j, t_j, π_2, f_2) and mp_c and mp_t
are the capital and labor time marginal products respectively.

The Derived Demand for Illegal Time

Accepting the postulates of the neoclassical theory of the firm
facing perfect competition in both the product and factor markets, we
obtain the input demand function, the *derived demand function for illegal
time,* as a necessary condition for profit maximization subject to the
production function.[9]

The jth firm has to choose the levels of inputs[10] that will maximize
profit:

$$\max_{t_j} \text{ profit} = Pf_j(t_j, \pi_2, f_2) - Wt_j$$

---

[9]Profit maximization can be replaced by utility maximization. This
utility reflects the decision maker's preferences regarding profit, interest
in nepotism, discrimination, ownership rights. For a review of this matter,
see Furubotn and Pejovich (1972). The firm could also minimize cost subject
to the production function.

[10]To simplify the analysis, we temporarily deleted capital services
from the inputs in the production function. The capital service input is
discussed at the empirical phase.

subject to $t_j \geq 0$. The first order condition is

$$\frac{\partial \text{ profit}}{\partial t_j} = \frac{P \partial f_j(.)}{\partial t_j} - W = 0$$

or

$$\frac{\partial f_j(.)}{\partial t_j} = W/P$$

Solving for t_j, we obtain the derived demand function for illegal time:

$$(2.3) \qquad t_j^d = h_j \ (P, \ W, \ \pi_2, \ f_2)$$

where t_j^d = demand for the illegal time by the jth firm, P = price of the output; W = nominal wage rate paid in the illegal labor market; π_2 = probability of unsuccessful illegal transaction in the crime production sector; and f_2 = real monetized fine for operating in the crime production sector.

Inserting the factor demand function into the production function yields the *output supply function* as a function of output price, input wage rate, probability of arrest and fine:

$$(2.4) \qquad q_j^s = x_j \ (P, \ W, \ \pi_2, \ f_2)$$

In real terms, the two equations become:
the jth firm's product supply curve

$$(2.5) \qquad q_j^s = x_j (p, \ w, \ \pi_2, \ f_2)$$

and the jth firm's derived time demand equation

(2.6) $t_j^d = h_j \ (p, \ w, \ \pi_2, \ f_2).$

Because the industry supply curve is the horizontal sum of the firm's supply curves, the aggregate supply curve with $Q^s = \sum_{j=1}^{\tau} q_j^s$ (τ = total number of firms in the crime industry) is written as

(2.7) $Q^s = x \ (p, \ w, \ \pi_2, \ f_2).$

Similarly, the aggregate derived demand equation for labor is given by

(2.8) $T^d = h \ (p, \ w, \ \pi_2, \ f_2).$

Further discussion of this labor demand equation is presented in section 2.2.1.

2.1.3.   The Market Clearing Equation

The crime product market is cleared with an equilibrium condition that supply equals demand, that is,

(2.9) $Nq^d = Q^s$

where N = population size. The equilibrium price at which the product market is cleared depends on N, the population size. We introduce this variable N explicitly in the aggregate supply curve by writing the supply curve in per capita terms:

(2.10) $q^s = \dfrac{Q^s}{N} = q \ (p, \ w, \ \pi_2, \ f_2, \ N).$

An increase in the price of the final product will, in the short run, *ceteris paribus*, induce a movement along the supply curve and increase the

supply of that product. Furthermore, an increase in the wage rate shifts
the supply curve to the left, that is, decreases the quantity supplied.
Similarly, an increase in the probability of arrest or fine will shift
the supply curve to the left.

2.2.   The Factor Market

The factor market for illegal time is characterized as a standard
competitive labor market of supply and derived demand. Most of the economics
of crime studies to date have developed a supply of illegal time equation and
evaluated behavioral implications of their supply models. However, a labor
demand equation has not been introduced explicitly, although several authors
seem aware of the need for such a demand equation.

In addition, on the supply side the optimal amount of time devoted
to illegal activities was not explicitly connected with the number of illegal
goods produced or the number of crimes committed. Ehrlich (1973) and others
assume   that the amount of time devoted to illegal activities is monotonically
related to the number of offenses one commits. Ozenne (1972, 1974), using
a transfer function between resources devoted to theft (factor inputs) and
the gain to thieves (output) - defined as returns from bank robberies - comes
the closest to our concept of a crime production function. Our model broadens
this analysis.

2.2.1.   The Supply of Illegal Time

The micro-theory of the supply of illegal time has been presented by
Ehrlich (1970, 1972, 1973), using a one-period uncertainty State Preference
model for the optimal allocation of time. Assuming two market activities,
illegal and legal, and with the amount of time allocated to (non-market)

consumption activities fixed, the objective of the individual is to maximize
the expected utility of a one-period consumption prospect associated with
two mutually exclusive "states-of-the-world", with the decision to be made
at the beginning of the period.

Ehrlich's model deals only with a one-period uncertainty. Also, the
State Preference approach analysis does not indicate the exact functional
form of the labor supply equation. An extension introducing more mutually
exclusive "states-of-the-world" and allowing for multiperiod decisions
has to be worked out. For a detailed evaluation of the State Preference
approach as it applies to labor supply to the illegal sector, see Block and
Heineke (1975).

Based on the State Preference analysis, but without justifying the
variables entering the supply equation in much detail from the microeconomic
point of view, we can now write the following aggregate illegal labor
supply equation:

$$(2.11) \quad T^S = g \ (w, \ w_\ell, \ \pi_3, \ f_3)$$

where T^S = time supplied to the illegal market; w = real wage rate in the
illegal labor market; w_ℓ = real wage rate in the legal labor market; π_3 =
probability of arrest and conviction in the illegal factor market; f_3 =
real monetized fine if convicted for operating in the illegal factor market.
Of course, (2.11) is only a general specification of the aggregate supply
equation. The specific aggregation procedure will be spelled out in detail
in Section 3.3.

Because the crime industry is a small sector of the economy, we assume
that w_ℓ is exogenously determined. The unemployment rate for the legal sector
could be an additional variable entering the supply equation, as the legal

earnings are not known with certainty but are influenced by the possibility

of being unemployed.[11] In addition, the relationship (2.11) can contain

other variables that shift the supply function, such as the age distribution

of the population, white-nonwhite population composition, and labor force

participation rate. In the empirical section, the importance of these

variables will be analyzed.

We anticipate that an increase in either π_3 or f_3, with no change

in the other variables entering (2.11), should reduce the incentive to enter

the illegal market as well as the amount of labor time spent there. Similarly,

if the other variables remain constant, a reduction in the return from illegal

activity, w, or an increase in the legal wage rate, w_ℓ, is expected to de-

crease the supply of illegal time.[12]

---

[11] It could also be argued that the probability of being unemployed
in the illegal sector is a variable in the supply equation. We assume that
there is no unemployment in the illegal sector. Similarly, we neglect the
possibility of a backward-bending supply curve of illegal time, assuming
that the substitution effect of the wage rate between leisure and illegal
activity dominates the income effect over the range of available data.

[12] From a theoretical point of view it is not possible to establish
unambiguously the direction of the effect of all variables in (2.11), unless
preferences are strongly restricted. See Block and Heineke (1975), Heineke
(1978). For example, the effect of a change in w is composed of a substitution effect and a wealth effect. Although the direction of the substitution
effect is clear, the final effect on T will depend upon the wealth effect.
See also previous footnote.

2.2.2.   The Market Equilibrium Condition

The market equilibrium condition in the illegal labor market is
the equality of demand and supply:

(2.12) $T^d = T^s$.

This completes the factor market of our crime model. Next we will develop
the crime prevention sector.

2.3.   The Crime Prevention Sector

For a legal product, the product market, the production sector, and
the factor market form a complete industry supply and demand model. However,
dealing in stolen cars is considered illegal.[13] Society's decision to categorize
commodities as legal and illegal implies an attempt to eliminate illegal goods
via public and private protection. A society can finance a public body to prevent the commission of crimes and to arrest and convict criminals for crimes
committed. Individuals can also try personally to protect property and life,
or they can buy insurance in order to minimize the loss due to a crime.[14]

In this section we analyze the aggregate public protection sector[15]

---

[13] The fact that economic agents may not always be aware that
they are transacting illegal goods is of no importance. Indeed, a car dealer
can resell a stolen car as a used car.

[14] In the insurance literature, a distinction is made between
self-insurance - a reduction in the size of a loss - and self-protection -
a reduction in the probability of a loss. For a theoretical analysis of the
demand for insurance, emphasizing the interaction between market insurance,
self-insurance, and self-protection, see Ehrlich and Becker (1972). When we
discuss insurance, we mean market insurance unless explicitly stated otherwise.

[15] For an analogous model of the private protection sector, see
Vandaele (1975). For a general analysis of the choices between private and public
modes of protection, see Clotfelter (1977). Clotfelter illustrates his model
using data for U.S. states in 1970.

but the allocation of public protection across precincts, the structure
of the court system, etc.[16] will not be examined.

The structure of the prevention sector is as follows. Individuals
have a demand for protective services[17] that are produced by the prevention
sector using both labor and capital as factor inputs. These inputs are
characterized as public or private, according to their origin. The probability of arrest and conviction links the protection sector with the
product market.

Therefore, we set up a production function producing protective
services; major factor inputs are the number of police officers and the
capital services used by the police departments. From this production
function we obtain the derived demand for police officers, which is then
combined with the supply function of police officers to obtain a market
equilibrium in this factor market.

---

[16] Individuals must determine how much to spend on the criminal
justice system. Further, the influence of the large number of pretrial
settlements, the bail system or court delay system on the crime index
cannot be disposed of without a careful examination of the data. However,
in our model we assume that the court system is fixed. For an "Economic
Analysis of the Courts" see Landes (1971, 1973). See also Gould (1973),
and Posner (1972).

[17] Rather than assume that households directly value units of publicly
provided goods per se, we claim it to be more realistic to view households
as valuing the ultimate output to which public goods and services contri-
bute. This output is here the level of protective services. For a
similar strategy, see Clotfelter (1977).

2.3.1 The Demand for Police Officers

In modeling the public protection sector, we make the following three assumptions.[18] First, majority rule decides the total amount to be spent on public protection. The platform selected is identical to the optimal position of the median voter. Second, output is produced at minimal cost. And third, we select for mathematical convenience a constant-return-to-scale Cobb-Douglas (CD) production function.[19]

---

[18] See also Borcherding and Deacon (1972), Ohls and Wales (1972).

[19] See Darrough and Heineke (1978) for a more detailed study of the law enforcement output explicitly allowing for multi-output, such as a service output (traffic control, first aid), several property crimes clearances and clearance of crimes against the person. In this study a more flexible functional form is advocated for the production function. However, by estimating a production function for auto theft in isolation from all other crimes, we have implicitly assumed that the output is nonjoint. For a discussion of nonjoint production functions, see Hall (1973). In Darrough and Heineke (1978), empirical evidence is also presented that auto theft cannot be aggregated with other crimes in forming an aggregate index of police department output.

This CD production function can be written as

$$(2.14) \qquad T = \gamma PU^{\alpha} S^{1-\alpha} Z^{\beta}$$

where T = level of protective services; PU = per capita number of police; S = per capita capital services; and Z = a vector[20] of other variables affecting the output of the production function, such as measures of the aggregate crime rate,[21] etc.

Minimizing the costs of providing protection subject to the production function and solving the first-order conditions, we obtain

$$(2.15) \qquad W_p = \frac{\alpha C}{PU} \qquad \text{or} \qquad PU = \frac{\alpha CT}{W_p}$$

$$(2.16) \qquad W_s = \frac{(1-\alpha)CT}{S} \qquad \text{or} \qquad S = \frac{(1-\alpha)CT}{W_s}$$

where C = marginal cost of output, W_p = wage rate for police officers, and W_s = factor price for capital services.

Substituting (2.15) and (2.16) into the production function (2.14), we obtain the marginal cost of protection services

$$(2.17) \qquad C = \gamma^{-1} \left(\frac{W_p}{\alpha}\right)^{\alpha} \left(\frac{W_s}{1-\alpha}\right)^{1-\alpha} Z^{-\beta}.$$

---

[20] The notation Z means $z_1^{\beta_1}, z_2^{\beta_2}, \ldots, z_m^{\beta_m}$, where z_i and β_i are components of the Z and β vectors respectively.

[21] The inclusion of the offense level in a police production function can be justified from two different arguments: because of police resource capacities and because of a so-called "fisheries argument." This argument runs as follows: if the number of offenses is high, then *ceteris paribus*, it should be easier to apprehend a fixed number of criminals than if there are but few offenses. There is, however, considerable debate as to whether the aggregate crime rate belongs in a police production function in general or in a protective services production function in particular. We will come back to this in Section 3.

This expression can also be written as

$$(2.18) \qquad C = \gamma' \; w_p^{\alpha} \; w_s^{(1-\alpha)} \; z^{-\beta}, \; \text{with} \; \gamma' = \left\{ \gamma \alpha^{\alpha} \; (1-\alpha)^{(1-\alpha)} \right\}^{-1} .$$

The marginal cost function (2.18) represents a supply function dependent on factor prices and Z variables. In real terms, (2.18) can be written as

$$(2.19) \qquad c = \gamma' \; (w_p)^{\alpha} \; (w_s)^{(1-\alpha)} \; z^{-\beta}$$

where $c = \dfrac{C}{P_0}$, $w_p = \dfrac{W_p}{P_0}$, $w_s = \dfrac{W_s}{P_0}$, and the variable P_0 is the general price level.

Specifying a log-linear demand function for public protective services depending on price and income as

$$(2.20) \qquad PU = \delta_1 \; c^{\varepsilon} \; y^{\eta}$$

with the marginal cost, c, as price variable, and y as per capita income. Income is introduced, reflecting the budget constraint.[22]

The function (2.20) is chosen in preference to a linear relationship because we would expect on *a priori* grounds that the marginal increase of an increase in income would decrease with income. A linear relationship between the logarithms gives a good fit to the data without requiring

---

[22]The demand for protective services, equation (2.20), indicates that after correcting for the crime levels, a rich community could prefer a higher level of protective services because of differences in perceived income utilities. However, as income increases, there may be a shift from public to private protection. The total effect of an increase in income is therefore uncertain. A more complete model would also explicitly include an index of prices of private protection. Because of data availability, the total private protection sector has been neglected. For a more detailed analysis, see Vandaele (1975).

additional parameters.

Substituting this demand equation in the real terms version of (2.15), we obtain

$$(2.21) \qquad PU^d = \alpha\delta_1 \, c^{1+\varepsilon} \, y^\eta \, /w_p.$$

After replacing c by (2.19), the per capita derived demand for police officers is obtained as

$$(2.22) \qquad PU^d = \delta w_p^{(1+\varepsilon)\alpha-1} \, w_s^{(1+\varepsilon)(1-\alpha)} \, z^{-(1+\varepsilon)\beta} y^\eta$$

with

$$\delta = \delta_1 \, \alpha \, \gamma'^{(1+\varepsilon)}.$$

This per capita derived demand for police officers can also be summarized as:

$$(2.23) \qquad PU^d = d_1(w_p, \, w_s, \, y, \, q^a)$$

where PU^d = per capita demand for police officers; w_p = real wage rate for police officers; w_s = real factor price for capital services; y = real per capita income; and q^a = a measure of the aggregate crime index in the community. This variable q^a is one of the variables in the vector Z. We could introduce two separate indexes, allowing the derived demand for police officers to respond differently to the level of crime against property and to the level of crime against persons. The educational level and racial composition of the population could also influence the demand

function for police officers.

If all other variables remain constant, an increase in real wage rate

for police officers, w_p, or a decrease in real factor price for capital

services, $w_{\wedge s}$, is expected to reduce the per capita demand for police officers.

Ceteris paribus, we expect an increase in the per capita demand for police

officers when the aggregate crime index or the real per capita income increases.

2.3.2   The Supply of Police Officers

Economic theory of occupational choice[23] is used to derive a supply

function of police officers. Assuming that an individual has a choice between

two occupations, one of which is police officer, it can be shown that an

individual will select the occupation with the highest real return (real wage

rate plus real nonmonetary returns). Therefore, an individual will enter the

police force if

$$(2.24) \qquad r_p > r_\ell$$

where r_p = real return for a police officer an r_ℓ = real return from another

occupation. Factors such as the relative danger of the two occupations, the

location of the two jobs, etc., will influence the nonmonetary returns. We

will assume that the crime index is a good proxy for some of these nonmonetary

returns.

---

[23]For an application to college-trained manpower, see Freeman (1971),
and for military manpower, see Oi (1967), Fisher (1969, 1970), Klotz (1970),
Altman and Barro (1970), and Lightman (1972). For a survey of military
manpower studies, see Gilman (1970).

An individual will also consider the probability of being unemployed. It is assumed, however, that for a police officer the probability of being unemployed is negligible, so that only the unemployment rate in the alternative occupation is relevant.

Next, we include real income in the per capita supply of function of police officers to take into account the effect of income on labor force participation. Under appropriate assumptions it can be shown[24] that an increase in property income[25], without a change in wage rates, would induce a decrease in time spent at work. An increase in wage rates compensated by a decline in property income would increase the time spent at work. However, an uncompensated increase in the wage rate, i.e., an increase in wage rate, holding property income constant, would induce substitution effects toward, and income effects away from hours worked, with an ambiguous net effect.

Summarizing, we write the supply function of police officers as

$$(2.25) \qquad PU^S = s_1 \ (w_p, \ w_\ell, \ y, \ q^a, \ UR)$$

where PU^S = per capita supply of police officers; w_p = real wage rate for police officers; w_ℓ = real wage rate paid in the alternative occupation (for example, the average real earnings in manufacturing industries); y = real per capita income; q^a = aggregate crime index; and UR = unemployment rate in the alternative employment.

We expect an increase in the real wage rate for police officers to

---

[24]See Becker (1965) and (1971), pp. 45-50, 162-165.

[25]We use real income, y, as a proxy for property income.

cause a movement along the supply curve and so to increase the per capita supply of police officers. Similarly, an increase in the real wage rate for alternative employment or a decrease in the unemployment rate, all other variables held constant, will shift the supply function downward. Next, an increase in real income and an increase in the aggregate crime index will^ decrease the supply of police officers.

2.3.3. The Equilibrium Condition

The public prevention sector is completed with the following equilibrium condition:

$$(2.26) \qquad PU^d = PU^s.$$

2.3.4. The Probability of Arrest and Conviction

The probability of arrest and conviction links the prevention sector with the three other sectors of the crime industry – the factor market, the production sector, and the product market. We view protective services as an input in a production function with the probability of arrest and conviction as an output.

As indicated in section 2.3.1., protective services are produced utilizing factor inputs from the protection sectors. Indirectly, then, the probability[26] of arrest and conviction production function uses factor inputs from the public protection sector. Therefore, the probability of arrest and

---

[26]This probability is an aggregate probability over the three market probabilities: the probability of arrest and conviction in the product market, π_1; in the production sector, π_2; and in the factor market, π_3.

conviction production function depends on PU, the per capita number of
police officers; S, the per capita capital services used by the police
departments; and other variables such as population density[27], education
level of the population, the race and age composition of the population,
and the community crime level as measured by the aggregate crime index, q^a.

The number of arrests[28] made by a police officer is assumed to be higher
at a high crime level than at a low crime level. This has sometimes been
called the "fisheries argument" : the total number of fish in the ocean
is a determinant of the number caught. However, given an optimal utilization of the police officer's time, we expect that the marginal increase
in the number of arrests as a function of the number of crimes would increase
at first and thereafter decrease. With the probability of arrest constant,
however, the number of arrests has to increase when the crime level increases.
Therefore, we expect that the marginal physical product of police officers,
that is, the marginal increase in the probability of arrest, will first
increase and then decrease as the crime level increases.

Therefore we write the probability of arrest production function as

(2.27) $\pi = f$ (PU, S, q^a, PD, NW, ED, A)

where π = probability of arrest and conviction; PU = per capita number of
police officers; S = per capita capital services; q^a = aggregate crime index;
PD = population density; NW = nonwhite population as a percentage of the
total population; ED = educational level of the population; and A = percentage

---

[27]See Ohls and Wales (1972), p. 424.

[28]In equation (3.30), section 3.5, we have introduced an arrest
producing production function as an intermediate step.

of the total population from 14 to 24 years of age.

An increase in a factor input such as the per capita number of police officers, all other variables held constant, should increase the probability of arrest. However, an increase in the aggregate crime index, *ceteris paribus*, could reduce the probability of arrest. We also expect that an increase in the population density will decrease the probability of arrest. An increase in the percentage of teenagers or nonwhites is assumed to increase the probability of arrest.

Some of these algebraic signs of the elasticities are tentative. For example, if the educational level of the population expands and leads to a better, more efficient crime reporting, the probability of arrest could increase. However, if criminals also become better educated, an increase in the educational level could cause the probability of arrest to decrease.

2.4   Summary

We have developed an economic model of crime capable of explaining criminal behavior in a community. This model is set up as an industry supply and demand model and is in no way restricted to one particular crime type. The interactions between the different types of crime have been neglected. As mentioned above, Darrough and Heineke (1978) have empirically analyzed these interactions.

We tried to be as general as possible in developing the model, without paying particular attention to the availability of the data; we are convinced that data limitations should not completely dictate theory. Later data may make it possible to test other aspects of the model. At least the theoretical foundations are established.

3.   The Empirical Analysis of the Structural Model

In this section we explain the estimated equations derived from the theoretical model developed in section 2, and discuss the empirical findings[29] in an attempt to iterate in on an acceptable model specification.

3.1. The Economic Model of Crime - Summary

The aggregate economic model of crime developed in section 2 can be summarized with the following equations [30]:

1.)   Product Market

(3.1) Demand $q_t^d: p_t, p_t^c, y_t, \pi_{1t}, f_{1t}$

(3.2) Supply $q_t^s: p_t, w_t, \pi_{2t}, f_{2t}, N_t$

(3.3) Equilibrium Conditon $q_t = q_t^d = q_t^s$

2.)   Factor Market

(3.4) Demand $T_t^d: p_t, w_t, \pi_{2t}, f_{2t}$

(3.5) Supply $T_t^s: w_{\ell t}, w_t, \pi_{3t}, f_{3t}$

(3.6) Equilibrium Condition $T_t = T_t^d = T_t^s$

---

[29] We performed the calculations on an IBM 360/65 and 370/168 at the University of Chicago Computation Center, using the Econometric Software Package (ESP). See Cooper (1973). Some of the 2SLS estimates have been obtained using the "Program for Computing Two- and Three-Stage Least Squares Estimates and Associated Statistics," developed by Stroud, Zellner and Chau, and subsequently modified by Thornber and Keesey. See Vandaele (1973).

[30] The subscript "t" on the variables denotes the value of that variable in the tth year. The period covered is 1935 to 1969, a total of 35 years. Initially, we indicate only which variables appear in the different equations. To the left of the colon we have the "dependent variable", and to the right the "independent variables". The symbols for the variables are defined in 3.1.1.

3.)   Crime Prevention Sector

3.1.)   Public Prevention Sector

(3.7)   Demand $PU_t^d : w_{pt}, w_{st}, y_t, q_t^a, A_t$

(3.8)   Supply $PU_t^s : w_{pt}, w_{\ell t}, y_t, q_t^a, UR_t$

(3.9)   Equilibrium Condition $PU_t = PU_t^d = PU_t^s$

3.2)   The Probability of Arrest and Conviction

(3.10) $\pi_{it} : PU_t, S_t, q_t^a, NW_t, A_t$

for the product market, i = 1; the production sector,

i = 2; and the factor market, i = 3.

3.3)   Definitional Equations

$q_t^a : q_t^v, q_t^p$

$q_t^v : q_{1t}, q_{2t}, q_{3t}$

$q_t^p : q_{4t}, q_{5t}, q_{6t}, q_{7t}$

with murder = 1, rape = 2, assault = 3, robbery = 4,

burglary = 5, larceny = 6, and auto theft = 7.

3.1.1.   Theoretical Variables

Endogenous

q_t = per capita number of stolen cars transacted in the crime product market, with q_t^d = quantity demand and q_t^s = quantity supplied,

p_t = real market price of a stolen car,

T_t = total number of man-hours used per year in the illegal sector, with T_t^d = quantity demanded and T_t^s = quantity supplied,

w_t = real wage rate paid in the illegal factor market,

PU_t = per capita number of police officers, with PU_t^d = quantity demanded and PU_t^s = quantity supplied,

w_{pt} = real wage rate for police officers,

π_{it} = probability of arrest and conviction; in the product market (i = 1),

    in the production sector (i = 2), and in the factor market (i = 3),

q_t^a = aggregate crime index,

q_t^p = property crime index.

Exogenous

p_t^c = a vector of real prices of commodities closely related to the

    illegal product,

y^t = real per capita income,

N_t = population size,

π_{it}^c = probability of conviction if charged; in the product market (i = 1),

    in the production sector (i = 2), and in the factor market (i = 3).

PR_t = labor force participation rate,

$w_{\ell t}$ = real legal wage rate,

w_{st} = real rental price for police capital services,

f_{it} = real average cost of punishment to the criminal when apprehended and

    convicted in the product market (i = 1), in the crime industry (i = 2)

    and in the factor market (i = 3),

NW_t = nonwhites as a percentage of the total population,

UR_t = unemployment rate,

A_t = population 14 to 24 years of age as a percentage of total population,

q_t^v = index of crimes against the person.

3.2.   The Demand for Stolen Cars

Writing the demand for stolen cars equation (3.1) in log-linear

form, we obtain[31]

$$(3.11) \quad \ln q_t^d = \alpha_0 + \alpha_1 \ln p_t + \alpha_2 \ln p_t^c + \alpha_3 \ln y_t$$
$$+ \alpha_4 \ln \pi_t + \alpha_5 \ln \pi_t^c + \varepsilon_{1t}$$

Rather than construct one compound measure of the probability of arrest and

conviction, we use two variables, π, the probability of arrest (the percentage

of offenses cleared by arrest), and π^c, the probability of convictions (the

number of persons found guilty for offenses charged, as a percentage of total

number charged). A change in the probability of arrest and a change in the

probability of conviction, given arrest, can deter potential criminals differently.[32]

Next, assume a log-linear relationship between the per capita number

of stolen cars, q_t, and the reported crime index[33], r_t, as

$$(3.12) \quad \ln q_t = \beta_0 + \beta_1 \ln r_t.$$

---

[31] As no time series is available for time served, the fine variable
is omitted. For π_t, see also footnote 1, p. 23, and footnote 3, p. 30.

[32] Evidence for murder also suggests an unequal effect of π and π^c
(see Ehrlich 1975b).   In particular, Ehrlich found that the effect of π on
the murder index was about three times as large as the effect of π^c. The underlying economic model is, however, not entirely comparable.

[33] The reported crime index is the ratio of the total number of
offenses reported to the police, to the total civilian resident population in
thousands.

Finally, we use also a log-linear relationship between the price of stolen

cars, p, and the price of used cars, p^c, as [34]

(3.13) $\ln p_t = \gamma_0 + \gamma_1 \ln p_t^c$ with $\gamma_1 > 0$.

Combining (3.11), (3.12), and (3.13) and solving for $\ln r_t$, we obtain

(3.14) $\ln r_t = a_0 + a_1 \ln p_t^c + a_3 \ln y_t + a_4 \ln \pi_{1t} + a_5 \ln \pi_{1t}^c + v_{1t}$

where $a_0 = (\alpha_0 - \beta_0 + \alpha_1)/\beta_1$, $a_1 = (\alpha_1\gamma_1 + \alpha_2)/\beta_1$, and $a_i = \alpha_i/\beta_i$

for $i = 3, 4, 5$. Notice that the price coefficient a_1 represents a combin-

ation of the price elasticity of the demand for stolen cars and the price

elasticity of the demand for used cars in the legal market. [35]

We expect in (3.14) the following coefficient signs: a_1 negative if

the own price elasticity is larger in absolute value than the cross elasticity;

a_3 positive; a_4 negative; and a_5 negative, with $|a_4| \geq |a_5|$. For the proof

of the latter inequality, see Ehrlich (1975b).

---

[34]We were unable to collect a price series for stolen cars. For
pragmatic reasons we assume that the changes in the stolen car price are
related to changes in the used car price, resulting in a constant elasticity
between the two variables. As described in Vandaele (1975), additional
assumptions had to be introduced to construct a complete used car price
time series for the period 1933-1972.

[35]With the own price elasticity α_1 negative and the price elasticity
of the substitute α_2 positive, the sign of a_1 depends on the relative magnitude of the two elasticities. If the other commodity is a complement rather
than a substitute, α_2 would be negative, and therefore a_1 also.

Estimating (3.14) using the 2SLS estimation method[36], we obtain

$$\ln q_t = 3.709 - .5856 \ln p_t + .6600 \ln y_t$$

(3.15) λ $\begin{pmatrix} \text{ln of Auto} \\ \text{Theft Index} \end{pmatrix}$ $SE\hat{\beta}$ 1.71   .424   .161

$\hat{\beta}/SE\hat{\beta}$ 2.17   -1.38   4.11

$$-1.302 \ln \pi_t - .3220 \ln \pi_t^c$$

.250   .0886

-5.20   -3.64

NOB = 35; SE = .1316; $\hat{\rho}_1$ = .590, $\hat{\rho}_2$ = .187, $\hat{\rho}_3$ = -.055, with standard error[37] = .169.

Note that the negative point estimate for the price coefficient implies that the own elasticity, in absolute terms, is larger than the cross-elasticity, a result expected to hold. Further, both the probability of arrest[38] and the probability of conviction for offense charged[39] have a significant negative effect on the demand for stolen cars, with point estimates of -1.302 and

---

[36] The following variables are included in the reduced form: A, LA, LN, LNW, LPCC, LQO, LREM, LRY, LUR, NW, T, and an intercept. For an explanation of these symbols, see Appendix A.

[37] In equation (3.15) estimated by 2SLS, we indicate the first-, second-, and third-order structural residual autocorrelation by $\hat{\rho}_1$, $\hat{\rho}_2$, and $\hat{\rho}_3$ respectively, as well as its large sample standard error = $1/\sqrt{NOB}$, with NOB = 35.

[38] Data on the probabilities of arrest and conviction for offense charged are available for the whole crime economy and not for each major subsector separately. We assume therefore that the sector probabilities are related to the overall probability as $\pi_i = A\pi^{\alpha}i$, with π the overall probability and π_i the probability specific to the ith sector. After taking the logarithm of this equation, we obtain $\ln \pi_i = \alpha_0 + \alpha_i \ln \pi$. Using this relationship will only change the intercept of the equation.

[39] We also checked on the effect of using the probability of conviction variable PCA, that is, the percentage of persons charged found guilty for offense charged or lesser offense. The point estimates were somewhat larger in absolute value, but these values had broader confidence intervals.

-.3220 and standard errors of .50 and .0886 respectively.

The values of the elasticities estimated in semilog[40] form and calculated at the mean value of the auto theft index are -1.09 for the price
elasticity, 1.08 for the income elasticity, -1.91 for the probability of
arrest elasticity, and -.300 for the probability of conviction elasticity.
These values are of the same magnitudes as the coefficients of (3.15).
Because all other equations are estimated in log-linear form[41], we have
selected the log-linear equation (3.15) for uniformity.

Comparing these results with a data-based prior obtained from related
studies[42], we remark:

1.) A price elasticity of -1 in the demand for stolen cars is highly
probable. The elasticity obtained is -.5856 with standard error of .424.
Note that the estimated price elasticity is a combination of the own price
elasticity and the cross-elasticity. Therefore, the implied point estimate
of the own price elasticity is larger when the legal car is a complement
and smaller when the legal car is a substitute.

---

[40]The equation estimated is:

$$r_t = b_0 + b_1 \ln p_t^c + b_3 \ln y_t + b_4 \ln \pi_t + b_5 \ln \pi_t^c.$$

[41]The results show great consistency across different functional forms.
There are also assumptions which make the log=linear form more acceptable.
Indeed, we assume that the stolen car price variable is a log-linear function
of the used car price, and that a sector-specific probability of arrest is a
log-linear function of an overall probability of arrest. Also, it is easier
to defend the assumption that the percentage of joyriding of the total number
of cars stolen has been constant over time, rather than the absolute level of
joyriding. All these assumptions affect the constant term, but not the
individual elasticities in a log-linear form.

[42]This data-based prior is based on studies of the demand for legal
cars; see Roos and von Szeliski (1939), Atkinson (1952), Chow (1957, 1960),
Suits (1958), Dyckman (1965), and Ackerman (1970). It can be shown that
under fairly general conditions, the price elasticity in the demand for
stolen cars has to be lower in absolute value than in the demand for legal
cars. See Vandaele (1975), Chapter III.

2.) The data-based prior - based on empirical studies of the demand

for legal cars - suggests a maximum value of 2 for the income elasticity.

The income elasticity with point estimate of .6600 and standard error of

.161 is on the low side.[43]

3.) For the demand for illegal products, there is no data-based prior

for the elasticities of the probability of arrest and the probability of

conviction given arrest. We find that the elasticity of the probability of

arrest is larger in absolute value than the elasticity of the probability

of conviction given arrest. For the supply of murder equation, Ehrlich (1975b)

obtained similar results.

The results of (3.15) indicate some evidence of first-order serial

correlation in the structural disturbances. This also happened when esti-

mating the demand equation using classical least-squares (CLS). Reestimating

the equation in first differences did not improve the results. Both the

coefficient of the price of stolen cars and the real per capita permanent

income variable were less precisely estimated. The coefficient of a time

trend, introduced as a proxy for omitted variables such as the fine, was

not significantly different from zero [44]. At the same time the Durbin-Watson

(DW) statistic still showed evidence of positive autocorrelation. Assuming

that the true relationship has autocorrelated disturbances, we applied the

---

[43]Using per capita real disposable income rather than permanent income,
and based on CLS results, we obtained a point estimate of the coefficient
of disposable income slightly higher and more precise. The point estimate
and standard error are .6365 and .146 as compared to .5737 and .150.

[44]Notice that the above methods of selecting variables are defective
as due to autocorrelation the standard errors of the coefficients are
incorrectly estimated; and due to the presence of endogenous variables
the CLS estimates are inconsistent.

Cochrane-Orcutt (CORC) method (1949) to correct for first-order auto-correlation[45]. The changes in the estimated regression coefficients were large. Although each coefficient had the same sign, magnitudes changed by more than 50 percent.[46]

The demand for stolen cars was also specified as a demand for durables, allowing an adaptive behavior.[47] This specification required as additional variable the stock of illegal cars, approximated by the per capita stock of legal cars.[48] As the results were inconclusive for the stock adjustment coefficient, we did not pursue this model specification.

---

[45] Blattberg (1973) showed that the power of the DW statistic for a second-order autoregressive process and a first-order moving average process can be greater than for a first-order autoregressive process. This implies that a Cochrane-Orcutt correction, which assumes a first-order autoregressive process for the error term, may be inapplicable.

[46] More detailed results are reported in Vandaele (1975).

[47] Including the per capita stock of legal cars is a way to take into account the interactions with the legal auto market.

[48] For an analysis of a *Do-Nothing-Do-All* random stock adjustment model, see Vandaele (1975). In this model the adjustment coefficient measures the probability that search and adjustment costs are less than the loss incurred for being out of equilibrium, given that no purchase is made.

3.3.   The Factor Market: Aggregate Illegal Time Supply

The aggregate supply of illegal time equation has the following general form, see equation (3.5):

$$T^S : w, w_\ell, \pi_3, f_3$$

where T^S = time supplied to the illegal market; w = real wage rate in the illegal market; w_ℓ = legal wage rate; π_3 = probability of arrest in the factor market; and f_3 = monetized fine when convicted for illegal activity in the factor market. As mentioned in Section 2.2.1, in writing down the equation (2.11) we did not evaluate the aggregation procedure involved in going from the micro level to the aggregate level, but only restated the variable already present at the micro level. We will now formally work out one aggregation scheme.

Suppose, as indicated in Section 2, that the variables reflecting age and white-nonwhite population composition enter into the labor supply equation, and that specifically we have the following two-by-two cross-tabulations: teenage versus older and white versus nonwhite, with the total population divided as N_1 = the number of nonwhite teenagers, N_2 = the number of white teenagers, N_3 = the nonwhite nonteenagers and N_4 = the white nonteenagers, with $N = N_1 + N_2 + N_3 + N_4$. Also, the variable $A = (N_1 + N_2)/N$ and $NW = (N_1 + N_3)/N$. Furthermore, each individual in each category receives a different wage rate and has a different probability of arrest and fine. All individuals in the same category face the same unemployment rate and labor force participation rate. Selecting a log-linear form, we can write the time supplied to the illegal market by the jth individual in the ith category as

$$(3.16) \quad \ln T_j^i = a_{i0} + a_1 \ln x_j^i + b_1 \ln z^i + u_j^i$$

where x_j^i are variables specific to the jth individual in the ith category, such as $w_j^i, w_{\ell j}^i, \pi_{3j}^i, f_{3j}^i$, and z^i represents category-related variables such as unemployment rate. Notice that all individuals have the same elasticities.

Summing (3.16) over all individuals in each of the four categories, and then over all categories, we obtain

$$(3.17) \quad \ln \bar{T} = a_{40} + (a_{10} - a_{30})A + (a_{10} - a_{20})NW$$
$$+ a_1 \ln \bar{x} + b_1 \ln \bar{z} + \bar{u}$$

where A = percentage of teenagers in the population, NW = percentage of non-whites in the population, and $\bar{T}$, $\bar{x}$, $\bar{z}$ and $\bar{u}$ = arithmetic means of the individual specific variables, with averages taken relative to the total population. Because only arithmetic means are available, we have substituted in (3.17) $\bar{T}$, $\bar{x}$ and $\bar{z}$ for their geometric mean. However, the aggregations of (3.18) would require the use of geometric means. For positive numbers, the geometric mean is less than or equal to the arithmetic mean. Notice that the distribution of the error term $\bar{u}$ now refers to the distribution of the mean of the underlying individual error distribution.

The total supply is obtained as (3.18) $\ln T^s = \ln \bar{T} + \ln N$, suggesting that among the right-hand side variables we should include the variable ln N, with a coefficient equal to one. Equation (3.18), incorporating (3.17), cannot be estimated because no data is available on two endogenous variables - the (dependent) supply of illegal time and real illegal wage rate. In the next section, we will combine this equation with the demand for illegal time equation and the supply of stolen cars equation, and then estimate a reduced form supply of stolen cars.

3.4.   The Factor Market and the Supply of Stolen Cars

Because it is impossible to estimate the factor supply equation (3.18) - no data on T_i, time spent in the illegal market, and on w, the real illegal wage

rate - we use the supply and demand equation of illegal time to solve for the
equilibrium wage rate. We can then substitute this into the supply function of
stolen cars.

The factor market, summarized with the equations (3.4), (3.5), and
(3.6), is restated here as

(3.19) Demand T^d : p, w, π_2, f_2
(3.20) Supply T^s : w, w_ℓ, π_3, f_3
(3.21) Equilibrium Condition $T = T^d = T^s$

In the previous section we introduced other variables, such as age
distribution and white-nonwhite population composition in the supply of illegal
time, and explicitly worked out the aggregation process; see equations (3.17)
and (3.18).

We will not calculate the reduced form industry supply schedule[49], and
for convenience, we omit all nonessential[50] variables. As a result, (3.19) and
(3.20) can be rewritten in logarithmic form, and taking into account the aggregation procedure discussed above, as

(3.22) $\ln T^d = \gamma_0 + \gamma_1 \ln p + \gamma_2 \ln w + v_3$
(3.23) $\ln T^s = \alpha_0 + \alpha_1 \ln w + v_4$.

---

[49] For a similar analysis, see Muth (1964).

[50] As the objective of this reduced form calculation is primarily to evaluate the implied coefficient of the price variable, we have omitted such variables
as π_2, π_3, A, NW, w_ℓ. It is, however, straightforward to include these variables.
See also Vandaele (1975). The equations estimated in (3.29) thus include these
variables, with the exception of π_2 and π_3, for which we only have an aggregate
probability of arrest available pertaining to the product market, production
sector and factor market.

Solving the systematic part of these two equations for ln w, the equilibrium
real wage rate in the illegal factor market, we obtain

(3.24) $\ln w = \xi_0 + \xi_1 \ln p$

with $\xi_0 = (\alpha_0 - \gamma_0)/\gamma$, $\xi_1 = -\gamma_1/\gamma$, and $\gamma = \gamma_2 - \alpha_1$.

Next, we write the essential variables of the product supply
equation (2.10) as

(3.25) $\ln q^S = \eta_0 + \eta_1 \ln p + \eta_2 \ln w + v_2$

Substituting (3.24) into (3.25), we have [51]

(3.26) $\ln q^S = \theta_0 + \theta_1 \ln p + v_2$

with $\theta_0 = \eta_0 + \eta_2\xi_0$ and $\theta_1 = \eta_1 + \eta_2\xi_1$.

This equation expresses the per capita number of stolen cars supplied
to the product market per unit of time. To make (3.26) operational, we
assume that the actual per capita number of stolen cars transacted, q_t, is
related to the reported crime index, r_t, as

$\ln q = \beta_0 + \beta_1 \ln r.$

---

[51] The disturbance term v_2 in (3.26) should really be v_2', as it is
a combination of v_2 in (3.25), v_3 in (3.22), and v_4 in (3.23).

Solving (3.26) for the observable variable, $\ln r$, we obtain [52]

$$(3.27) \qquad \ln r = \frac{\theta_0 - \beta_0}{\beta_1} + \theta_1' \ln p + v_2$$

$$\text{with } \theta_1' = \theta_1/\beta_1.$$

Based on information presented in Section 2 about the probable algebraic signs of the coefficients in the supply equation of stolen cars, we know that the algebraic sign of θ_1' is ambiguous and depends on the relative magnitudes of the constituent parts. The relationship with the structural coefficients is

$$(3.28) \qquad \theta_1' = \frac{\theta_1}{\beta_1} = \frac{\eta_1 + \eta_2 \xi_1}{\beta_1}$$

---

[52] Notice that perfect reporting would make the value of the coefficents β_1 and β_0 equal to one and zero respectively, and as such (3.27) would simplify to (3.26), with $\ln r$ as dependent variable.

with $\xi_1 = -\gamma_1/\gamma > 0$, $\eta_1 > 0$, $\eta_2 < 0$, where η_1 is the price elasticity in the supply function of stolen cars, η_2 the illegal wage elasticity in the supply equation of stolen cars, and γ_1 the price elasticity in the derived demand for the illegal time equation, and γ has been defined in (3.24).

After estimating the supply equation of stolen cars by 2SLS, we obtain the results reported in equation (3.29).

$$\ln q_t = -3.629 - .4383 \ln p_t - .5409 \ln w_{\ell t}$$

$$\begin{pmatrix} \ln \text{ of Auto} \\ \text{Theft Index} \end{pmatrix} \quad \text{SE}\hat{\beta} \quad 2.15 \quad .257 \quad .398$$

$$\hat{\beta}/\text{SE}\hat{\beta} \quad -1.68 \quad -1.70 \quad -1.36$$

(3.29)

$$-.4487 \ln \pi_t + 65.36 \, NW_t + 4.192 \, A_t$$

$$.202 \qquad 12.6 \qquad 1.13$$

$$-2.22 \qquad 5.18 \qquad 3.71$$

NOB = 35; SE = .07450, $\hat{\rho}_1$ = .199, $\hat{\rho}_2$ = −.314, $\hat{\rho}_3$ = −.115, with standard error = .169.

Less precise results were obtained when the supply equation was estimated in first difference form. In particular, both the coefficients of the price of stolen cars and the legal wage rate were very imprecisely estimated.

Remember also that the coefficients of the estimated supply equation are reduced form coefficients of a subsector of the industry supply and demand model, composed of the factor market and production sector. The economic interpretation is that the coefficients represent the anticipated changes in the supply of stolen cars due to changes in the "independent" variables after the indirect effect of such a change in the labor market has been considered.

The following remarks are also appropriate:

1.) The supply of stolen cars is negatively influenced by the probability of arrest[53] with a point elasticity of -.4487 and standard error of .202. The point elasticities of the probability of arrest elasticity in Ehrlich (1973) are between -.409 and -.495.

2.) The elasticity of supply of the legal wage rate has the expected negative sign, with a point estimate of -.5409 and standard error of .398.

3.) The price of stolen cars has a negative coefficient. The sign of this reduced form coefficient is ambiguous, however, and depends on the relative magnitudes of price and wage elasticities in the product supply equation and of the price elasticity in the illegal time derived demand equation.

4.) The age and race variables, A and NW, are highly significant with elasticities, measured at the mean value[54], of .7353 and 7.1961 respectively.[55]

5.) We also introduced a time variable, possibly capturing a crime reporting effect or the influence of omitted variables such as the fine variable. The results indicate that the point estimate does not differ significantly from zero.

6.) Unemployment rate, UR, labor force participation rate, PR, and population size, N, have an insignificant impact on the supply of stolen cars.

---

[53] The probability of conviction for offense charged, LPCC, was not retained in the supply equation, as its point estimate was accompanied by a very broad confidence interval, which also included positive values. With LPCC included, the effect of the other variables did not change noticeably, whereas the coefficient value of LPCC was .049 with standard error of .072.

[54] The mean of the age variable is .1754 and of nonwhite .1101.

[55] As suggested by the aggregation procedure, these two variables are introduced in absolute rather than in logarithmic terms.

7.) We also estimated this equation in combining our time series data
with the 1960 cross-section data as reported in Ehrlich (1973), and encountered
no major differences in the estimates. For more detailed results, see Vandaele
(1975), chapter V.

3.5.   The Probability of Arrest Production Function

The probability of arrest production function links the prevention
sector with the illegal factor market, the production sector, and product
market. In section 2, we derived the probability of arrest as a production
function with as inputs both labor and capital as well as other variables
affecting the efficiency of its technology.
Let A be the number of arrests made during some time period, and let
L and K be the labor and capital inputs during the same period. Suppose that
output is related to these inputs by the following Cobb-Douglas (CD) production
function[56]:

$$(3.30)   A = L^{\alpha_1} K^{\alpha_2}$$

In addition, the production function is influenced by the number of
crimes committed[57]. First, when no crimes are committed, no arrests can be made.
Second, with labor and capital constant, the fraction of the crimes cleared by
arrest will be smaller during riots than at other times. We therefore expect
that as the number of crimes committed increases, the number of arrests would
increase at a decreasing rate. Writing equation (3.30) as a fraction of Q,

---

[56] In section 2, we introduced a probability of arrest production
function without formally stating an arrest production function.

[57] See also section 2.3.3.

the total number of crimes committed[58], we obtain the probability of arrest

production function:

$$(3.31) \qquad \pi = \frac{A}{Q} = \alpha L^{\alpha_1} K^{\alpha_2} (Q^a)^{\alpha_3}$$

We expect the value of α_3 to be between 0 and -1.

As mentioned in Section 2.3.3., arguments are put forward debating

the appropriateness of the variable Q^a in the arrest production function.

See Darrough and Heineke (1978). In addition, empirical evidence based on

Ehrlich (1973) and Votey and Phillips (1972), suggest that α_3 in (3.31)

was not significantly different from minus one. We adopt this more general

specification which permits testing of this hypothesis.

Variables such as age and white-nonwhite composition of the population

could influence output. Arresting adults may be more time consuming than

arresting teenagers.[59] All these variables are grouped together in an

exponential trend; we therefore write the probability of arrest function

as

$$(3.32) \qquad \pi = \alpha L^{\alpha_1} K^{\alpha_2} (Q^a)^{\alpha_3} e^{\alpha_0 t}$$

---

[58] Should Q be a measure of all crimes in a community (a source of
external economies in a criminal activity), or just auto theft? If the
police force were highly specialized according to crime type and other
duties, then Q should only measure auto theft. However, because each
police officer performs highly diversified tasks, we include in the production
function the variable Q^a measuring total aggregate crime.

[59] Other variables that could enter the probability of arrest production
function are population density and education level of the population.
Whether population density and education level of the population would increase or decrease the probability of arrest is a question of fact that cannot be answered conclusively here. Although when a community is composed of
more educated people, the police may receive more useful information for
apprehending offenders, also criminals are better educated and therefore
more able to protect themselves from being arrested. See Ehrlich (1975a).
See also section 3.7 where we discuss the identification.

or in per capita terms,

$$(3.33) \qquad \pi = \alpha l^{\alpha_1} k^{\alpha_2} (q^a)^{\alpha_3} N^{\alpha_4} e^{\alpha_0 t}$$

where $l = L/N$, $k = K/N$, $q^a = Q^a/N$, and N the population size. Deriving (3.33) from (3.32), we would expect that $\alpha_4 = \alpha_1 + \alpha_2 + \alpha_3$. However, the population size is possibly another efficiency characteristic of the probability of arrest technology, negatively related to π because of the relative ease with which an offender could elude the police in densely populated areas.

No annual statistics are available on capital utilization by police departments and therefore we neglect capital services in estimating (3.33)[60].

After taking logarithms of both sides of (3.33), we obtain

$$(3.34) \qquad \ln \pi = \ln \alpha + \alpha_0 t + \alpha_1 \ln l + \alpha_3 \ln q^a + \alpha_4 \ln N.$$

The effect of excluding the variable ln k is that the expectation of the estimates of the included coefficients equals [61]

$$E \hat{\alpha}_i = \alpha_i + \delta_i \alpha_2 = \beta_i \qquad i = 0, 1, 3, 4$$

where the δ_i's are the coefficients in the regression of the omitted variable on the included ones, also called the auxiliary regression:

$$(3.35) \qquad \ln k = \delta + \delta_0 t + \delta_1 \ln l + \delta_3 \ln q + \delta_4 \ln N + v.$$

---

[60]Although the more recent _Municipal Year Book_ contains data on capital outlay by selected police departments, it is not possible to construct a consistent time series for the period 1935 to 1969. In addition, there are specification problems when using a measure of the capital stock rather than capital services when in fact the rate of utilization of the stock is not constant. In particular, if capital services grew significantly faster than the gross stock, using the capital stock as capital input would underestimate the elasticity of output with respect to capital.

[61]For an analysis of the specification bias due to omitted variables see Theil (1971), p. 548 ff.

With $\alpha_2 > 0$, the sign of δ_i will determine if a particular $\hat{\alpha}_i$ will under-estimate or overestimate the corresponding parameter of (3.34). In parti-cular, keeping output (the probability of arrest) constant, we expect a negative association between capital services and labor output. Hence, excluding∧the capital input will introduce a negative bias in the estimated elasticity of output with respect to labor.

In conclusion, we estimate the following probability of arrest production function:

$$(3.36) \qquad \ln \pi_t = \beta + \beta_0 t + \beta_1 \ln PU_t + \beta_3 \ln q_t^a + \beta_4 \ln N_t$$
$$+ \beta_5 \ln A_t + \beta_6 \ln NW_t + \varepsilon_t$$

where π = probability of arrest; t = time trend; PU = per capita number of police officers; q^a = aggregate crime index; N = population size; A = population 14 to 24 years of age as a percentage of the total population; NW = nonwhites as a percentage of the total population. Note that we also added the age and nonwhite variables to the model.

Based on interpretation and statistical significance of the estimates, we retained the following equation, estimated by 2SLS, to represent the probability of arrest production function:

$$\ln \pi_t = 5.114 + .3511 \ln PU_t - .07475 \ln q_t^a$$

$\begin{pmatrix}\ln \text{ of Prob.} \\ \text{of Arrest}\end{pmatrix}$ $SE\hat{\beta}$ 2.47   .460   .0313

$\hat{\beta}/SE\hat{\beta}$ 2.07   .762   −2.39

(3.37)

$$+ 1.548 \ln NW_t - .5887 \ln \hat{A}_t$$

1.06   .208

1.46   −2.84

NOB = 35; SE = .09567; $\hat{\rho}_1$ = .479; $\hat{\rho}_2$ = .303; $\hat{\rho}_3$ = .065, with standard error =

The major findings are:

1.) The crime level, measured by the aggregate crime index, q^a, has
the expected negative effect on the probability of arrest production function,
although its coefficient is rather small in absolute value.

Notice that this coefficient is significantly different from minus one.
This implies that the aggregate crime rate is not superfluous in the arrest
production function and the resulting probability of arrest function (3.31).
Recall that the inclusion of aggregate crime rate implies a departure from
the neoclassical production literature.

2.) The age distribution has a negative effect on the probability of
arrest, that is, as the percentage of young people in the population increases,
the probability of arrest will decrease. Our prior belief about the nonwhite
coefficient in inconclusive. Nonwhites may spend less resources on legal
counsel and defense and they may also be prime suspects in a crime, two
possible explanations for the positive relation between NW and the probability
of arrest. However, nonwhites could also be more skilled in stealing and
transacting stolen cars, and thus a negative relation between NW and probability of arrest could result.

3.) The probability of arrest elasticity with respect to the per
capita police force is inconclusive. The results show a positive relationship
between the per capita police force and the probability of arrest. However,
the estimate is imprecise, possibly because arrest is only one part of the
diversified output of a police·department. [62] The police also prevent crimes.

---

[62] A major function of the police department is the general service
function: directing traffic, supplying emergency first aid, etc., which
currently accounts for over 80% of total man-hours. For an analysis
allowing for a heterogeneous police department input, see Darrough and
Heineke (1978).

Obtaining a measure of the number of crimes prevented by the presence of police officers on the street is a difficult but important problem. Furthermore, a police force may respond to a change in variables omitted from the model, such as changes in courtroom procedure. Adverse changes in these variables, resulting in increases in the amount of crime and in the number of police officers, could cause the probability of arrest to decrease while the police force is increasing. Also, according to the FBI, certain police departments have, due to manpower limitations and other demands on their time[63], shifted their emphasis from property crimes toward crimes against the person. All these factors could account for the low and imprecise estimate of .3511 for the police force elasticity. However, the omission of capital services in the production function is likely to bias the estimate of labor share downward.

4.) We also estimated (3.37) using a logit model to take into account that the dependent variable is not continuous over the whole real line, but can only take on values between zero and 100. The empirical findings showed hardly any differences between the log-linear and the logit formulation.

---

[63]There are indications that the police spend greater efforts on developing a reputation for fairness, civility, and integrity that wins the respect of all citizens.

3.6.   The Demand for and the Supply of Police Officers

The police demand and supply equations and the equilibrium condition, as derived in section 2, have been summarized in the beginning of this section 3 with the following equations:

(3.38)   Demand PU^d : w_p, w_s, y, q^a, A

(3.39)   Supply PU^s : w_p, w_ℓ, y, q^a, UR

Equilibrium Condition $PU = PU^d = PU^s$

where PU = per capita number of police officers, PU^d and PU^s the quantity demanded and supplied respectively; w_p = police officers' real wage; w_ℓ = real wage rate in the alternative occupation; w_s = real rental price for police capital services; y = real income; q^a = aggregate crime index; UR = unemployment rate; and A = the age composition of the population. NW, the percentage nonwhites in the population, could also be added to the model.

3.6.1.   The Demand for Police Officers

The 2SLS estimates of the demand for police officers are:

$$\ln PU_t \quad = \quad -8.144 + .3285 \ln w_{pt} + .3252 \ln y_t$$

$$\begin{pmatrix} \ln \text{ of per} \\ \text{capita} \\ \text{police} \end{pmatrix} \quad SE\hat{\beta} \quad 3.93 \quad .173 \quad .123$$

$$\hat{\beta}/SE\hat{\beta} \quad -2.07 \quad 1.90 \quad 2.64$$

(3.40) $+ .01555 \ln q_t^a - 1.521 \ln NW_t - .1285 \ln A_t$

                        .0134   .813   .0928

                        1.16   -1.87   -1.38

NOB = 35; SE = .04111; β_1 = .317, β_2 = -.238, β_3 = -.551, with standard error = .169.

All the estimates in (3.40), with the exception of the coefficient of the police officer's real wage rate, have the expected algebraic sign.[64] In the derived demand equation for police officers, equation (2.22), the real wage rate coefficient is equal to

$$(3.41) \qquad (1 + \varepsilon)\alpha - 1$$

where α is the labor coefficient in the probability of arrest production function and ε the price elasticity in the demand function for the probability of arrest [equation (2.20)]. The wage coefficient can only be positive if $|\varepsilon| < 1$ and $\alpha > 1$. This last condition implies that the probability of arrest prodution function exhibits increasing returns to scale, contradicting the estimates of the probability of arrest production function in equation (3.37). The real capital rental price, w_s, is not used in the equation because of lack of data. We included a time trend as a proxy, but found its estimate to be insignificantly different from zero.

3.6.2.   The Supply of Police Officers

The estimates for the supply of police officers are not entirely in agreement with the theoretical model; several have incorrect signs, although with large standard errors. We expected that the coefficient[65] of $\ln w_p$ (LRWP) and $\ln w_1$ (LREM) would have the opposite algebraic sign, and therefore were surprised that an increase in w_p creates a decrease in the supply of police officers.

---

[64] There is no strong prior about the sign of the age and nonwhite variables.

[65] We used as a proxy for the wage rate in the legal sector the real wage rate in the manufacturing industry and as proxy for w_p an index of maximum salary scales for police officers in cities of 100,000 or more inhabitants.

Even after constructing the ratio of the real wage rate in the alternative occupation to the real police wage rate, and therefore ensuring that
these two earnings coefficients have the same absolute value, the CLS estimate
of the ratio coefficient is .2285 with standard error of .2070. Notice that
this coefficient still has the incorrect sign.

As proxy for the relative taste factor of an alternative occupation
versus a police job, we introduced the aggregate crime index, q^a. We
expected that the elasticity for q^a would be negative.

The following equation represents the supply of police officers
function, estimated by 2SLS:

$$\ln PU_t \quad = \quad 3.241 \quad -.2375 \;\ln w_{pt} + .3475 \;\ln_{w\ell t}$$

$$\left(\begin{array}{c} \ln \text{ of per} \\ \text{capita} \\ \text{police} \end{array} \right)$$

	$\widehat{SE\beta}$	3.51	.229	.241
	$\hat{\beta}/\widehat{SE\beta}$	.924	-1.04	1.44

$$-.1019 \;\ln y_t + .02496 \;\ln q_t^a + .01473 \;\ln UR_t$$

.246	.0175	.0229
$-.415$	1.43	.644

NOB = 35; SE = .04194; $\hat{\rho}_1$ = .375, $\hat{\rho}_2$ = -.195, $\hat{\rho}_3$ = .446, with standard
error = .169.

This concludes the prevention sector. Several results do not confirm
the economic theory or involve imprecisely estimated coefficients. We
therefore feel the need for more detailed analysis of this sector with a
different body of data involving time series and cross-section information
at the city levels. There are several possible explanations for these
results. First, in the last decade much of the increase in public spending
for police has been used to expand office staffs and to reduce working hours

rather than to increase police patrols. Second, manpower limitations and
other demands on their time have prompted certain police departments to
shift their emphasis from property crimes toward crimes against the person.
Third, we have neglected direct interactions among crimes by analyzing only
auto theft. Fourth, the effect of the interaction of the private and public
protection is omitted.

3.7.   Model Identification and Model Specification

One of the requirements for building an estimable simultaneous equation
model is that the equations are identified. The problem of identification
is logically prior to the estimation problem and would still exist even if
our samples were infinitely large. A necessary condition for the identification
of the jth equation is that the number of excluded endogenous variables from the
j^{th} equation be at least as great as the number of exogenous variables included
in the jth equation less one[66] (the order condition). This restriction is less
serious than it may seem because the number of exogenous variables tends to
increase with the number of equations, whereas the number of unknown parameters
in any particular equation is typically small. In Appendix B we have worked
out the identification of the auto theft model.

A more difficult problem is the model specification. For any equation in
an economic model, we can always ask why certain variables, and in particular
why certain socioeconomic variables, are not included. For example, in a consumption function, we can ask why besides income, there are no other variables
such as white-nonwhite variable, a rural-urban variable, an age variable. Quite

---

[66]See e.g., Theil (1971), P. 448 ff. A necessary and sufficient condition
for identification of the jth equation is that the rank of the matrix of
coefficients in the other equations of the endogenous and exogenous variables
excluded from the jth equation equals the total number of endogenous variables
in the model less one (or total number of equations less one).

often the scope of the study will dictate the level of detail the investi-
gator wants to go into. In general, e.g., an age variable may not be included when estimating an aggregate consumption function.

Within a simultaneous equation model this model specification problem
has often been defined to be synonymous with the identification problem.
Possibly so because the order condition for identification will be violated,
as soon as a sufficient number of exogenous variables are added to a particular
equation. However, as mentioned above, in general the order condition is not
stringent and before the order condition would fail, quite a number of the
variables would have to be added. Therefore, the use of the name model specification would be more appropriate when discussing the inclusion or exclusion
of variables.

In the construction of the auto theft model, we have primarily been guided
by the theoretical model. We are aware that for each equation we could evaluat
several alternative specifications distinguishing each other by the particular
exogenous variables included. Indeed, in Vandaele (1975), Appendix VI, for eac
equation of the model several alternative specifications have been evaluated.[67]
The equations reported above were selected based on a combined criterion of
economic justification and statistical reliability.

Several alternative versions, not necessarily all with good economic
justification, could still be evaluated. We have not done so because we
view our auto theft model as a first step in the validation of the
theoretical model. Given the limited number of observations and the
quality of the data, we find it preposterous to try to claim that any
particular estimate should be taken at face value. Furthermore, the annual
data used do not allow sharp policy suggestions. What we did show is that
the theoretical model applied to auto theft seems to be natural and is
supported by the data. The next step would be to evaluate the model

---

[67] For a detailed analysis along these lines of the Ehrlich (1973) model
specification, see Vandaele (1978).

with micro (city) data and to extend the model to include interactions with other crimes, rather than trying to exhaust all possible model specifications with the current data set.

3.8 The Auto Theft Model: Summary and Forecasts

Table 1 summarizes the 2SLS estimates of the Auto Theft Model. This model is meant to be analyzed as a whole because an evaluation of an individual equation does not tell us much about how the variables interact as a complete system. Understanding this requires mathematical analysis as well as simulation of the model.

This section presents the results of a simulation[68] for the period 1935 to 1972, and gives ex post forecasts which are based on realized values of the exogenous variables, with no constant adjustment factors.[69] Note that the forecasts for the years 1970, 1971, and 1972 are outside the sample period and are therefore important for the model validation. The simulation results of all the endogenous variables are shown in figures 2 through 6, and table 2 contains forecast summary statistics. Finally, figure 7 contains the forecasting errors, that is, the differences between forecast and realized values.[70]

---

[68] Basically, the simulation involves taking the point estimates of the model as given in table 1 and then solving the model for each endogenous variable. We used the NBER TROLL system for the simulation.

[69] It has become general practice to adjust the forecast of a model by changing the values of the constant terms in the equations to capture special events. See, for example, Haitovsky and Treyz (1972).

[70] In keeping with current forecasting practice, we use point estimates for the parameters of the model. Since the coefficients of the models are estimated on the basis of a sample, these parameters are only known in a probabilistic sense. We agree that forecasts of the distribution of possible outcomes for the endogenous variables might be more appropriate and informative than the point projections currently made. If ex ante forecast distributions were available for the endogenous variables, we could use these distributions as a standard for accepting of rejecting the structural model specifications.

TABLE 1

ESTIMATES OF THE AUTO THEFT MODEL USING   2SLS

Demand for Stolen Cars

$\ln q_t$ = 3.709 - .5856 $\ln p_t$ + .6600 $\ln y_t$ - 1.302 $\ln \pi_t$ - .3220 $\ln \pi_t^c$
SE$\hat{\beta}$ 1.71   .424   .161   .250   .0886

Supply of Stolen Cars

$\ln q_t$ = -3.629 - .4383 $\ln p_t$ - .5409 $\ln w_{\ell t}$ - .4487 $\ln \pi_t$ + 65.36 NW_t + 4.192 A
SE$\hat{\beta}$ 2.15   .257   .398   .202   12.6   1.13

Probability of Arrest Production Function

$\ln \pi_t$ = 5.114 + .3511 $\ln PU_t$ - .07475 $\ln q_t^a$ + 1.548 $\ln NW_t$ - .5887 $\ln A_t$
SE$\hat{\beta}$ 2.47   .460   .0313   1.06   .208

Demand for Policemen

$\ln PU_t$ = -8.144 + .3285 $\ln W_{pt}$ + .3252 $\ln y_t$ + .01555 $\ln q_t^a$
SE$\hat{\beta}$ 3.93   .173   .123   .0134
                  -1.521 $\ln NW_t$ - .1285 $\ln A_t$
                  .813   .0928

Supply of Policemen

$\ln PU_t$ = 3.241 - .2375 $\ln w_{pt}$ + .3475 $\ln w_{\ell t}$ - .1019 $\ln y_t$
SE$\hat{\beta}$ 3.51   .229   .241   .246
                  + .02496 $\ln q_t^a$ + .01473 $\ln UR_t$
                  .0175   .0229

Endogenous:
              $\ln q$, $\ln p$, $\ln \pi$, $\ln PU$, $\ln w_p$

Definition:
              $\ln q^a$: $\ln q^a \equiv \ln q + \ln QO$, with QO the product of all other
index crimes. See also Appendix A for a definition of the variables.

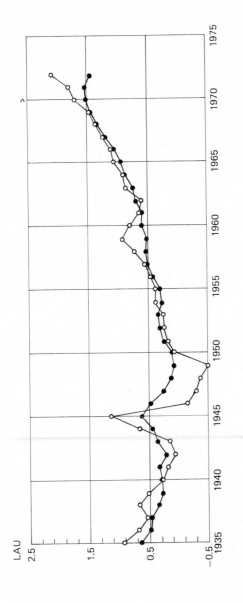

Fig. 2.—LAU: ln of the Auto Theft Index
Simulation output

Symbol: ● Realized
         ○ Simulated

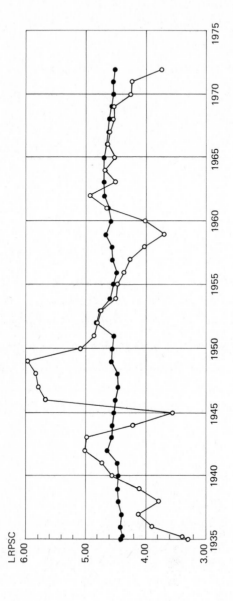

Fig. 3.--LRPSC: ℓn of the Real Price of Stolen Cars
Simulation output

Symbol: ●Realized
          ○Simulated

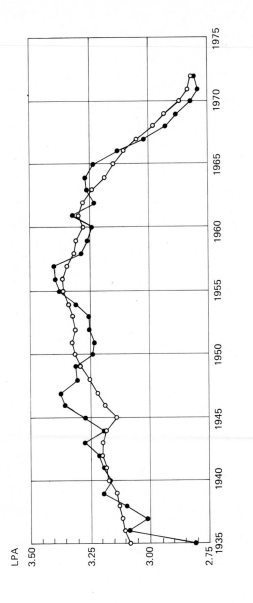

Fig. 4.—LPA: ℓn of the Probability of Arrest
        Simulation output
        Symbol: ● Realized
                 ○ Simulated

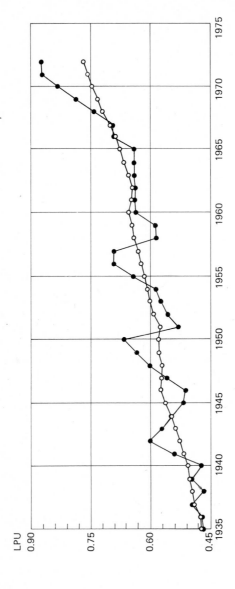

Fig. 5.--LPU: ℓn of the Per Capita Policemen
Simulation output

Symbol: ● Realized
          ○ Simulated

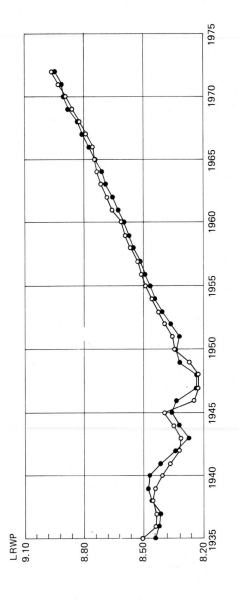

Fig. 6.—LRWP: ℓn of the Real Wage Rate of Policemen
Simulation output

Symbol: ● Realized
         ○ Simulated

Fig. 7.-- Forecasting Errors

7.1. LAU: LN OF THE AUTO THEFT INDEX

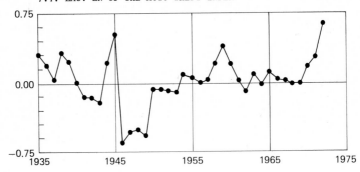

7.2. LRPSC: LN OF THE REAL PRICE OF STOLEN CARS

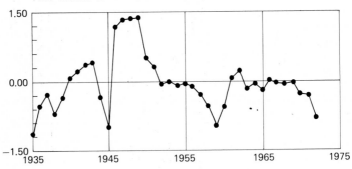

7.3. LPA: LN OF THE PROBABILITY OF ARREST

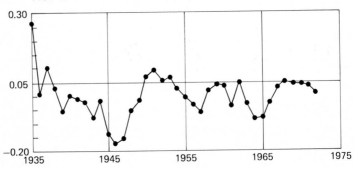

7.4. LPU: LN OF THE PER CAPITA POLICEMEN

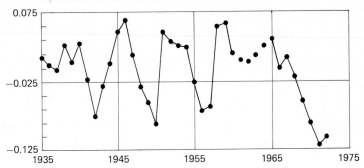

7.5. LRWP: LN OF THE REAL WAGE RATE OF POLICEMEN

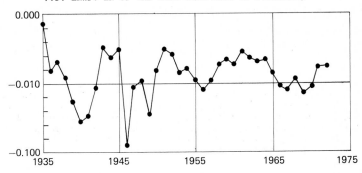

TABLE 2

FORECAST ERRORS STATISTICS

Endogenous Variables	1935–1969 RMS [71]	1935–1972 RMS	Percentage Differences [72]		
			1970	1971	1972
ln q	.256	.272	19.6	32.2	90.4
ln y	.607	.600	−24.2	−26.6	−54.5
ln π	.0791	.0766	4.64	4.13	1.23
ln PU	.0388	.0474	− 8.29	−11.0	−10.2
ln w_{ℓ}	.0308	.0298	− 1.55	1.15	1.22

[71] $RMS = \sqrt{\frac{1}{N} \Sigma (F_t - R_t)^2}$, F_t and R_t are, respectively, the fore-casted and realized values in period t.

[72] The percentage differences are calculated as a percentage of the realized values, after taking antilogs of the log forecasts. In calculating the antilogs, we did not introduce a correction factor, and therefore we are using the median forecasts rather than the mean. A positive value of the precentage difference indicates that the forecast is larger than the realized value.

The results show that ln of auto theft index (ln q), ln of probability of arrest (ln π), and ln of real police wage rate (ln w_p), track the historical time series quite closely. The largest forecasting errors for ln q_t occur immediately after the Second World War for the years 1946 through 1949. Basically the forecast overshoots the trough in the auto theft index during those years. The same years also cause forecasting problems for the probability of arrest series. Although the forecast catches most of the turning points in the historical series of this last variable, it misses the increase of probability in 1945. Indeed, the forecast value involves a decrease in the probability of arrest, and it then takes three years to correct this forecasting error. As might be expected ln of real wage rate of police officers tracks the historical time series quite closely since 1950 because this variable followed a trend which was fairly steady then. However, this variable also catches the turning points before 1950.

The price of stolen cars, ln p, is a weak variable in the model. Although the historical series shows a fairly constant growth, the simulated values constantly over- and undershoot the realized values. Again the largest forecasting errors occur during the years 1946 through 1949. The performance is somewhat better after 1952, when the price index of used cars was explicitly available.

The behavior of the per capita police officers variable, ln PU, leaves something to be desired. Although the historical series indicates a pronounced zigzag movement, the forecasted series somehow seems to smooth out all these values. It is possible, however, that some of the peaks could be an artifact of the per capita police data.

Figures 2 through 6 also contain the ex post forecasts for the years 1970, 1971, and 1972. The data for these three years were not used when estimating

the model. Basically, the endogenous variables forecasted well within the
sample period are also quite accurately predicted in the immediate future.
Notice that our model predicted that the auto theft index would continue
to increase, whereas since 1970, the actual auto theft index has decreases
slightly.

Keeping in mind the inherent difficulties of modeling the criminal
sector and the quality of available data, we think that the auto theft industry
model performs rather well. Furthermore, it should be apparent that this auto
theft model has not been developed primarily for forecasting, but rather to
explain the different forces governing the auto theft industry. Further analysis
would be needed to evaluate the structural properties as well as the forecasting
behavior. It should also be calibrated against naive forecasting, claiming
that the best forecast for next year is the present observed value, and against
transfer function analysis exploiting the dynamic structures of the model.

4.   Policy Implementation

4.1.   Introduction

Although the primary objective of this paper is to develop an economic
model capable of explaining crime in general and auto theft in particular, we
want to use the model for some aggregate policy implementation by answering some
"what if?" questions. We warn the reader that no single result obtained in this
section should be carried over to reality without additional careful study. This
section is only intended to illustrate what kind of questions could be ascertained
with the model if more detailed micro (city) data were available.

We will first evaluate the effects of changes in the probability of
arrest and the probability of conviction for offense charged. Next, we will
report on changes in unemployment rate and in the age composition of the population. For more detailed results about these police implementations, see Vandaele
(1975), Chapter VI.

4.2.   Changes in Deterrence Probabilities

To evaluate the effect of changes in the probability of arrest and
conviction on the total number of cars stolen, we used the reduced form equations
of a simplified model, in which the prevention sector is exogenous to the product
market, production sector and factor market. As a result, the probability of
arrest is an exogenous variable under control of a policy maker.

The historical data on the probabilities of arrest and convictions
(figures 8 and 9) show a sizeable drop toward the end of the sample period.
In the experiment evaluated, the value for the probability of arrest variable
was trended downward from its 1957 value along a path that lies halfway between
the high 1957 value and the historically observed values. We also modified
the values of the probability of conviction independently, so that the policy

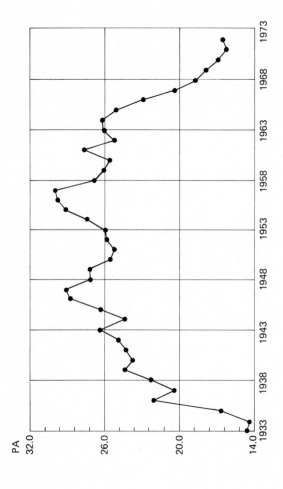

Fig. 8.--PA: Probability of Arrest
Time bounds: 1933-1972

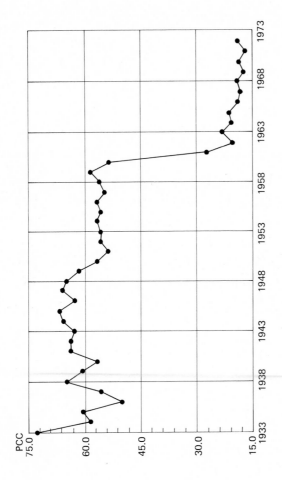

Fig. 9.--PCC: Probability of Conviction for Offense Charged
Time bounds: 1933-1972

values are similarly positioned halfway between the 1959 value and the historically observed values.

Table 3 shows the results of this simulation for the last five years
of the sample period. Focusing on 1969, we observe that with a 34 percent
increase in the probability of arrest, from 17.9 to 24, the number of cars
stolen would decrease to 573,072, a decrease of about 300,000 or 34 percent.
When increasing the probability of conviction independently from 17.6 to
38.15 (an increase of 117 percent), the decrease is auto theft would only be
24 percent or about 200,000 cars. The 75 percent confidence limits for the
change in the probability of arrest for 1969 are 479,500 and 648,900. We
therefore conclude that changes in the probabilities would induce large
changes in the number of cars stolen.[73]

4.3. Changes in Unemployment and Age Composition

Next we used the complete model, as given in table 1, to investigate
the effects of changes in the unemployment rate and in the percentage of the
total population 14 to 24 years of age. Given the abrupt increase in the unemployment rate, from 3.5 at the end of 1969 to 8.6 in June of 1975, we are
interested in evaluating the effect of similar changes in unemployment rate
on the number of cars stolen. We have therefore run the following simulation.
After changing the actual unemployment rates for 1967, 1968, and 1969 from
3.8, 3.6, and 3.5 to 6, 7, and 8 respectively, we calculated the change in
the number of cars stolen, keeping all other exogenous variables at the
historically observed levels. The analysis shows only small increases in
the number of cars stolen of 1,692, 2,827 and 3,962 in 1967, 1968, and 1969
respectively.

---

[73]More detailed discussion of this and other experiments is given in
Vandaele (1975). An analysis of the optimal ratio between probability of
arrest and probability of conviction suggests that the probability of arrest
should increase and the probability of conviction decrease.

TABLE 3

EFFECTS OF CHANGES IN DETERRENCE PROBABILITIES

Year	Actual Number of Cars Stolen in Thousands	Predicted Number of Cars Stolen in Thousands	
		Probability of arrest[a]	Probability of conviction[b]
1965	493.1	412.4	392.2
1966	557.0	461.7	458.7
1967	654.9	510.6	544.5
1968	777.8	543.2	618.0
1969	871.9	573.1	661.6

The reduced form contains the following variables: T, LREM, LRY, LUR, LPA, LPCC, and a constant.

[a]Trending the value of the probability of arrest variable downward from its 1957 value along a path that lies halfway between the 1957 value and the historically observed values.

[b]Trending the value of the probability of conviction given arrest downward from its 1959 value along a path that lies halfway between the 1959 value and the historically observed values.

For the age simulation[74], we kept the percentage of young persons
(14 to 24 years of age) constant at 16 for 1962 and later, and used the
historically observed values for all other exogenous variables in the model.
The maximum change introduced in the young age group was for the year 1969
with a decrease from 19.35 to 16. For that year the number of cars stolen
would decrease by about 210,000. In 1966, for a 2.19 percent decrease in the
percentage of young persons, the decrease in cars stolen would be 95,241.
This simulation experiment suggests that a change in the percentage of the
population 14 to 24 years of age has a large impact on the number of cars
stolen.

4.4.   Summary

Our analysis rests on the presumption that offenders, as a group,
respond to incentives in much the same way as those who engage in strictly
legitimate activities do. We therefore developed for the economics of crime
a theoretical model analogous to a standard economic industry supply and
demand model. This crime industry model is composed of a market for factors
of production, including illegal labor services, a production sector that
produces illegal goods and services, and a product market for these goods
and services. In addition there is a crime prevention sector that forms an
important link among the different sectors. This model has been summarized
in figure 1, section 2.

The empirical analysis of auto theft is presented in section 3.
Due to data unavailability, we only estimated the following five equations:

---

[74]The census projections for the percentage of young persons indicate
a gradual decrease from 20.36 in 1973 to 16.20 in 1985. This percentage was
16.34 in 1962 and increased to 20.39 in 1972.

the demand for stolen cars, the supply of stolen cars, the probability of
arrest production function, the demand for police officers, and the supply
of police officers. The results are summarized in table 1 and are not
inconsistent with the basic economic model. Despite the shortcomings in
the crime statistics used, and the somewhat stringent econometric specification of the functional relationships, the algebraic signs and point estimates
of the coefficients are remarkably consistent with the theoretical predictions.
The demand for stolen cars is found to be positively related to real income
and negatively related to the price of stolen cars. In the demand equation,
the deterrent effect of the probability of arrest is much larger than the
effect of the probability of conviction. In the supply of stolen cars, the
probability of arrest is significant, but in absolute magnitude its coefficient
is much smaller than in the demand for stolen cars equation. The effect of
the probability of conviction is insignificant. We find that the number of
police officers per capita is positively related to the probability of arrest,
although its coefficient is not very precisely estimated. Also, the probability
of arrest exhibits a decreasing scale effect: as the aggregate crime index
increases, the probability of arrest decreases. Furthermore, an increase in
the percentage of nonwhites in the population and a decrease in the young age
group increase the probability of arrest. The results for the public prevention
sector are not very conclusive. Possible reasons for this are changes in crime
mix over time, changes in police department's emphasis on certain crimes, and
neglect of the private protection influence.

We have also used the model to make forecasts within and outside the
sample. The model appears capable of predicting the observed auto theft index,
probability of arrest, per capita police force, and the real police wage rate.
The price of stolen cars is less well forecasted.

In section 4, the model has been used for policy implementations. First, we evaluated the effect of changing the probability of arrest and the probability of conviction separately. The experiments indicate that the reduction in the number of cars stolen would be considerable for reasonable increases the probability of arrest or the probability of conviction. Second, we simulated the effect on the number of cars stolen of changes in the unemployment rate and changes in the percentage of the population 14 to 24 years of age.

Harvard University

APPENDIX A

Index to the Variables[75]

A = Young Age Group: the percentage of the total resident population 14 to 24 years of age.

AU = Auto Theft Crime Index: The yearly national index of crime, as measured by the ratio of the total number of auto thefts reported to the police to the total civilian resident population in thousands. The other crime indexes have been calculated similarly.

CARS = Per Capita Number of Passenger Cars: The number of passenger cars as of December 31 of each year, expressed per 1,000 civilian residents.

CPI = Consumer Price Index: 1957-1959 = 100.

EM = Earnings in Manufacturing: Average gross hourly earnings of production and nonsupervisory workers in manufacturing.

N = Civilian Resident Population: estimates as of July 1 of each year.

NW = Nonwhite Population as a percentage of the total resident population.

PA = Probability of Arrest for Auto Theft: The percentage of auto theft cleared by arrest during a particular year, irrespective of when they were committed.

PCA = Probability of Conviction: Percentage of persons charges, found guilty (for offense charged or for lesser offense).

PCC = Probability of Conviction for Offense Charged: Persons found guilty for offense charged, as a percentage of total charged.

---

[75]A detailed description of the data used is given in Vandaele (1975), Chapter III and Appendix IV. See also Vandaele (1977).

PR = Total Labor Force Participation Rate: Annual estimates of average
monthly figures for persons 14 years of age and over. PR is calculated as the ratio of civilian labor force to civilian non-institutional
population.

PSC = Price of Stolen Cars: Where possible, the price of stolen cars was
related to the consumer price index for used automobiles. Otherwise,
the consumer price index for new automobiles and private transportation
has been used.

PU = Full-time Police Department Employees including civilians; rate per
1,000 inhabitants.

QA = Aggregate Crime Index: calculated as the product of the seven FBI
crime indexes: murder, rape, assault, robbery, burglary, larceny
and auto theft.

QO = Aggregate Crime Index, without auto theft.

T = Time Variable (1933 = 1).

UR = Total Unemployment Rate: (unemployment as a percentage of total
civilian labor force), annual averages.

WP = Index of Maximum Salary Scales for Police Officers: in cities of
100,000 or more. Data are based on maximum rates in effect on January
1 of each year. The salaries pertain to police officers engaged in
general police duties, including traffic control.

YP = Per Capita Permanent Income: Permanent income constructed according
to Friedman (1957) and in particular using methods explained in
Darby (1972). See also Vandaele (1975), p. 100 ff.

To simplify the understanding of the symbols, we adopted the following
rules for indicating transformed variables. Say the untransformed variable
has the symbol X. Then LX = natural logarithm of X; X1 = the variable X lagged
one period; DX = differencing the variable; DX = X - X1; RX = the real value
of X, obtained by deflating X with the consumer price index (CPI).

Table 4 contains summary statistics for the variables.

TABLE 4

VARIABLES USED IN THE AUTO THEFT MODEL--SUMMARY STATISTICS

Name	Symbol	Mean	Standard Dev.	Trend Regression* Intercept	Slope	R^2	Symbol	Mean	Standard Dev.	Trend Regression* Intercept	Slope	R^2
Auto theft crime index	AU	1.825	.7666	.816	.0504	.454	LAU	.5371	.3413	.0847	.0226	.461
Real price of stolen cars	RPSC	97.77	9.880	85.6	.609	.399	LRPSC	4.577	.09336	4.45	.00635	.433
Probability of arrest	PA	25.09	3.270	24.7	.0202	.004	LPA	3.213	.1408	3.20	.000743	.004
Per capita police officers	PU	1.822	.1487	1.57	.0124	.728	LPU	.5967	.08090	.461	.00678	.738
Real wage rate police officers	RWP	4.995	929.8	3,550	72.2	.633	LRWP	8.500	.1785	8.23	.0136	.613
Real per capita permanent income	RY	1,778	406.8	1,026	37.6	.896	LRY	7.454	.2554	7.00	.0229	.843
Probability of conviction	PCC	49.55	17.62	76.8	-1.37	.632	LPCC	3.812	.4754	4.54	-.0366	.622
Real earnings manufacturing	REM	1.843	.4194	1.03	.0407	.986	LREM	.5846	.2372	.128	.0228	.971
Percentage nonwhite population	NW	.1101	.006882	.0971	.000649	.935	LNW	-2.208	.06200	-2.33	.00585	.941
Percentage population, 14-24 years of age	A	.1754	.02027	.196	-.00102	.265	LA	-1.747	.1167	-1.634	-.00567	.248
Civilian resident population	N	157,569	25,018	109,650	2,396	.963	LN	11.96	.1608	11.7	.0152	.966
Aggregate crime index							LQA	-3.747	2.205	-7.64	.194	.817
Unemployment rate	UR	6.631	5.118	12.6	-.293	.355	LUR	1.663	.6627	2.21	-.0272	.177
Labor force participation rate	PR	.5723	.01277	.557	.000786	.403	LPR	-.5583	.02216	-.586	.00137	.404

* This is a simple regression of the variable indicated in the symbol column on trend: y= a + bt, with y the different variables indicated in the symbol column. The sample period used in 1935 - 1969.

APPENDIX B

IDENTIFICATION OF THE AUTO THEFT MODEL

B.1 The Auto Theft Model

Given that the auto theft model is linear in the parameters, we can represent the full model as

$$(B.1) \qquad \underline{y}_t' \Gamma = \underline{x}_t' B + \underline{u}_t'$$

with $\underline{y}_t$ a 6 x 1 vector of endogenous variables, $\underline{x}_t$ a 10 x 1 vector of exogenous variables, $\underline{u}_t'$ a 6 x 1 vector of errors and Γ and B are a 6 x 6 and 10 x 6 matrix of endogenous and exogenous coefficients.

We can also write (B.1) as

$$(B.2) \qquad (\underline{y}_t' \vdots - \underline{x}_t') \begin{bmatrix} \Gamma \\ B \end{bmatrix} = \underline{u}_t'$$

and compactly as

$$(B.3) \qquad \underline{z}_t' A = \underline{u}_t'$$

In the auto theft model (B.1) takes the following form

$$\underline{y}_t' = (\ln q_t, \ln p_t, \ln \pi_t, \ln PU_t, \ln w_{pt}, \ln q_t^a)$$

$$\underline{x}_t' = (\text{constant}, \ln y_t, \ln \pi_t^c, \ln w_{\ell t}, \ln NW_t, NW_t, \ln A_t, A_t, \ln UR_t, \ln QO_t)$$

$$(B.4) \qquad \Gamma = \begin{bmatrix} \gamma_{11} & \gamma_{21} & & & & \gamma_{61} \\ \gamma_{12} & \gamma_{22} & & & & \\ \gamma_{13} & \cdot \gamma_{23} & \gamma_{33} & & & \\ & & \gamma_{34} & \gamma_{44} & \gamma_{54} & \\ & & & \gamma_{45} & \gamma_{55} & \\ & & \gamma_{36} & \gamma_{46} & \gamma_{56} & \gamma_{66} \end{bmatrix}$$

and

$$(B.5) \quad B = \begin{bmatrix} b_{11} & b_{21} & b_{31} & b_{41} & b_{51} & & & & & \\ b_{12} & & & b_{42} & b_{52} & & & & & \\ b_{13} & & & & & & & & & \\ & b_{24} & & & & b_{54} & & & & \\ & & b_{35} & b_{45} & & & & & & \\ & b_{26} & & & & & & & & \\ & & b_{37} & b_{47} & & & & & & \\ & b_{28} & & & & & & & & \\ & & & & & b_{59} & & & & \\ & & & & & & b_{6,10} & & & \end{bmatrix}$$

where zeros in the matrices Γ and B are indicated by blanks. The following remarks are appropriate.

1) The full reduced form is composed on the exogenous variables
    specified in vector $\underline{x}_t$ together with the variables t, $\ln N$ and $\ln PR$.

2) The definition

$$(B.6) \qquad \ln q^a = \ln q + \ln QO$$

    is explicitly left in the model. We could have eliminated this defi-
    nition by substituting for $\ln q^a$ resulting in a 5 x 5 matrix Γ and
    a 5 x 10 matrix B.

Neither of these remarks in any way affects the identification of the model as
explained below.

B.2.   Order and Rank Condition

The standard[76] identification conditions are composed of an order and
a rank condition.

---

[76] See, e.g., Theil (1971).

Order Condition. A necessary (but not sufficient) condition for the
identification of a particular equation under exclusion restrictions[77] is that
the number of exogenous variables excluded from the equation must be at least
as great as the number of endogenous variables included in the equation with
coefficients non-zero, minus one.

Rank Condition. A necessary and sufficient condition for the identification of a particular equation under exclusion restrictions is that it be
possible to form at least one nonvanishing determinant of order m-1 from the
rows of A corresponding to the variables excluded *a priori* from that equation,
where m is the total number of endogenous variables in the model.

Finally, a model is identified if all the equations are identified.

B.3.   Identification of the Auto Theft Model

Let us now evaluate both conditions on each equation of the auto
theft model. As remarked above, the last equation does not have to be evaluated as this is a definition. As can be seen from the matrix Γ, in each equation there are three endogenous variables included, requiring that in each
equation there would be at least two exogenous variables excluded. Examining
matrix B, we notice that in each equation there are at least six exogenous
variables excluded. Therefore, each equation satisfies the order condition.

The rank condition is more tedious to verify. We will therefore
only explicitly evaluate the rank condition of demand for illegal car equations
equation 1.

The submatrix we have to examine is composed of all rows for which
there is a zero in the first column of matrix A. This submatrix, denoted by $\bar{A}$,
is given below.

---

[77]Exclusion restrictions on the jth equation imply that some of the
coefficients in the jth column of Γ or B are equal to zero.

$$(B.6) \quad \bar{A} = \begin{bmatrix}
\gamma_{34} & \gamma_{44} & \gamma_{54} & \\
 & \gamma_{45} & \gamma_{55} & \\
\gamma_{36} & \gamma_{46} & \gamma_{56} & \gamma_{66} \\
b_{24} & & b_{54} & \\
 & b_{35} & b_{45} & \\
b_{26} & & & \\
 & b_{37} & b_{47} & \\
b_{28} & & & \\
 & & b_{59} & \\
 & & & b_{6,10}
\end{bmatrix}$$

The rank condition requires that we find at least one nonvanishing determinant of order 5. One such nonvanishing determinant can be calculated from the following submatrix of $\bar{A}$:

$$(B.7) \quad \begin{bmatrix}
b_{24} & & b_{54} & \\
 & b_{35} & b_{45} & \\
 & b_{37} & b_{47} & \\
 & & b_{59} & \\
 & & & b_{6,10}
\end{bmatrix}$$

Therefore, equation 1 is identified. Similarly, it can be shown that the rank condition for all other equations is satisfied. As a result, the auto theft model is identified.

Ackerman, S.R. (1970). "The Demand for Used Automobiles in the United States - 1954-1966." Ph.D. dissertation, Yale University. Pp.145.

Ahamad, B. (1967). "An Analysis of Crimes by the Method of Principal Components." *Applied Statistics (Journal of the Royal Statistical Society, (Series C). 16,* 1, 17-35.

Altman, S.H., and R.J. Barro (1971). "Officer Supply - The Impact of Pay, the Draft, and the Vietnam War." *The American Economic Review, 61,* 4 (September), 649-664.

Atkinson, L.J. (1952). "Consumer Markets for Durable Goods." *Survey of Current Business,* U.S. Department of Commerce, Office of Business Economics, *32,* (April), 19-24.

Avio, K.L. and C.S. Clark (1976). *Property Crime in Canada: An Econometric Study.* Toronto: University of Toronto Press for the Ontario Economic Council. Pp. vii+ 86.

Bartel, A.P. (1974). "The Demand for Private Protection." Ph.D. dissertation, Columbia University.

_____ (1975). "An Analysis of Firm Demand for Protection against Crime". *Journal of Legal Studies, 4,* 2 (June), 443-478.

Becker, G.S. (1965). "A Theory of the Allocation of Time." *The Economic Journal, 75,* 299 (September), 493-517. Reprinted in Becker, G.S. (1976). *The Economic Approach to Human Behavior.* Chicago: The University of Chicago Press. Pp. 89-114.

_____ (1968). "Crime and Punishment: An Economic Approach." *Journal of Political Economy, 76,* 2 (March/April), 169-217. Reprinted in Becker, G.S. and W.M. Landes, Eds. (1974). *Essays in the Economics of Crime and Punishment.* New York: Columbia University Press for National Bureau of Economic Research. Pp. 1-54. Reprinted in Becker, G.S. (1976). *The Economic Approach to Human Behavior.* Chicago: The University of Chicago Press. Pp. 39-85.

_____ (1971). *Economic Theory.* New York: Alfred A. Knopf. Pp. xii + 222.

_____ (1976). *The Economic Approach to Human Behavior.* Chicago: The University of Chicago Press. Pp. 314.

Becker, G.S. and W.M. Landes, Eds. (1974). *Essays in the Economics of Crime and Punishment.* New York: Columbia University Press for National Bureau of Economic Research. Pp. xvii + 268.

Becker G.S. and G.J. Stigler (1974). "Law Enforcement, Malfeasance, and Compensation of Enforcers." *Journal of Legal Studies, 3,* 1 (January), 1-18.

Blattberg, R. C. (1973). "Evaluation of the Power of the Durbin-Watson Statistic for Non-First Order Serial Correlation Alternatives." *The Review of Economics and Statistics, 55,* 4 (November), 508-515.

Block, M. K. and J. M. Heineke (1975). "A Labor Theoretic Analysis of the Criminal Choice." *The American Economic Review, 65,* 3 (June), 314-325.

Block, M. K. and R. C. Lind (1975a). "Crime and Punishment Reconsidered." *Journal of Legal Studies, 4,* 1 (January), 241-247.

_____.(1975b). "An Economic Analysis of Crimes Punishable by Imprisonment." *Journal of Legal Studies, 4,* 2 (June), 479-492.

Blumstein, A., Cohen, J. and D. Nagin, Eds. (1978). *Deterrence and Incapacitation: Estimating the Effects of Criminal Sanctions on Crime Rates.* Washington, D.C.: National Academy of Sciences, The National Research Council, Panel on Research on Deterrent and Incapacitative Effects. Pp. ix + 431.

Borcherding, T. E., and R. T. Deacon (1972). "The Demand for the Services of Non-Federal Governments." *The American Economic Review, 67,* 5 (December), 891-901.

Carr-Hill, R. A., and N. H. Stern (1971). "Variations in Recorded Statistics of Police Work, Offender Behaviour and Judicial Activity in England and Wales in the Early 1960's," University of Sussex (September). Mimeographed. Pp. 38.

_____.(1973). "An Econometric Model of the Supply and Control of Recorded Offences in England and Wales." *Journal of Public Economics, 2,* 4 (November), 289-318.

Chow, G. C. (1957). *Demand for Automobiles in the United States, A Study in Consumer Durables.* Contributions to Economic Analysis, XIII. Amsterdam: North-Holland Publishing Company. Pp. xii + 110.

_____. (1960). "Statistical Demand Functions for Automobiles and Their Use for Forecasting." In Harberger, A. C. Ed., *The Demand for Durable Goods.* Chicago: The University of Chicago Press. Pp. 149-186.

Church, A. M., III. (1970). "An Econometric Model of Crime in California." Ph.D. dissertation, Claremont Graduate School and University Center.

Clotfelter, C. T. (1977). "Public Services, Private Substitutes, and the Demand for Protection Against Crime." *The American Economic Review, 67,* 5 (December), 867-877.

Cochrane, D., and G. H. Orcutt (1949). "Application of Least Squares Regression to Relationships Containing Auto-Correlated Error Terms." *Journal of the American Statistical Association, 44,* 245 (March), 32-61.

Cooper, T. Ph. (1973). "Econometric Software Package Users Manual." University of Chicago (May 1).

Darby, M.R. (1972). "The Allocation of Transitory Income Among Consumers'
Assets." *The American Economic Review, 62,* 5 (December), 928-941.

Darrough, M.N. and J.M. Heineke (1978). "The Multi-Output Translog Production
Cost Function: The Case of Law Enforcement Agencies," present volume.

Dyckman, T.R. (1965). "An Aggregate-Demand Model for Automobiles." *Journal
of Business, 38,* 3 (July), 252-266.

Ehrlich, I. (1967). "The Study of Illegitimate Activities," Columbia
University. (Mimeographed.)

_____ (1970)."Participation in Illegitimate Activities: An Economic
Analysis." Ph.D. dissertation, Columbia University. Pp.151.

_____ (1972). "The Deterrent Effect of Criminal Law Enforcement."
Journal of Legal Studies, 1, 2 (June), 259-276.

_____ (1973). "Participation in Illegitimate Activities: A Theoretical
and Empirical Investigation." *Journal of Political Economy, 81,* 3 (May/
June), 521-566. Article reprinted with some corrections and supplemented
with appendixes from Ehrlich (1970) as "Participation in Illegitimate
Activities: An Economic Analysis." In Becker, G.S., and W.M. Landes, Eds.
(1974). *Essays in the Economics of Crime and Punishment.* New York:
Columbia University Press for National Bureau of Economic Research.
Pp. 69-134.

_____ (1975a) "On the Relation Between Education and Crime." In Juster,
F.T., Ed. (1975). *Education, Income, and Human Behavior.* New York:
McGraw-Hill Book Company, 313-337.

_____ (1975b) "The Deterrent Effect of Capital Punishment: A Question
of Life and Death." *The American Economic Review, 65,* 3 (June), 397-417.

_____ (1977). "Capital Punishment and Deterrence: Some Further Thoughts
and Additional Evidence." *Journal of Political Economy, 85,* 4 (August),
741-788.

Ehrlich, I. and G.S. Becker (1972). "Market Insurance, Self-Insurance, and
Self-Protection." *Journal of Political Economy, 80,* 4 (July/August),
623-648.

Fisher, A.C. (1969). "The Cost of the Draft and the Cost of Ending the Draft."
The American Economic Review, 59, 3 (June), 239-254.

_____ (1970). "The Cost of Ending the Draft: Reply." *The American
Economic Review, 60,* 5 (December), 979-983.

Fleisher, B.M. (1963). "The Effect of Unemployment on Juvenile Delinquency."
Journal of Political Economy, 71, 6 (December), 543-555.

_____ (1966a). "The Effect of Income on Delinquency." *The American
Economic Review, 56,* 1 (March), 118-137.

_____ (1966b). *The Economics of Delinquency.* Chicago: Quadrangle
Books. Pp. 127.

Freeman, R. B. (1971). *The Market for College-Trained Manpower: A Study in the Economics of Career Choice*. Cambridge, Mass.: Harvard University Press, Pp. xxvi + 264.

Friedman, M. (1957). *A Theory of the Consumption Function*. NBER General Series nr. 63. Princeton: Princeton University Press for National Bureau of Economic Research. Pp. xvi + 243.

Furubotn, E. G., and S. Pejovich (1972). "Property Rights and Economic Theory: A Survey of Recent Literature." *Journal of Economic Literature, 10*, 4 (December), 1137-1162.

Gilman, T. (1970). "Supply of Volunteers to the Military Services." U.S. President's Commission on an All-Volunteer Armed Force. *Studies Prepared for the President's Commission on an All-Volunteer Armed Force*. Vol. 1 Washington, D.C.: U.S. Government Printing Office. (November).

Gould, J. P. (1973). "The Economics of Legal Conflicts." *Journal of Legal Studies, 2*, 2 (June), 279-300.

Haitovsky, Y. and G. Treyz (1972). "Forecasts with Quarterly Macroeconomic Models: Equation Adjustments, and Benchmark Prediction: The U. S. Experience." *The Review of Economics and Statistics, 54*, 3 (August), 317-325.

Hall, R. E. (1973). "The Specification of Technology with Several Kinds of Output." *Journal of Political Economy, 81*, 4 (July/August), 878-892.

Heineke, J. M. (1978). "Sustitution Among Crimes and the Question of Deterrence: An Indirect Utility Function Approach to the Supply of Legal and Illegal Activity," present volume.

Klotz, B. P. (1970). "The Cost of Ending the Draft: Comment." *The American Economic Review, 60*, 5 (December), 970-978.

Landes, W. M. (1971). "An Economic Analysis of the Courts." *Journal of Law and Economics, 14*, 1 (April), 61-107. Reprinted in Becker, G. S. and W. M. Landes, Eds. (1974). *Essays in the Economics of Crime and Punishment*. New York: Columbia University Press for National Bureau of Economic Research. Pp. 164-214.

_____. (1973). "The Bail System: An Economic Approach." *Journal of Legal Studies, 2*, 1 (January), 79-105. Reprinted in Becker, G. S. and W. M. Landes, Eds. (1974). *Essays in the Economics of Crime and Punishment*. New York: Columbia University Press for National Bureau of Economic Research. Pp. 135-163.

_____. (1978). "An Economic Study of U.S. Aircraft Hijacking, 1960-1976."

Lightman, E.S. (1972). "The Economics of Military Manpower Supply in Canada." Ph. D. dissertation, University of California, Berkeley. Distributed by U.S. Department of Commerce National Technical Information Service, Springfield, Va. Pp. 224.

Luce, R. D., and D. H. Krantz (1971). "Conditional Expected Utility."
   Econometrica, 39, 2 (March), 253-271.

The Municipal Year Book. Washington, D. C.: International City Management
   Association (Annual).

Muth, R. F. (1964). "The Derived Demand Curve for a Productive Factor and the
   Industry Supply Curve. " *Oxford Economic Papers, New Series, 16,* 2 (July),
   221-234.

Nagin, D. (1978). "General Deterrence: A Review of the Empirical Evidence."
   In Blumstein, A. et al., Eds., *Deterrence and Incapacitation: Estimating
   the Effects of Criminal Sanctions on Crime Rates.* Washington, D. C.:
   National Academy of Sciences, The National Research Council, Panel on
   Research on Deterrent and Incapacitative Effects. Pp. 95-139.

Ohls, J. C., and T. J. Wales (1972). "Supply and Demand for State and Local
   Services." *The Review of Economics and Statistics, 54,* 4 (November), 424-
   430.

Oi, W. Y. (1967). "The Economic Cost of the Draft." *The American Economic
   Review, 57,* 2 (May), 39-62.

Ozenne, T. O. (1972). "The Economics of Theft and Security Choice." Ph. D.
   dissertation, University of California, Los Angeles. Pp. x + 99.

_____. (1974). "The Economics of Bank Robbery." *Journal of Legal
   Studies, 3,* 1 (January), 19-52.

Palmer, J. (1977). "Economic Analyses of the Deterrent Effect of Punishment:
   A Review." *Journal of Research in Crime and Delinquency, 14,* 1 (January),
   4-21.

Parkin, J. M. and S. Y. Wu (1972). "Choice Involving Unwanted Risky Events
   and Optimal Insurance." *The American Economic Review, 62,* 5 (December),
   982-987.

Pashigian, B. P. (1975). "On the Control of Crime and Bribery." *Journal of
   Legal Studies, 4,* 2(June), 311-326.

Phillips, L., H. L. Votey, Jr., and D. Maxwell (1972). "Crime, Youth, and
   the Labor Market." *Journal of Political Economy, 80,* 3, Part I (May/June),
   491-504.

Posner, R. A. (1972). "The Behavior of Administrative Agencies." *Journal of
   Legal Studies, 1,* (June), 305-347. Reprinted in Becker, G. S. and W. M.
   Landes, Eds. (1974). *Essays in the Economics of Crime and Punishment.*
   New York: Columbia University Press for National Bureau of Economic
   Research. Pp. 215-261.

Press, S. J. (1971). *Some Effects of an Increase in Police Manpower in the
   20th Precinct of New York City.* New York: The New York City RAND
   Institute. R-704-NYC (October). Pp. xiii + 158.

Robert, P. and J.-P. Bombet (1970). "Le coût du crime en France." *Annales Internationales de Criminologie, 9,* 2, 599-655.

Roos, C. F. and V. von Szeliski (1939). "Factors Governing Changes in Domestic Automobile Demand." In *The Dynamics of Automobile Demand.* New York: General Motors Corporation. Pp. 21-95.

Smigel-Leibowitz, A. (1965). "Does Crime Pay? An Economic Analysis." M.A. thesis, Columbia University.

Suits, D. (1958). "The Demand for New Automobiles in the United States, 1929-1956." *The Review of Economics and Statistics, 40,* 3 (August), 273-280.

Swimmer, E. R. (1972). "Measurement of the Effectiveness of Urban Law Enforcement—A Simultaneous Equations Approach." Ph. D. dissertation, Cornell University (August). Pp. vii + 138.

_____. (1974). "Measurement of the Effectiveness of Urban Law Enforcement—A Simultaneous Approach." *Southern Economics Journal, 40,* 4 (April), 618-630.

Theil, H. (1971). *Principles of Econometrics.* New York: John Wiley and Sons, Inc. Pp. xxxi + 736.

Tobin, J. (1950). "A Statistical Demand Function for Food in the U.S.A." *Journal of the Royal Statistical Society, Series A, 113,* 2, 113-149 (with discussion).

Vandaele, W. (1973). "Seemingly Unrelated Regression and Two- and Three-Stage Least Squares Program." University of Chicago (October). Pp. 44.

_____. (1975). "The Economics of Crime: An Econometric Investigation of Auto Theft in the United States." Ph. D. dissertation, University of Chicago (December). Pp. xi + 263.

_____. (1977). "The Economics of Crime: An Econometric Investigation of Auto Theft in the United States - Data References, " Harvard University, Graduate School of Business Administration, Division of Research, Report HBS 77-30 (December). Pp. 38.

_____. (1978). "Participation in Illegitimate Activities: Ehrlich Revisited." In Blumstein, A. et al., Eds. *Deterrence and Incapacitation: Estimating the Effects of Criminal Sanctions on Crime Rates.* Washington, D.C.: National Academy of Sciences, The National Research Council, Panel on Research on Deterrent and Incapacitative Effects. Pp. 270-335.

Votey, H. L., Jr. and L. Phillips (1972). "Police Effectiveness and the Production Function for Law Enforcement." *Journal of Legal Studies, 1,* 2 (June), 423-436.

Wolpin, N. (1971). "An Economic Analysis of Crime and Punishment in England and Wales: 1894-1967." Yale University, (April), Pp. 60.   :

Zeegers, J. (1971). "Analyse Economique des Dépenses Publiques Belges en Matière Repressive de 1950 à 1967," Université Catholique de Louvain, Centre de Recherches Interdisciplinaires Droit-Economie, Document de travail No. 771. Pp. 45.

NAMES AND ADDRESSES OF CONTRIBUTORS

MASAKO M. DARROUGH — *Department of Economics,*
University of Santa Clara,
Santa Clara, California

J.M. HEINEKE — *Department of Economics,*
University of Santa Clara,
Santa Clara, California

CHARLES F. MANSKI — *Department of Economics,*
Carnegie-Mellon University,
Pittsburgh, Pennsylvania

LLAD PHILLIPS — *Department of Economics,*
University of California,
Santa Barbara, California

NICHOLAS H. STERN — *Department of Economics,*
University of Warwick,
Coventry, England

JOHN B. TAYLOR — *Department of Economics,*
Columbia University,
New York City, New York

WALTER VANDAELE — *Graduate School of Business*
Administration,
Harvard University,
Boston, Massachusetts